Intention, Plans, and Practical Reason

Intention, Plans, and Practical Reason

Michael E. Bratman

Harvard University Press
Cambridge, Massachusetts, and London, England

Library of Congress Cataloging-in-Publication Data

Bratman, Michael.
   Intention, plans, and practical reason.

   Bibliography: p.
   Includes index.
   1. Intentionalism.   2. Planning.   I. Title.
BF619.5.B73   1987   128'.3   87-8702
ISBN 0-674-45818-4 (alk. paper) (cloth)
ISBN 0-674-45819-2 (paper)

To my mother and father, Anne and Harry Bratman

Preface

What happens to our conception of mind and rational agency when we take seriously future-directed intentions and plans and their roles as inputs into further practical reasoning? This question drives much of this book. My initial efforts with it resulted in a quintet of papers published between 1981 and 1985: "Intention and Means-End Reasoning," *The Philosophical Review* 90 (1981): 252–265; "Castañeda's Theory of Thought and Action," in *Agent, Language, and the Structure of the World: Essays Presented to Hector-Neri Castañeda, with His Replies,* ed. James E. Tomberlin (Indianapolis: Hackett, 1983); "Taking Plans Seriously," *Social Theory and Practice* 9 (1983): 271–287; "Two Faces of Intention," *The Philosophical Review* 93 (1984): 375–405; and "Davidson's Theory of Intention," in *Essays on Davidson: Actions and Events,* ed. Bruce Vermazen and Merrill B. Hintikka (Oxford: Oxford University Press, 1985). (Material from "Two Faces of Intention" is included here in Chapter 8 with the permission of *The Philosophical Review.*) In this book I develop further some of the main themes of these essays and also explore a variety of related ideas and issues. Although, no doubt, much remains to be said, my hope is that I have made the overall outlines of my answer to my question sufficiently clear that its general merit and usefulness for further research can reasonably be assessed.

Work on this book was made possible in part by a Fellowship from the American Council of Learned Societies, under a program funded by the National Endowment for the Humanities, during the academic year 1984–85. My work during that academic year was also supported by Stanford University, through its sabbatical leave program. During the past several years my work has benefited from the generous support and computer facilities provided by the Center for the Study of Language and Information, made possible in part through an award from the System

Development Foundation. And I could not have written this book had it not been for the stimulating and supportive intellectual environment provided both by the Stanford University Philosophy Department and by the Center for the Study of Language and Information.

Donald Davidson first awakened my interests in the theory of action, and John Perry helped me develop these interests through many years of conversation as my colleague at Stanford. Most recently I have learned from an ongoing interdisciplinary seminar on rational agency conducted at the Center for the Study of Language and Information and from an informal graduate seminar based on an early draft of this book. Daniel Farrell and David Velleman both provided extensive and helpful comments on parts of earlier drafts.

I am also indebted to many others. Among them are Robert Audi, Lawrence Becker, Ned Block, David Brink, Hector-Neri Castañeda, Mark Crimmins, Arnold Davidson, Alan Donagan, Charles Dresser, John Dupré, John Etchemendy, John Fischer, Allan Gibbard, Gilbert Harman, David Hilbert, David Israel, Hugh McCann, Julius Moravcsik, Adrian Piper, Martha Pollack, Peter Railton, Jean Roberts, Kwong-loi Shun, Michael Slote, Holly Smith, Michael Stocker, Patrick Suppes, Howard Wettstein, and George Wilson. Ingrid Deiwiks kindly helped prepare the bibliography.

Susan Gross Bratman, Gregory Bratman, and Scott Bratman each provided support in her or his own special way and made my work on this book a lot more fun than it might have been.

Contents

Intention, Plans, and Practical Reason

chapter 1

Introduction

MUCH of our understanding of ourselves and others is rooted in a commonsense psychological framework, one that sees intention as central. Within this framework we use the notion of intention to characterize both people's actions and their minds. Thus, I might *intentionally* pump the water into the house, and pump it *with the intention* of poisoning the inhabitants. Here intention characterizes my action. But I might also *intend* this morning to pump the water (and poison the inhabitants) when I get to the pump this afternoon. And here intention characterizes my mind.[1]

Such characterizations are important to us in many ways. First, they are tied tightly to a wide range of emotional reactions, moral attitudes, and legal institutions. If I poison the inhabitants, but do not do so intentionally and do not act with the intention of poisoning them, you will react very differently to me than if I had acted with that intention and poisoned them intentionally; and so will our legal institutions. Second, these characterizations provide a basis for our everyday attempts to predict what others will do, explain what they have done, and coordinate our projects with theirs. You can predict my actions with some accuracy if you know of my prior intention to poison the inhabitants, and a later appeal to that intention might play an important role in an attempt to explain my actions at the pump. And your knowledge of my intention to poison the inhabitants may play a significant role in our joint attempt to steal the gold from the building they are in.

In this book I take some steps toward providing a systematic framework within which to understand these ways of characterizing mind and action in terms of intention. In doing this I am led to discuss a range of issues about intention, action, and practical rationality. Throughout, however, I am guided by a simple but, I think, powerful idea. This is the idea that our commonsense conception of intention is inextricably tied to the phenomena of plans and planning. It is my view that an adequate theory of intention needs to take seriously these phenomena and their relation to intention. In this chapter I want briefly to clarify this underlying theme, and contrast it with a variety of ideas common to much recent philosophy of mind and action. This will lead me to touch briefly on several ideas that will be receiving detailed treatment in the chapters to follow. But in this introduction my main concern is to set out the general picture that will be guiding these later, more detailed discussions.

1.1 Plans

Begin with plans and planning. The central fact is that we are planning agents. We frequently settle in advance on more or less complex plans concerning the future, and then these plans guide our later conduct. So much, anyway, is included in our commonsense understanding of the sort of beings we are. As planning agents, we have two central capacities. We have the capacity to act purposively; and we have the capacity to form and execute plans. The latter capacity clearly requires the former; but it is plausible to suppose that the former could exist without the latter. Indeed, it is natural to see many nonhuman animals as having only the former capacity, and to see our possession of both capacities as a central feature of the sort of beings we are.

Our need for plans concerning the future is rooted in two very general needs. We are rational agents, to some extent. For us this means in part that deliberation and, more generally, rational reflection help shape what we do. If, however, our actions were influenced only by deliberation at the time of action, the influence of such deliberation would be rather minimal. This is so because deliberation requires time and other limited resources, and there is an obvious limit to the extent to which one may successfully deliberate at the time of action.[2] So we need ways to allow deliberation and rational reflection to influence action beyond the present.

Second, we have pressing needs for coordination. To achieve complex goals I must coordinate my present and future activities. And I need also to coordinate my activities with yours. Anyone who has managed to write a lecture, pick up a book at the library, attend a committee meeting, and then pick up a child at school will be familiar with the former type of *intra*personal coordination. And anyone who has managed to arrange and participate in a committee meeting with several colleagues will be familiar with the latter sort of *inter*personal coordination. Of course, as the examples make clear, we are typically in need of both sorts of co-ordination; for we are both temporally extended and social agents. And as we all learn to our chagrin, neither sort of coordination happens effortlessly.

So we need ways for deliberation and rational reflection to influence action beyond the present; and we need sources of support for coordination, both intrapersonal and interpersonal. Our capacities as planners help us meet these needs. We facilitate coordination in part by constructing larger plans for the future, plans that help coordinate both our own activities over time and our activities with the activities of others. And by settling now on a plan for later I enable my present deliberation to influence my later conduct; I thereby extend the influence of my deliberation beyond the present moment.

We do not, of course, promote coordination and extend the influence of deliberation by means of plans that specify, once and for all, everything we are to do in the future. Such total plans are obviously beyond our limits. Rather, we typically settle on plans that are *partial* and then fill them in as need be and as time goes by. This characteristic *incompleteness* of our plans is of the first importance. It creates the need for a kind of reasoning characteristic of planning agents: reasoning that takes initial, partial plans as given and aims at filling them in with specifications of appropriate means, preliminary steps, or just relatively more specific courses of action.

These facts about the roles of such garden-variety plans in our lives are in need of further elaboration and clarification. I will be trying to do just that in the coming pages. But the crucial point for now is that these roles of plans in our lives are central for a theory of intention. In particular, they are central to an account of the nature of intention that avoids a skepticism about future-directed intention into which one is easily led. I proceed to explain.

1.2 Intention

As I have noted, our commonsense psychological scheme admits of intentions as states of mind; and it also allows us to characterize actions as done intentionally, or with a certain intention. A theory of intention must address both kinds of phenomena and explain how they are related. A natural approach, the one I will be taking here, is to begin with the state of intending to act. We try to say what it is to intend to do something. Then we try to explain what it is to do something intentionally, or with a certain intention, in part in terms of the notion of having an intention to do something.

This approach must confront a variety of problems. But its most general problem concerns the very idea of intending to act. Looked at in a certain way, the idea of intending to do something can seem quite puzzling. When we talk of an intention to do something, we frequently have in mind intentions concerning the future. When I am actually pumping the water, for example, it may seem natural to say that I no longer *intend* to pump it, I *am* pumping it.[3] This should not lead us to doubt the existence of present-directed intentions: intentions concerning what to do beginning now. But it should lead us to see the future-directed case as central. If we are going to make sense of the notion of intending to do something, we must make sense of the notion of a future-directed intention. But here is where the trouble starts.

I now intend to take a United flight to Boston tomorrow. It seems that in so intending I do not merely want or desire today to take that flight tomorrow. Rather I am in some sense *committed* today to taking that flight tomorrow.[4] But what could such commitment amount to? Commitment to present action may seem a relatively clear idea: I am committed to acting in those ways in which I am presently trying or endeavoring to act. But what is it to be committed now to some *future* action?

Behaviorist sympathies might lead one to look to present action and to try to see future-directed intention as always embedded in present intentional activity. One might try saying that to intend now to A at some future time, one must now be doing something as a means or as a preliminary step to one's A-ing later. I might now, for example, be on my way to the ticket office in order to get my ticket for tomorrow's flight. On this approach, commitment to future action is always embedded in present action.[5] But this is oversimplified. I might intend now to take the United flight tomorrow while doing nothing now as a means or as a preliminary step to taking that flight then. Perhaps I am just reading a novel. Granted, if I really do intend to go to Boston tomorrow, my present activity will normally conform to certain constraints. I will not knowingly get on a boat to Hawaii. But my present activity will be, as far as I know or believe, compatible with an enormous range of future conduct. Yet only some small part of that range of future conduct is within the scope of what I intend—it is only to some small part of that range of future conduct that I am now committed.

So it seems that my commitment to future action is not merely implicit in my present intentional activity. But then in what, over and above my present intentional activity, does my commitment to future action consist?

When we try to answer this question, we are quickly faced with a puzzling trilemma. My intention today does not reach its ghostly hand over time and control my action tomorrow. Commitment is one thing, action at a distance another. But my intention must *somehow* influence my later action; otherwise why bother today to form an intention about tomorrow? It will be suggested that, once formed, my intention today to take a United flight tomorrow will persist until tomorrow and then guide what will then be present action. But presumably such an intention is not irrevocable between today and tomorrow. Such irrevocability would clearly be irrational; after all, things change and we do not always correctly anticipate the future. But this suggests that tomorrow I should continue to intend to take the United flight only if it would be rational of me then to form such an intention from scratch. But then why should I bother deciding today what to do tomorrow?[6] So it seems that future-directed intentions will be (1) metaphysically objectionable (since they involve action at a distance), or (2) rationally objectionable (since they are irrevocable), or (3) just a waste of time.

Such puzzles lead to suspicion about the very notion of future-directed intention; and this suspicion, once generated, quickly spreads to the general notion of intending to act. After all, as I noted, the central case of intending to act is just that of future-directed intention. If the latter leads us into action at a distance, or a choice between seeing such intentions as either irrevocable or a waste of time, then we should be skeptical about the very idea of intending to act.

This skepticism suggests an alternative approach to intention, one that has, in fact, been a main tradition in recent philosophy of mind and action. I will characterize this approach in terms of four theses. My claim is not that these theses precisely characterize any single philosopher's view (though they do come quite close in a variety of cases). Rather, I think these four theses succeed in describing a certain general approach to intention, one that can naturally be motivated by skepticism about future-directed intention, and one with which it is useful to contrast the approach I will be taking in this book.

The first move is methodological. Instead of beginning with the state of intending to act, we turn immediately to intention as it appears in action: we turn directly to acting intentionally and acting with a certain intention. We adopt

(1) The methodological priority of intention in action.

This is, for example, the strategy followed by Elizabeth Anscombe in her ground-breaking monograph, *Intention*.[7] It is a strategy that is, I think, implicit in Alvin Goldman's book, *A Theory of Human Action*,[8] as well as in Donald Davidson's important series of essays on intention and action.[9] When we follow this strategy we are naturally led to a second idea. This is the idea that what makes it true that an action was performed intentionally, or with a certain intention, are just facts about the relation of that action to what the agent *desires* and what the agent *believes*. For example, what makes it true that I intentionally move the pump is that my so acting is appropriately related to my desire to poison the inhabitants and my belief that I would poison them by moving the pump. And these same facts make it true that I move the pump with the intention of poisoning the inhabitants. Thus we are led to

> (2) The desire-belief theory of intention in action: we understand intentional action, and action done with an intention, in terms of the agent's desires and beliefs, and actions standing in appropriate relations to those desires and beliefs.

According to (2) the underlying structure of our commonsense conception of intention in action involves two basic types of mental states: those that play the role of beliefs, and those that play the role of desires or evaluations. These types of states are to be understood broadly. Belief may be all-or-none or may come in degrees. Desires include a wide range of "pro-attitudes"—wanting, judging desirable, caring about, and so on—and also may admit of degrees. It is standing in an appropriate relation to such states that makes an action intentional, or done with a certain intention.

Here, again, we can cite Anscombe, Goldman,[10] and—in his early work—Davidson as, among others, subscribers to this view. Granted, Davidson and Goldman do differ from Anscombe in their account of just what relation between desires and beliefs, on the one hand, and action, on the other hand, makes for intentional action: Davidson and Goldman insist, while Anscombe emphatically denies, that the appropriate relation is in some significant sense a causal relation. But that difference does not touch the present point, which is that all three at some stage accept a version of (2).[11]

Once we embrace (1) and (2), how should we think about future-directed intention? Here it will be natural, given (1), to suppose that there will be a fairly straightforward extension of the account of intention in action to an account of future-directed intention. The idea here is that once we have an adequate account of acting intentionally and acting with a certain intention we can expect to have available all the main materials needed for a satisfactory treatment of future-directed intention. This is

(3) The strategy of extension.

When we combine (2) and (3), however, we are led to

(4) A reduction of future-directed intention to appropriate desires and beliefs.

A classic statement of such a reductive approach can be found in the work of the nineteenth-century philosopher John Austin, who would have suggested that for me to intend to take the United flight to Boston tomorrow is just for me both to want to get to Boston and to believe that I will take that flight then in order to get there.[12] More recent versions of such a reductive approach are presented by Robert Audi, Monroe Beardsley, Paul Churchland, and Wayne Davis.[13] On these approaches there is no special state or attitude of intending to act; our commonsense characterizations of mind and action need only the two-parameter, desire-belief framework.

Of course, one might accept some elements of this quartet of theses while rejecting others. For example, one might accept (1) but reject (2) because one supposes that we need some special notion of present-directed intention or volition, distinct from ordinary desires and beliefs, to understand intentional action. One might then accept (3), but not be led thereby to (4) given one's rejection of (2). In different ways, this is the sort of view that George Wilson takes in his monograph[14] and Donald Davidson turns to in his later work.[15] The nineteenth-century Austin, for his part, accepted pretty much all of (1)–(4), with the qualification that a present-directed desire to move one's body in a certain way now has a privileged relation to action, a relation because of which it merits the title of *volition*. And Anscombe, whose views are quite close to (1) and (2), does not say enough about future-directed intention for us to be sure about her attitude toward (3) and (4).

Theses (1) and (3) express strategies for research. They lead naturally to (2) and (4) as substantive views about mind and action. Theses (2) and (4) together amount to a *desire-belief model* of intention and intentional action, a dominant view in contemporary philosophy of mind and action. On this model intention *in* action is a matter of the relation of the action to the agent's desires and beliefs, while intention *to* act is to be identified with some desire-belief complex.

I think, however, that we should reject all four of these theses, and so the desire-belief model. The source of the problem is the same in each case. Our understanding of intention is in large part a matter of our understanding of future-directed intention. But, to return to a question raised earlier, Why do we bother forming intentions concerning the future? Why don't we just cross our bridges when we come to them? An adequate answer to this question must return to the central fact that we are planning creatures. We form future-directed intentions as parts of larger plans, plans which play characteristic roles in coordination and ongoing practical reasoning; plans which allow us to extend the influence of present deliberation to the future. Intentions are, so to speak, the building blocks of such plans; and plans are intentions writ large.[16]

If we ignore plans and planning, focus on intentional action, and then try to recognize future-directed intentions that are not embedded in present action, we are likely to see such intentions as having little to do with ongoing rational agency. But this would be a mistake. Such a mistake can even be built into the terminology we employ. For example, in his well-known paper "Intention and Punishment,"[17] H. L. A. Hart writes: "Intention is to be divided into three related parts ... The first I shall call 'intentionally doing something'; the second 'doing something with a further intention,' and the third 'bare intention' because it is the case of intending to do something in the future without doing anything to execute this intention now." This scheme forces us to see most future-directed intentions merely as "bare" intentions. But it is only by ignoring the complex roles of such intentions in larger, coordinating plans that this terminology will seem apt.

The problem with the strategies expressed in (1) and (3) is that they are unlikely to shed much light on the planning dimension of intention. These strategies lead us to focus on intentional action; and such actions may well involve the execution of prior plans. But plans are not merely executed. They are formed, retained, combined, constrained by other plans, filled in, modified, reconsidered, and so on. Such processes and activities are central to our understanding of plans, and so to our understanding of intention. Yet it seems unlikely that the strategies expressed in (1) and (3) will lead us to do justice to these processes and activities.

Seen as natural upshots of (1) and (3), theses (2) and (4) are chickens come home to roost. By following the strategy of beginning with intention in action and then seeking a conservative extension to future-directed intention we can naturally be led to endorse an overly simple, desire-belief psychology. This psychology has no room for a distinctive attitude of intending to act. But, as I will be arguing, we are unlikely to do justice to the central phenomena of plans and planning without recognizing some such distinctive attitude. The problem with (1)–(4) is that they are more appropriate for an understanding of agents who are not also *planning* agents—dogs and cats, perhaps. Yet we see ourselves, and rightly so, as planning agents.

Let us briefly review. We were led to theses (1)–(4) by skeptical worries about the very idea of future-directed intention and its characteristic commitment. Yet (1)–(4) are unlikely to do justice to our conception of ourselves as planning agents. To do justice to this self-understanding, then, we must confront skepticism about future-directed intention head on. And that is what I will be trying to do.

1.3 Intention and Plans

1.3.1 The Planning Theory

My approach to intention is, broadly speaking, within the functionalist tradition in the philosophy of mind.[18] I take it that our commonsense understanding of various types of mental states depends on the supposition of appropriate, underlying regularities within which these states are embedded. These regularities connect these various states with each other, with associated psychological processes and activities, and with characteristic "inputs" and "outputs": perception and action.[19] These regularities may sometimes involve fairly straightforward dispositions to behave in certain ways. Thus, there is a connection between an intention to raise one's arm now and one's actually raising it. But these regularities may also concern dispositions to think or reason (or, indeed, to refrain from reasoning) in characteristic ways. Belief, for example, will involve characteristic tendencies toward inference.

I will be arguing that these last sorts of dispositions and regularities—those concerning reasoning—are critical to our understanding of intention. If we concern ourselves exclusively with dispositions to behave in various ways, we will find ourselves hard put to avoid skepticism about future-directed intention. But such an exclusive focus on behavioral dispositions is a mistake inherited from the behaviorist tradition and need not be embraced by a functionalist philosophy of mind. Avoiding this mistake is a key to understanding intention.

Many of the regularities central to our commonsense psychology involve associated norms or standards. For example, when we recognize that we hold beliefs that are, taken together, jointly inconsistent, we normally have some disposition to change them in the direction of consistency. Associated with this regularity is a norm enjoining consistency of belief. As we will see, a similar point can be made about intention: associated with our tendency to adjust in the direction of jointly consistent intentions is a norm enjoining such consistency. In articulating the web of regularities within which an element of our commonsense framework is embedded we need, in part, to say what these associated norms or standards are.[20]

The way to confront skepticism about intention—in particular, future-directed intention—is to show that intentions can be embedded in such a web of regularities and norms. We demystify intention, and its characteristic commitment, by showing that it can be at least as successfully embedded in such a web as can other commonsense psychological states—especially desire and belief. In this way we show that we have as much reason to talk of an agent's intentions to act as we have to talk of her desires and beliefs. And in this way we can also support the claim that our commonsense framework sees intention as a distinctive attitude, not to be conflated with or reduced to ordinary desires and beliefs. We do this by showing how the nexus of regularities and norms in terms of which we understand intention differs in systematic and important ways from those in terms of which we understand desire and belief.

The regularities and norms that are characteristic of intention essentially include those which are characteristic of the roles of partial plans in the ongoing practical reasoning and action of limited rational agents like us. So my defense of intention as a distinctive attitude goes hand in hand with an analysis of what is involved in being limited, planning agents. In particular, it will involve an account of the structure of the practical reasoning characteristic of such planning agents, namely: reasoning aimed at adjusting and completing prior but partial plans. And it will involve an account of the norms of rationality that are appropriate for agents for whom such planning plays a central role. In focusing on such planning concerning future action we abandon the methodological priority given to intentional action by the strategies sketched in (1) and (3). Thus we not only reject the substantive conclusions of (2) and (4)—the desire-belief model—but we also reject the methodological assumptions that lie behind them. This is the *planning theory* of intention.

Such a planning theory brings together two issues. First, there is the problem of how to avoid skepticism about intention. Second, there is the problem of understanding what practical rationality consists in for agents who, like us, have limited resources for use in attending to problems, deliberating about options, determining likely consequences, performing relevant calculations, and so on. This is the problem of understanding what Herbert Simon calls "bounded rationality."[21] We solve the first problem in large part by reflecting on the roles of intentions and partial plans in the ongoing practical reasoning and planning of limited rational agents. So reflection on Simon's problem is a key to solving our problem about intention; and a solution to our problem about intention will also be a contribution to the theory of bounded rationality.[22]

1.3.2 The Importance of Buridan

This planning approach to intention returns us to the two main grounds for being planning agents at all: our resource limitations and our needs for coordination, both social and intrapersonal. It will be useful at this point to stop and ask just how these two grounds are related.

It is clear that our need for plans to support coordination is at least in part attributable to our resource limitations: we cannot strive for coordination by determining at each moment what it is best for us to do given our up-to-date assessment of what others are likely to think is best for them to do (given their up-to-date assessment of what we are likely to think is best to do . . .). But does our need for coordination also introduce independent pressures for being planning agents?

I think it does. My reason for this derives from consideration of the sort of case famously attributed to Jean Buridan. Buridan seems to have worried that a rational ass placed midway between two equally attractive piles of hay would starve, for he would have no reason to go left rather than right, and he would have no reason to go right rather than left. Of course, he would have overwhelming reason to go either left or right; but that is a different matter.

Let us call such cases of forced choice between options that seem to the agent equally desirable *Buridan cases*. Following Edna Ullmann-Margalit and Sidney Morgenbesser[23] I suspect such Buridan cases are common in the lives of rational agents like us. Just consider choosing one of the many boxes of Cheerios from the supermarket shelves,[24] or one of two equally attractive routes to San Francisco. I conjecture that we have an ability that is basic at the level of commonsense psychology: an ability to decide in the face of equidesirability. Which box of Cheerios I choose may not be explainable by my other desires, beliefs, and intentions; though it will, presumably, be explainable at some other—perhaps, neurophysiological—level.

This has implications for coordination. If I want to coordinate with you, I need to know not just the desires and beliefs in light of which certain alternatives are seen by you as equally desirable; I also need to know your intentions. And a similar point can be made about my efforts to coordinate my own activities over time. My conjecture, then, is that the need for decision in the face of equidesirability, when tied to our needs for coordination, provides independent pressure for being a planning agent, pressure that would exist even if we were not subject to the resource limitations I have been emphasizing.[25]

1.3.3 Ordinary Intentions

I turn now to another point about the planning theory of intention. In developing such a theory we focus on ordinary, humdrum cases in which future-directed intentions and partial plans lead without great difficulty from prior deliberation to later conduct. Such cases contrast with certain special kinds of cases in which we form intentions concerning the future as a way of responding to complex issues about self-control. I might know that tonight I will be sorely tempted to drink too much, or to gamble too much, and so this morning resolve not to. In such cases we might be struck by the impotence of such resolves in the face of later temptation. This might lead us to emphasize the need for external sources of what Jon Elster calls "precommitment," for example: locking up the liquor cabinet or making a side bet with someone else that one will not gamble later on.[26]

Such examples are quite fascinating. But I think we get a distorted view of future-directed intention if we take them as paradigmatic of intention. It is best, I think, to begin with ordinary, garden-variety cases in which, without major psychological resistance, future-directed intentions and partial plans support coordination in the lives of limited agents like us. It is here that we need to look to get at the major regularities, roles, and norms in terms of which we can understand intention and its associated commitment.

1.4 Coming Attractions

I will proceed as follows. In Chapters 2–7 I try to make good on the promise made here, namely, to locate intention to act and its characteristic commitment in the web of regularities and norms associated with our nature as limited, planning agents. Many of these regularities and norms are associated with the roles of partial plans as inputs into further practical reasoning. An exploration of these roles leads me to distinguish several different kinds of judgment of practical rationality and to develop a historical theory of "agent rationality," one that tries to take seriously the roles of partial plans in the lives of limited agents like us.

In Chapter 8 I return to intention in action. I explore the consequences of my planning approach for our understanding of intentional action and its relation to the state of intending to act. This relation turns out to be more complex than many have thought. Its examination sheds light on different ways in which our interests in prediction and explanation, on the one hand, and in the ascription of responsibility, on the other hand, shape our commonsense psychological framework. I argue that it is important to recognize these differences, for otherwise the very idea of intention as a distinctive attitude will be in jeopardy.

In Chapter 9 I extend my approach to the phenomenon of acting with an intention. This leads me to a discussion of what, following Roderick Chisholm,[27] I call *endeavoring*. In a normal case in which an agent like us acts intentionally there will be something he is endeavoring to do and something he intends to do. Our actions normally involve a standard triad of intention, endeavoring, and intentional action. There will sometimes be divergence, however, between what one does intentionally, what one endeavors to do, and what one intends to do; and I try to discern the reasons for these possibilities of divergence. I argue that in some cases the possibility of such divergence is grounded in the appropriateness of different strategies for dealing with practical conflict.

Finally I turn, in Chapter 10, to the idea that there is an important distinction to be made between intending to bring about some effect and merely expecting to bring it about as a result of something else one intends. This distinction is, of course, crucial to the principle of double effect—the view that it can sometimes be morally permissible knowingly to cause (or allow) a harm it would not have been permissible to have caused (or allowed) in executing an intention to cause (or allow) it. Reflection on this distinction, and the criticisms it naturally elicits, leads to a better understanding of the ways in which intentions function as outputs of practical reasoning.

This book raises more questions than it answers. At most it is an incomplete first step toward an approach to intention and action that takes plans and our limits seriously, an approach that differs significantly from standard accounts in terms of a desire-belief psychology. I confess to being more confident about the main outlines of this approach than I am about the details I have been able to provide. But progress requires an attempt to provide such details, with all its risks. So that is what I have done.

chapter 2

On the Way to the Planning Theory

IN THIS chapter I note two aspects of the desire-belief model, describe several features of intention that will be central to later discussion, argue for the need to take intentions seriously as distinctive states of mind, and describe certain problems that will shape later discussion.

2.1 Two Aspects of the Desire-Belief Model

It will be useful to begin by saying more about the desire-belief model. On this view what makes an action intentional, or done with a certain intention, is the fact that it stands in an appropriate relation to the agent's relevant desires and beliefs. The relation in question is typically taken to be explanatory in some way. Suppose, for example, that Eve intentionally turns on the air conditioner. This action is intentional because it is explained, at least in part, by the fact that Eve wants to cool off and believes in the efficacy of air conditioners. Such an explanation of Eve's action has an important feature, one that distinguishes it from an explanation of Eve's sweating by an appeal to the fact that she is hot. What is special about the former explanation is that Eve's desire and belief explain her action in part because they provide Eve with a *reason* so to act. In seeking such an explanation of Eve's intentional conduct we are trying to see that conduct as at least to some extent evidencing Eve's rationality; we are trying to see Eve and her action as at least to some extent rational.

In developing a model of intention and action we are quickly led into questions about practical rationality: What makes actions rational? What makes it rational of agents to act as they do? These questions are normative in nature: they are queries about how an agent ought, rationally speaking, to act. As commonly understood, the desire-belief model goes on to provide a powerful and plausible approach to such questions of practical rationality. The main idea is that the agent's desires and beliefs at a certain time provide her with reasons for acting in various ways at that time. What practical rationality requires is that her intentional action be at least as strongly supported by these desire-belief reasons as any of its supposed alternatives. On this view, then, the rationality of intentional action is primarily a function of the agent's desire-belief reasons for action: only these desire-belief reasons have *direct relevance* to the rationality of action; other considerations bear on the rationality of conduct only *in*directly, by way of their impact on the agent's desires and beliefs.

To change examples: My desire to get a copy of *Actions and Events,* together with my belief that I can do this by going to Tanner Library, provides me with a reason for going there. And my desire to watch the Giants on television, together with my belief that I can do this only by staying home, provides me with a reason for not going to Tanner. On the desire-belief approach just sketched my intentionally going to Tanner is rational only if it is supported by the balance of such reasons.

So the desire-belief model, as I will be understanding it here, has both descriptive and normative aspects. It attempts to capture the basic structure of the conception of mind implicit in our commonsense understanding of intention and action. And it also attempts to articulate an associated, normative conception of practical rationality.

2.2 Intention and Commitment

Return now to commitment. Intention, I have said, involves a characteristic kind of commitment. A full characterization of the commitment involved in intention is one of the main jobs of a theory of intention. Here I will provide just an initial characterization.

The first step is to distinguish two dimensions of commitment. The first concerns the relation between intention and action, and I will call it the *volitional* dimension of commitment (or, for short, volitional commitment). To explain what I have in mind here I need to introduce some terminology. Both intentions and desires are, but ordinary beliefs are not, *pro-attitudes*. Pro-attitudes in this very general sense play a motivational role: in concert with our beliefs they can move us to act. Thus, both a desire to go to Tanner Library and an intention to go could, in concert with a belief that a certain bus will take me there, lead to my taking that bus.

But we may go on to distinguish between two kinds of pro-attitudes. To change examples, suppose I desire a milk shake for lunch, recognize that the occasion is here, and am guilty of no irrationality. Still, I might not drink a milk shake; for my desire for a milk shake still needs to be weighed against conflicting desires—say, my desire to lose weight. My desire for a milk shake potentially influences what I do at lunchtime. But in the normal course of events I still might not even try to drink a milk shake.

In contrast, suppose that this morning I formed the intention to have a milk shake at lunch, lunchtime arrives, my intention remains, and nothing unexpected happens. In such a case I do not normally need yet again to tote up the pros and cons concerning milk-shake drinking. Rather, in the normal course of events I will simply proceed to execute (or, anyway, try to execute) my intention and order a milk shake. My intention will not merely influence my conduct, it will control it.

This example illustrates an important difference in the normal functioning of desires and intentions concerning what to do in present circumstances. Intentions are, whereas ordinary desires are not, conduct-*controlling* pro-attitudes. Ordinary desires, in contrast, are merely *potential influencers* of action. The volitional dimension of the commitment involved in future-directed intention derives from the fact that intentions are conduct controllers. If my future-directed intention manages to survive until the time of action, and I see that that time has arrived and nothing interferes, it will control my action then. As a conduct-controlling pro-attitude my intention involves a special commitment to action that ordinary desires do not.

Turn now to the second dimension of the commitment characteristic of future-directed intention. Here what are crucial are the roles future-directed intentions play in the period between their initial formation and their eventual execution. For reasons that will become apparent I will say that these roles constitute the *reasoning-centered* dimension of commitment, or simply, for short, reasoning-centered commitment.

There are two main facts here. The first is signaled by talk of being *settled* on a certain course of action. If I now intend to go to Tanner later today, I normally will not continue to deliberate about whether to go. I will normally see (or, anyway, be disposed to see) the question of whether to go as settled and continue so to intend until the time of action. My intention resists reconsideration: it has a characteristic *stability* or *inertia.*

Of course, given new information, or a change in what I want, I may well reopen the question and reconsider. As Austin emphasized, "Every intention . . . which regards the future, is ambulatory or revocable."[1] But revocability does not entail actual reconsideration. Lacking new considerations I will normally simply retain my intention up to the time of action. Retention of my prior intention and nonreconsideration is, so to speak, the "default option."

The second fact concerns the role my intention normally plays in my further reasoning between now and the time for going to Tanner. I will frequently reason from such a prior intention to *further* intentions. I will frequently reason from intended end to intended means or preliminary steps: as when I reason from my intention to go to Tanner to intentions concerning how to get there. And I will frequently reason from more general to more specific intentions: as when I reason from an intention to take a bus to Tanner, and my reflections on the bus schedule, to an intention to take a particular bus. Further, my prior intention to go to Tanner this afternoon will constrain the other intentions I form for the day, since I will seek to make my intentions consistent with one another and with my beliefs.

My intention to go to Tanner this afternoon involves, then, certain characteristic dispositions concerning my reasoning between now and this afternoon: a disposition to retain this intention without reconsideration, and a disposition to reason from this retained intention to yet further intentions, and to constrain other intentions in light of this intention. These dispositions partly constitute the reasoning-centered dimension of the commitment characteristic of future-directed intentions.

So there are two dimensions to the commitment characteristic of future-directed intention: volitional and reasoning-centered. Of course, these two dimensions of commitment are closely related. When I decide this morning to go to the basketball game tonight, my intention will play its volitional role only if it first plays its role in reasoning: I must retain this intention, go on to figure out how to get tickets and get to the game, and also be careful not to schedule incompatible activities. And it is because of its ultimate volitional role that the inertia of intention, and its role in further means-end reasoning, is so important to us. Thus the dispositions behind both kinds of commitment are more or less directly tied to action. But this should not lead us to ignore the fact that some of these dispositions are, in the first instance, dispositions concerning reasoning.

A related and important point is that the combination of both dimensions of commitment involves a kind of synergy: taken together these two dimensions of commitment help explain how intentions play their characteristic role in supporting coordination, both intrapersonal and social. Both the inertia of intention and the fact that it is a conduct-*controlling* pro-attitude provide support for the expectation that when the time for action comes, an agent will at least try to do what she intends to do.

Further, the dispositions to figure out how to do what one intends, and to settle on needed preliminary steps, provide support for the expectation that an agent will both be in a position to do what she intends and succeed in doing it. And it is such expectations as these that are central to coordination—both interpersonal and intrapersonal. Because my intention to go to Tanner supports your expectation that I will be there, you can go ahead and plan to meet me there. And because it also supports my expectation that I will be there, I can go ahead and plan the rest of my day on the assumption that I will be there. For example, I can plan on reading a book tonight that I can only get at Tanner. So both dimensions of commitment help explain why an intention to *A* normally supports a belief that the agent will *A*. And this belief helps facilitate coordination.[2]

2.3 The Initial Challenge to the Desire-Belief Model

These characterizations of volitional and reasoning-centered commitment are, so far, only partial. We have focused on the underlying regularities and dispositions associated with each dimension of commitment. We have not yet explored the implications of these phenomena for our normative conception of practical rationality. But even at this stage there is a challenge to the descriptive aspect of the desire-belief model; for it seems doubtful that these complex phenomena can be adequately described while staying strictly within the desire-belief framework.

At issue here is thesis (4), the reduction of future-directed intention to appropriate desires and beliefs. A natural first step in the direction of such a reduction might go by way of the notion of a predominant desire. I have a predominant desire to *A* if I desire to *A* strictly more than I desire to perform any option thought by me to be incompatible with my *A*-ing. But it seems clear that my intention, say, to go to Tanner, cannot be identified just with such a predominant desire; for such a predominant desire does not ensure either volitional or reasoning-centered commitment.

Consider reasoning-centered commitment. A crucial point here is that even if I now have a predominant desire to go to Tanner—and so prefer to go there—I still might not see the issue as *settled*: I might be disposed to continue to give serious consideration to the possibility of taking the afternoon off and going to a concert. But if I were to intend to go to Tanner, I would be disposed not to continue to deliberate in this way: this is what is involved in the resistance to reconsideration characteristic of intention. For similar reasons my predominant desire does not ensure that I have an appropriate disposition to reason about means to going to Tanner. After all, if I am still deliberating about whether or not to go to Tanner, I may well have as yet no disposition at all to reason about means to going.

Turning to volitional commitment, there is an analogous problem with the reduction of intention to predominant desire. An intention to *A* is a conduct-controlling pro-attitude. But my predominant desire to go to Tanner at noon does not guarantee that when I see that it is noon my desire will control my conduct. I might still be disposed to deliberate about what to do; for I might still not see the issue as settled.[3]

A final point is that if intention is seen as reducible to such a predominant desire, we will misdescribe the role of a prior intention in constraining other intentions, given the search for consistency. In requiring that I desire to go more than I desire to perform actions thought incompatible with going, the account makes it impossible to intend to perform actions thought incompatible. But while it is, other things equal, criticizably irrational to have such conflicting intentions,[4] it does seem possible to be guilty of such irrationality. And we want our theory to allow for this possibility.

Can these objections be overcome by the addition of further conditions? A natural proposal is that to intend to go to Tanner is not only to have a predominant desire to go, but also to believe that one will go because of this desire to go.[5] One worry here—one I will be discussing further in Chapter 3—is that it is too much to require that an intention to *A* involve a belief that one will. A second worry is that the addition of this other condition by itself does nothing to block the objection, already mooted, that we have made conflicting intentions impossible, rather than merely irrational. But here I want briefly to consider a different aspect of the question of whether such an account captures the commitment characteristic of intention.

Does the addition of the further belief condition guarantee that I see the issue of whether to go to Tanner as settled in the relevant sense—a sense that precludes a disposition for continued deliberation about whether to go? Suppose that I presently have a predominant desire to go to Tanner and (knowing my own work habits) expect that as a result of this desire I will go to Tanner. Could I nevertheless continue to be disposed to deliberate about whether to take the afternoon off? Suppose that I suspect that my predominant desire to go to Tanner is a result of my workaholic tendencies and want to reflect further on the matter. When I step back and try to make a prediction about what I will do, I continue to expect that I will end up going to Tanner. Still, I am suspicious of my motivation and want to think about it some more. Am I settled on going to Tanner, in the sense of being settled that is involved in reasoning-centered commitment? I am inclined to say no.

Another case. Suppose I have a fleeting craving for a chocolate bar, one which induces a fleetingly predominant desire to eat one for dessert. And suppose that just as fleetingly I notice this desire and judge (in a spirit of resignation, perhaps) that it will lead me so to act. But then I stop and reflect, recall my dieting plans, and resolve to skip dessert. On the present desire-belief account I had a fleeting intention to have a chocolate dessert. But I am inclined to say I had no such intention, for I was never appropriately settled in favor of such a dessert.

Such objections are not conclusive; nor do they do justice to all attempts to defend reductions along the lines I have sketched. But I do think such objections are plausible. And they help raise the basic question of why we should seek such a reduction in the first place. Presumably such a reductive approach to intention should be judged by its theoretical fecundity. But I believe that in the end such attempts at reduction do not promise to tell us a great deal about how intentions function in the lives of rational agents like us. I think we gain more insight into the kinds of agents we are by putting aside such attempts at reduction and taking seriously the idea that intentions are distinctive states of mind, on a par with desires and beliefs. Intentions are conduct-controlling pro-attitudes, ones which we are disposed to retain without reconsideration, and which play a significant role as inputs into reasoning to yet further intentions. I propose to consider this network of dispositions and functional roles on its own terms, without trying somehow to reduce it to ordinary desires and beliefs. In the end the main argument for this richer conception of mind and action lies in its theoretical usefulness: the proof of the pudding is in the eating. The main burden of much of this book is to demonstrate the theoretical fecundity of this more complex conception of mind and intelligent agency.

2.4 The Modest Extension of the Desire-Belief Model

Having departed this much from the desire-belief model, we are faced with a further issue, an issue about practical rationality. The issue arises because, as we have seen, the desire-belief model has both descriptive and normative aspects. In granting intentions status as distinctive attitudes, we reject as inadequate the descriptive aspect of the desire-belief model. But we do not yet reject its normative aspect: the powerful and extremely plausible conception of practical rationality as, roughly, a function of desire-belief reasons for action. Should our rejection of the descriptive aspect of the desire-belief model bring with it a rejection of its conception of practical rationality as well?

At this point a desire-belief theorist may be attracted to a conservative strategy. This is to grant intentions status as distinctive states of mind and yet hold onto the desire-belief conception of practical rationality. On this strategy one insists that, unlike desires and beliefs, an agent's intentions do *not* have direct relevance to the rationality of her actions. Intentions are distinctive states of mind, states that play distinctive causal roles in the connection between deliberation and action. These causal roles include those described in our discussion of the volitional and reasoning-centered dimensions of commitment. But in playing these roles intentions do not provide considerations that are directly relevant to the rationality of the actions in which they issue.

Of course, it can still be granted that intentions (like anything else) can be *indirectly* relevant to what it is rational to do. We may distinguish three ways in which this might happen. First, intentions may have indirect *practical* relevance. This would happen if the agent's desires concerned the realization of earlier intentions. For example, she might just desire to stick to her guns or to improve her reputation for steadfastness. Second, intentions may have an indirect *epistemic* relevance. The agent might see her prior intention to A as evidence that she will A, and so take her A-ing for granted (or, anyway, assign it a high probability) in her further reasoning. Third, intentions may have an indirect *second-order* relevance. The agent might see her prior intention to A as evidence that A-ing is in fact favored by the balance of her present desire-belief reasons; or as evidence that the costs of reconsidering that intention would not be worth it, from the standpoint of her present desires and beliefs. In all such cases, however, the view in question insists that the relevance of a prior intention to the rationality of action is at most *in*direct: it goes by way of the agent's desires and beliefs.

I call such a view a *modest extension* of the desire-belief model; for it retains that model's conception of practical rationality, even while rejecting the underlying psychology. While modifying the descriptive aspect of the model, it retains its normative aspect. I am going to argue, however, that this is an unstable compromise. Once we take seriously the roles of intentions as inputs to reasoning to yet further intentions, we are, I think, forced to complicate our normative account of practical rationality as well. But before explaining why, let me note a limitation of the present discussion.

There are various more traditional ways in which philosophers have challenged the idea that it is the agent's desires and beliefs that provide considerations that are directly relevant to the rationality of her actions.

For example, one might argue that only desires that would remain after full rational reflection on available information provide such direct considerations.[6] Or one might urge, in an Aristotelian spirit, that only facts about what things are part of or a means to an objectively good human life can provide such direct considerations. These challenges, and others in a similar spirit, are deep and important. But I shall put them to one side here; for they do not address the particular problems about practical rationality that I think are raised by taking intentions seriously. Even a person of Aristotelian practical wisdom, with only fully rational desires, will—if she is like us—form future-directed intentions of a sort that will raise the problem I want to focus on, a problem that challenges the modest extension of the desire-belief model.

So let me say what I think this problem is. Intentions, we are now supposing, are states of mind on a par with desires and beliefs. We have indentified three kinds of dispositions associated with such states. They are conduct-controlling—and not merely potentially conduct-influencing—pro-attitudes; they resist reconsideration, and so have a characteristic inertia; and they play characteristic roles as inputs into further practical reasoning to yet further intentions. In each case we could ask about the impact on our normative conception of practical rationality; and I will have a great deal to say later about such matters. But for now let me focus only on this third type of disposition: the disposition to enter as an input into further practical reasoning.

Consider my intention in January to go to Boston in April. Having formed this intention I might go on to reason from it to a more specific intention (for example, to go during the first week of April) or to a further intention concerning means (for example, to take a United flight) or to a further intention concerning preliminary steps (for example, to ask Jean to cover my teaching responsibilities). For simplicity let us focus on the case in which I reason to an intention concerning means. In such reasoning I begin with my intention to go to Boston and deliberate about how. I treat my intention to go to Boston as *directly* relevant to the rationality of the further intention concerning means that I reach in such reasoning. I see it, for example, as directly relevant to the rationality of my decision to take a certain United flight. And when I actually take the United flight, I see the fact that so acting is a means to what I intend (going to Boston) as directly relevant to its rationality. I see my prior intention to go to Boston as directly relevant to the rationality of both my later intention to take the United flight and my eventual action of taking that flight. But this understanding of the role of my prior intention is in conflict with the view that only desire-belief reasons could have such direct relevance.

The problem is particularly clear in Buridan cases, cases in which I arbitrarily form an intention in favor of one of several incompatible but (so far as I can see) equally desirable options. My desire-belief reasons in favor of taking route 101 to San Francisco may seem on reflection equal in weight to those in favor of route 280. Still I must decide. As it happens, I decide—albeit arbitrarily—in favor of 101.[7] Now I must figure out how to get there: I reason from my intention to take 101 to an intention to turn right at Page Mill Road. In this means-end reasoning I treat my prior intention to take route 101 as directly relevant to the rationality of my derivative intention to turn right at Page Mill. That is why I see my intention to turn right as rational and an intention to turn left (toward route 280) as irrational, whereas before I formed the intention to take route 101 this was not so. Having decided to take 101 I think that I ought to turn right at Page Mill; but before I decided to take 101 I did not think this. But my thought that my prior intention to take 101 is directly relevant to the rationality of my turning right is in conflict with the desire-belief conception of practical rationality.

There is, then, a serious tension between an agent's commonsense understanding of such means-end reasoning and this desire-belief conception. To the extent that we take this commonsense understanding seriously we should find the desire-belief approach problematic.

Here is another way of looking at the problem. Associated with the desire-belief conception of practical rationality is a model of practical reasoning as the weighing of desire-belief reasons for and against various options. And such weighing is doubtless one common form of practical reasoning. But once we take intentions seriously as distinctive attitudes, we must also come to terms with reasoning concerning means to intended ends.[8] In such reasoning we treat our prior intention as having a sort of direct relevance to the rationality of further intention and action that is, on the desire-belief approach, reserved to desire-belief reasons. We need a satisfactory theoretical account of how these two kinds of reasoning are related. Barring a successful demonstration that we are just confused in seeing prior intentions in this way, the search for such an overall account forces us to go beyond the modest extension of the desire-belief model.

2.5 The Intention-Based-Reasons View

How then are we to understand the way in which prior intentions provide considerations that are directly relevant to the rationality of derivative intentions and actions? One approach is just to build on the reasons-for-action structure provided by the desire-belief model, but to supplement its account of reasons for action with *intention-based reasons*. The idea is that not only do our desires and beliefs give us reasons for action; so also do our intentions (together with our beliefs). Just as there are desire-belief reasons for action, there are also intention-based reasons for action. Intentions are not only distinctive states of mind; they also provide reasons for action, reasons over and above ordinary desire-belief reasons. It is by providing these reasons for action that intentions provide considerations that are directly relevant to the rationality of the conclusions of means-end reasoning.[9]

For example, my intention to go to Boston provides a reason to take the United flight, a reason over and above my relevant desire-belief reasons. It is this reason that I recognize when I treat my prior intention as directly relevant to the rationality of an intention to take that flight. Again, in our Buridan case my intention to take route 101 gives me a reason in favor of turning right at Page Mill, a reason over and above my desire-belief reasons. And it is this reason I recognize when I see my prior intention as having direct relevance to the rationality of my turning right there.

Seeing intentions as reason-giving in this way would help explain how intentions could be directly relevant to the rationality of derivative intentions and actions. But as stated this view seems to me doubly flawed. The role it provides for prior intentions as inputs into further practical reasoning is in one way too weak, and yet in another way too strong.

First, it is too weak because it treats my intention to go to Boston as just one reason among many—including many desire-belief reasons—that weigh for and against taking the United flight. But when I reason from intended end to means I do not see my intended end in this way. Rather, I take this end as fixed (in a sense that needs to be made clear) for the purposes of my deliberation, and proceed to try to figure out how to achieve it. Of course, difficulties in discovering acceptable means may force me to give up or, anyway, reconsider my intended end. But unless and until I do give up or reconsider my prior intention, its role in my means-end reasoning will be to set an end for that reasoning and not just to provide one reason among many. As Alan Donagan once put it, to see my intention as providing just one reason among many is to fail to recognize the peremptoriness of reasoning-centered commitment.[10]

Second, the intention-based-reasons view is too strong; for it leads us to sanction unacceptable forms of bootstrapping. To see why, let me introduce an example I will be using quite a bit in the discussions to follow: the example of Walter Mondale before the second Presidential Debate with Ronald Reagan. Let us suppose that prior to the debate Mondale considers whether to attack Reagan's "Star Wars" plan. Mondale realizes there are serious political risks involved in such an attack. Indeed, let us suppose (what is probably contrary to fact) that Mondale should have seen that in light of his information it would be better to focus on Middle East policy instead; focusing on this different issue is better supported by Mondale's desire-belief reasons than is attacking Star Wars. But Mondale is so annoyed about Star Wars, and so susceptible to wishful thinking, that he gives in to temptation and irrationally decides to attack that plan in the debate. Mondale, however, leaves open which of three different questions to use to pursue this issue, waiting to see just how Reagan will act.

Now comes the debate. Mondale still intends to attack Star Wars and, after listening to Reagan, decides in favor of his third question. What are we to say about the rationality of this decision and the ensuing act of asking that third question? Asking the third question is, Mondale knows, a means to attacking the Star Wars program; and so it is supported by Mondale's various desire-belief reasons in favor of attacking that plan. But we may suppose that Mondale still has strong desire-belief reasons in favor of pursuing issues about Middle East policies, and so in favor of asking a different question. And these desire-belief reasons are stronger than those in support of attacking Star Wars. May we then conclude that just as the original decision to attack Star Wars was irrational, given Mondale's reasons for action, so is his later decision concerning means?

Surprisingly, the defender of the intention-based-reasons view may not reach this conclusion. When Mondale comes to decide about means, his situation has changed in a crucial respect from his situation prior to the debate when he reached his initial decision: Mondale now has the intention to attack Star Wars. On the intention-based-reasons view this intention—together with Mondale's means-end beliefs—gives Mondale yet a further reason for asking his third question, a reason over and above his various desire-belief reasons for so acting. So even if the balance of Mondale's desire-belief reasons presently favors asking a different question, once we "add in" his intention to attack Star Wars, the balance of *all* of Mondale's reasons for action may well favor his asking his third question. This means that Mondale's irrational earlier decision to attack Star Wars can bootstrap his later decision to ask his third question into a decision that is rational, all considered. But this seems to let his decision about means (and the ensuing intentional action) too easily off the hook of criticizable irrationality.

One way to appreciate the oddity of such bootstrapping is to note that if Mondale had, prior to the debate, decided *all at once* to attack Star Wars by asking his third question, this entire decision would have been, on balance, irrational. Yet, on the present view, by proceeding in two steps Mondale can make his later decision about means rational, all considered. And this seems odd.

We must, however, be careful here; for even the modest extension of the desire-belief model will support a kind of bootstrapping. This is because reconsidering and changing a prior intention typically has costs of its own. In certain circumstances these costs are obviously significant; and in the heat of the debate Mondale well knows that he is in such circumstances. In such debates time is quite limited, and audiences tend to interpret hesitation as a sign of weakness. Once in the debate Mondale already intends to attack Star Wars. For him to take a different tack he would have to reconsider and change that intention. And this itself might have—and be known by Mondale to have—nontrivial costs. So Mondale might have corresponding desire-belief reasons against reconsidering that intention. And these reasons might make it rational, relative just to Mondale's desire-belief reasons, for him to ask the third question.

In contrast, if prior to the debate Mondale had decided all at once to attack Star Wars by asking his third question, such desire-belief reasons against reconsideration would not have been available to support the decision to ask the third question. So even on a desire-belief conception of practical rationality we might get a kind of bootstrapping. By reaching his decision in two steps, Mondale might bring it about that his second decision—concerning means—is rational, all considered. And this might be so even if, had he decided prior to the debate and all at once to attack Star Wars by asking his third question, his total decision would not have been rational, all considered.

It is important to see, however, that the intention-based-reasons account justifies yet a *further* kind of bootstrapping. On this account Mondale's intention to attack Star Wars might bootstrap into rationality his intention to ask his third question, even if the latter intention fails to be rational relative to his desire-belief reasons, including those that reflect the expected costs of reconsideration and change of mind. On the intention-based-reasons view Mondale's decision to ask his third question and his intentional action of asking that question may be bootstrapped into rationality by an intention it was irrational to form. And this may happen even though this decision and action would not be desire-belief rational, even taking into account the costs of reconsideration. And this seems too easily to let this decision and action off the hook of criticizable irrationality.[11]

The desire-belief conception of practical rationality avoids sanctioning such unacceptable bootstrapping. But it fails to do justice to means-end reasoning and other kinds of practical reasoning in which one's prior intentions provide crucial inputs. The intention-based-reasons view attempts to take seriously the way an agent sees his prior intentions as directly relevant to the conclusions of his further practical reasoning. But this view itself faces two difficulties: it mistakenly sees a prior intention as providing just another reason among many, and it leads us into problems about bootstrapping. We need a view of intention that escapes both these objections to the intention-based-reasons view, and yet still goes beyond the modest extension of the desire-belief model in its account of the normative role of intentions in reasoning and action.

2.6 A Look Ahead

Let us take stock. We have isolated three central facts about intentions: they are conduct-controlling pro-attitudes, they have inertia, and they serve as inputs into further practical reasoning. These facts were a source for the challenge to the descriptive aspect of the desire-belief model. This challenge led us to see intentions as distinctive states of mind, on a par with ordinary desires and beliefs. We then turned to the normative aspect of the desire-belief theory. There I have argued that the role of intentions as inputs into further practical reasoning exerts pressure for a change in our normative conception of practical rationality. My conclusion was that the desire-belief conception of practical rationality could not stand unchanged. Yet it turned out not to be obvious how to change it. The most direct form of change—the introduction of intention-based reasons—led to significant problems of its own: especially problems about unacceptable bootstrapping.

We may cast these last problems in terms of the notion of commitment. Future-directed intention involves a characteristic commitment to later conduct. It is natural to interpret this to mean at least that the agent who intends now to *A* later thereby has a reason both for means to *A*-ing and for *A*-ing itself, a reason he would not have if he did not so intend. And it is natural to suppose that it is such a reason that one recognizes when one reasons from a prior intention to an intention concerning means. But we have seen that this approach to commitment is problematic.

In the next five chapters I will try to develop a framework within which we can solve this cluster of problems about intention, practical reasoning, practical rationality, and commitment. Much will depend on the basic idea, noted in Chapter 1, that intentions are typically elements in the larger, partial plans characteristic of limited agents like us. So I will begin by returning to this idea and providing some important detail.

chapter 3

Plans and Practical Reasoning

3.1 Plans

I have emphasized the fact that our intentions concerning our future actions are typically elements in larger plans, plans which facilitate co-ordination both socially and within our own lives, plans which help enable prior deliberation to shape later conduct. In the search for co-ordination and effective action we simply are not capable of constantly redetermining, without inordinate costs, what would be the best thing to do in the present, given an updated assessment of the likelihoods of our own and others' future actions. We are not frictionless deliberators. Rather, we settle in advance on prior, partial plans and tend to reconsider them only when faced with a problem. The ability to settle in advance on such plans enables us to achieve complex goals we would not otherwise be able to achieve. This ability to settle on coordinating plans is a kind of universal means: it is of significant use in the pursuit of goals of very different sorts. One of the legacies of the behaviorist tradition in the philosophy of mind is that contemporary theories of action—with some exceptions[1]—have tended to ignore the roles of such plans as inputs into further practical reasoning. But this has been a mistake.

Before proceeding I need to clarify what I have in mind when I talk about plans. The first distinction that needs to be made is between plans as abstract structures and plans as mental states. When I speak here of plans, I have in mind a certain kind of mental state, not merely an abstract structure of a sort that can be represented, say, by some game-theoretical notation. A more colloquial usage might reserve 'plan' for the notion of an abstract structure and 'having a plan' for the notion of a mental state. But this is frequently stylistically awkward. In any case, even after saying this there remains room for misunderstanding; for there are two significantly different cases of having a plan. On the one hand, I might have only a kind of recipe; that is, I might know a procedure for achieving a certain end. In this sense I can have a plan for roasting lamb whether or not I actually intend to roast lamb. On the other hand, for me to have a plan to roast lamb requires that I plan to roast it. It is the second kind of case that I intend when I speak of plans. Plans, as I shall understand them, are mental states involving an appropriate sort of commitment to action: I have a plan to A only if it is true of me that I plan to A.

Plans, so understood, are intentions writ large. They share the properties of intentions recently noted: they resist reconsideration, and in that sense have inertia; they are conduct controllers, not merely potential conduct influencers; and they provide crucial inputs for further practical reasoning and planning. But because of their increased complexity (as compared with relatively simple intentions) plans reveal other properties that are crucial to an understanding of reasoning-centered commitment. In particular, the plans characteristic of limited agents like us typically have two important features.

First, our plans are typically *partial*. Suppose I decide this morning to go to a concert tonight. I do not settle all at once on a complete plan for the evening. Rather, I decide now to go to a concert, and leave till later deliberation about which concert to go to, how to get tickets, how to get to the concert in ways consistent with my other plans, and what to do during intermission. Later, as time goes by, I fill in my plan with specifications of means, preliminary steps, and more specific courses of action. Of course I am aware when I first decide to go to a concert that my plan is importantly incomplete. But I know that for now only a partial plan is needed; I can fill it in later as required.[2]

Second, our plans typically have a *hierarchical structure*. Plans concerning ends embed plans concerning means and preliminary steps; and more general intentions (for example, my intention to go to a concert tonight) embed more specific ones (for example, my intention to hear the Alma Trio). As a result, I may deliberate about parts of my plan while holding other parts fixed. I may hold fixed certain intended ends, while deliberating about means or preliminary steps; and I may hold fixed a more general intention, while deliberating about how more specifically to realize it.

The strategy of settling in advance on such partial, hierarchically structured plans, leaving more specific decisions till later, has a deep pragmatic rationale. On the one hand, we need to coordinate our activities both within our own lives and socially, between lives. And we need to do this in ways compatible with our limited capacities to deliberate and process information. Further, given these same limitations we need a way to allow prior deliberation to shape later conduct. This argues for being planning creatures. On the other hand, the world changes in ways we are not in a position to anticipate; so highly detailed plans about the far future will often be of little use and not worth the bother. Partial, hierarchically structured plans for the future provide our compromise solution.

We not only have relatively specific plans; we also have quite general plans—for example, to pursue an academic career, to raise a family, to work for social justice. Such very general plans—projects, as we might say—structure our lives in a way analogous to the way in which more specific plans for a day structure deliberation and action that day. Of course, these very general plans are radically partial, and need to be filled in as time goes by. But that is a virtue of such plans.

Partiality and hierarchy combine with the inertia of plans to give many intentions and actions a *hybrid* character: at one and the same time, a new intention or action may be both deliberative in one respect and nondeliberative in another. An intention or action may be the immediate upshot of deliberation, and so deliberative. But that very deliberation may have taken as fixed a background of prior intentions and plans that are not up for reconsideration at the time of the deliberation. I may hold fixed my intention to earn a doctorate in philosophy while deliberating about what school to go to, what to write a thesis on, and so on.

It is by way of such plans—plans that are partial, hierarchical, resist reconsideration, and eventually control conduct—that the connection between our deliberation and our action is systematically extended over time. The partiality of such plans is essential to their usefulness to us. But on the other side of the coin of partiality are the patterns of reasoning I have been emphasizing: reasoning from a prior intention to further, more specific intentions, or to further intentions concerning means or preliminary steps. In such reasoning we fill in partial plans in ways required for them successfully to guide our conduct.

These connected phenomena of partial plans and reasoning aimed at filling in such plans are central to our understanding of intention. As I have said, a theory that approaches intention by way of these phenomena is a planning theory of intention. My aim is to sketch a plausible version of such a planning theory.

3.2 Demands on Plans

Plans support coordination and systematically extend the influence of deliberation on later conduct. Let us reflect on demands that plans, other things equal, need to satisfy to serve these roles well.

First, there are *consistency constraints*. To coordinate my activities over time a plan should be, other things equal, *internally consistent*. Roughly, it should be possible for my entire plan to be successfully executed. Further, a good coordinating plan is a plan for the world I find myself in. So, assuming my beliefs are consistent, such a plan should be consistent with my beliefs, other things equal. Roughly, it should be possible for my entire plan to be successfully executed given that my beliefs are true. This is a demand that my plans be *strongly consistent, relative to my beliefs*.[3] Violation of either of these consistency constraints tends to undermine the contribution of my plan to coordination in the world I am in. If I plan both to leave my car at home for Susan and also to drive my car to Tanner Library, all the while knowing that I have only one car, I am unlikely to succeed in my effort at coordination.

Second, there is a demand for *means-end coherence*. Although plans are typically partial, they still must be appropriately filled in as time goes by. My plans need to be filled in with subplans concerning means, preliminary steps, and relatively specific course of action, subplans at least as extensive as I believe are now required to do what I plan. My plan to go to Tanner Library will need at some point to be filled in with a specification of a means to getting there (car? bus? bike?), and may also need to include a specification of appropriate preliminary steps (for example, checking the bus schedule). And my plan to go to a concert tonight needs at some point to be filled in with a specification of which concert. Failure to fill in my plans as needed in these ways will leave them means-end *in*coherent.[4]

Of course, means-end coherence does not require that my plans specify what I am to do down to the last physical detail. Rather, my plans will typically be at a level of abstraction appropriate to my habits and skills. My plan to take the bus to Tanner Library need not include a detailed specification of the foot with which I am to step onto the bus when it comes. Again, my plans need not specify what I am to do in every conceivable future circumstance; for many circumstances will seem too unlikely to be worth planning for. So even means-end-coherent plans will remain partial in significant ways. But means-end coherence does require that my plans be filled in with specifications that are as detailed as is, on my view, needed for their successful execution. That is not to say that they need to be filled in all at once; it is enough that they be sufficiently filled in before it is, by my lights, too late.[5]

So we have two important demands on an agent's plans: they are to be both internally consistent and consistent with the agent's beliefs; and they are to be means-end coherent. Both these demands are rooted in a pragmatic rationale: their satisfaction is normally required for plans to serve well their role in coordinating and controlling conduct. Both these demands are also defeasible: there may be special circumstances in which it is rational of an agent to violate them. But they are nevertheless important demands, ones whose recognition is central to an understanding of the role of prior plans in ongoing practical reasoning and planning.

The recognition of these demands helps distinguish intentions and plans, on the one hand, from ordinary desires and valuations, on the other. First, we do not normally require our desires to be consistent in these ways. I might, without irrationality, both desire to play basketball today and desire to finish this chapter today, all the time knowing that I cannot do both. This is a sort of conflict that occurs countless times in the life of a rational agent. If, however, my *plans* include both actions then I *am* guilty of a criticizable form of inconsistency.

Second, simply desiring to go to Tanner this afternoon, or finding that prospect desirable, places me under no rational demand to settle on some means to getting there. But if I am planning to go there, I am subject to such a demand.

Intentions are the building blocks of larger plans. Of course, not all intentions are initially formed by way of a process of planning. We sometimes come to have intentions by way of very different sorts of psychological processes. Still, once I come to intend to *A*, my intention becomes part of my web of intentions and plans, a web subject to the plan-type demands of consistency and coherence. Perhaps I simply find myself with the intention to solve a chess puzzle I stumble on while glancing through the newspaper; I do not arrive at this intention through deliberation or planning.[6] Nevertheless, if I really do intend to solve the puzzle, I am subject to a demand to figure out how to solve it in a way that satisfies the demands of consistency on my total web of intentions.

3.3 The Framework of Prior Plans

So we have two major rational demands on intentions and plans. Associated with these two demands are two direct roles intentions and plans play as inputs in practical reasoning. First, given the demand for means-end coherence prior intentions not up for reconsideration frequently *pose problems* for further deliberation. For example, given my intention to go to Tanner later today I need soon to fill in my plan with a specification of some means for getting there. And to do this I might well deliberate between alternative, conflicting means. Second, given the need for strong consistency prior intentions not up for reconsideration *constrain* further intentions; in particular, they constrain the solutions to the problems posed by the demand for means-end coherence. If I am already planning to leave my only car at home for Susan to use, and if I do not reconsider this prior plan, then I cannot settle on driving my car to Tanner without violating the demand for consistency. So my intention to leave the car at home constrains the solutions to my problem about means. The option of driving my car to Tanner is, given my prior intentions and beliefs, not an admissible option.

The demand for means-end coherence provides rational pressure for the addition of further intentions. In contrast, considerations of consistency do not by themselves provide pressure for the addition of further intentions. Rather, the need for strong consistency only provides constraints on what further intentions may be introduced.[7]

My prior intentions and plans, then, pose problems for deliberation, thereby establishing standards of *relevance* for options considered in deliberation. And they constrain solutions to these problems, providing a *filter of admissibility* for options. In these ways prior intentions and plans help make deliberation tractable for limited beings like us. They provide a clear, concrete purpose for deliberation, rather than merely a general injunction to do the best. They narrow the scope of the deliberation to a limited set of options. And they help answer a question that tends to remain unasked within traditional decision theory, namely: where do decision problems come from?[8]

They can also force us to consider more complicated options.[9] For example, suppose I intend to lose three pounds by tomorrow and consider drinking a milk shake for dessert. I know that if I have this milk shake I will only be able to lose the three pounds if I skip lunch tomorrow. So considerations of consistency force me to consider the more complex option of drinking a milk shake and skipping tomorrow's lunch.

All this is equally true of intentions formed in Buridan cases. Once I form the intention to take route 101, I am faced with a problem about means, and must filter my other options accordingly. My turning right at Page Mill is an admissible, relevant solution to this problem; my turning left (toward route 280) is not. The fact that my prior intention was in a way arbitrary does not prevent it from playing these roles.

Note that it is not merely that prior intentions in fact tend to lead us to consider certain options and not consider others. Such a causal role might be played by a variety of sensitivities. But in addition to this causal role prior intentions provide a kind of rationale for considering some options but not others, a rationale rooted in the demands for consistency and means-end coherence.[10]

Prior intentions and plans, then, provide a *background framework* against which the weighing of desire-belief reasons for and against various options is to take place. This framework helps focus deliberation: it helps determine which options are relevant and admissible. Prior intentions provide this background framework directly: the framework does not depend on the agent's seeing her intentions as evidence for something else, or on the presence of some special desire—for example, to stick to her guns. Nevertheless, in playing these roles intentions do not provide reasons for action to be placed on the scale with desire-belief reasons in determining what to do. Their role is to help determine which options are to be considered in the process of weighing conflicting reasons for action, rather than to provide reasons to be weighed in favor of one considered alternative over another. The reasons to be weighed in deliberation remain desire-belief reasons. In this way we go beyond the modest extension of the desire-belief model, giving intentions a direct role as inputs in practical reasoning, just as common sense would suppose. But we do this without following the intention-based-reasons view in supposing that intentions provide reasons for action analogous to those provided by one's desires and beliefs.

So, do intentions provide reasons for action or not? On the one hand, intentions do provide—by way of demands for coherence and consistency—considerations that are directly relevant in deliberation to the rationality of the ensuing intention and action. On the other hand, intentions do not provide reasons that are to be weighed along with desire-belief reasons in favor of one considered alternative over another. The best thing to say is that intentions provide special kinds of reasons—*framework reasons*—whose role is to help determine the relevance and admissibility of options. These reasons do not compete with desire-belief reasons, but rather structure the process of weighing such reasons. Further, this role of intentions in providing a background framework for the weighing of desire-belief reasons is itself grounded in pragmatic considerations concerning the satisfaction of (rational) desire.[11]

A complication is that I may well intrinsically desire to act in a way I also intend to act. This is frequently true about those general intentions and plans—for example, my intention to work for social justice—that are naturally describable as projects. But it can also be true of relatively specific intentions—my intention to hear Pavarotti at the Opera House tonight, for example. In many contexts it may not be important to separate these two attitudes toward so acting. But for the purpose of understanding the structure of practical reasoning we need to make this distinction. My intention to hear Pavarotti partly constitutes the background framework of my further reasoning, whereas my desire to hear him can provide reasons for relevant and admissible options.

As I noted at the end of Section 2.4, a central problem for a theory of intention is to provide a satisfactory model of the relation between two kinds of practical reasoning: the weighing of desire-belief reasons for and against various options, and reasoning from a prior intention to intentions concerning means, preliminary steps, or more specific courses of action. My solution to this problem is to see prior intentions as elements of plans which provide a background framework within which the weighing of desire-belief reasons is to occur—a framework that poses problems for such further reasoning and constrains solutions to those problems.

Practical reasoning, then, has two levels: prior intentions and plans pose problems and provide a filter on options that are potential solutions to those problems; desire-belief reasons enter as considerations to be weighed in deliberating between relevant and admissible options. This two-level structure is an essential part of the way in which intentions and plans play their coordination-facilitating role, and so part of the way in which intentions enable us to avoid being merely time-slice agents— agents who are constantly starting from scratch in their deliberations. So this two-level structure of practical reasoning has a pragmatic rationale, one grounded in its long-run contribution to our getting what we (rationally) want—given our limits and our complex needs for coordination. We need not leave a broadly instrumental conception of practical reason in order to allow intentions to have direct relevance to the rationality of action.

It is commonly noted that sometimes in means-end reasoning one sees a certain means as necessary to one's intended end, whereas at other times one must choose among several means, each of which would suffice but no one of which is necessary for one's end. Our model of practical reasoning provides a unified treatment of these two types of cases. In both cases one settles on an option so as to avoid a threatened incoherence in one's plans. In the case of reasoning to a necessary means one is presented with what is (at the appropriate level of abstraction) a unique solution to the problem of avoiding this incoherence. In the latter sort of case one is presented with several solutions to this problem, and one needs to appeal to one's desire-belief reasons to determine the best solution. But in both cases one's prior intentions play the same role, namely: the role of posing a problem of coherence and of constraining admissible solutions to that problem.

3.4 Intention and Belief

This discussion of plans and their role in practical reasoning raises a cluster of issues about belief, its relation to intention, and its role in the background framework against which further planning takes place. Though some of these issues go beyond the scope of this book, I proceed to a brief discussion of some relatively pressing matters.

3.4.1 Flat-out Belief

In explaining the role of intentions and plans in the background framework I have been assuming that there is such a thing as flat-out belief (or, as it is sometimes called, acceptance), not just degrees of confidence or "subjective probabilities" ranging from 0 to 1. Recall my planning concerning how to get to Tanner. My planning proceeds against a background that includes intentions to go there and to leave my only car with Susan. But this background also includes a variety of relevant beliefs, for example: that Tanner Library is not in my house and that I have only one car. It is important to my treatment both of option admissibility and of means-end coherence that these beliefs can be all-or-nothing, flat-out beliefs. If I just assigned a high probability (less than 1) to the proposition that I have only one car and did not simply believe that I have only one car, then a plan to leave a car of mine at home with Susan while driving a car of mine to Tanner would not run into problems of inconsistency. It is my flat-out belief that I have only one car that combines with my prior plans to make inadmissible the option of driving a car of mine to Tanner. And it is because of my flat-out belief that I will not get to Tanner unless I decide between car, bus, and bike that my plan to go to Tanner is threatened with means-end incoherence.

The background framework against which practical reasoning and planning typically proceeds includes not only prior intentions and plans but also such flat-out beliefs. Together these attitudes structure the decision problem addressed in the reasoning. Of course, just as I can always stop and reconsider some prior intention, I can also stop and reconsider some background belief. I might stop and ask whether there is some serious chance that I have more than one car, or that Tanner Library is no longer in the Philosophy Department. And in each case it is possible for such reconsideration to lead to revision. Still, in a normal case in which there is no such reconsideration my planning will be framed in part by my flat-out beliefs that I have but one car and that Tanner is in the Philosophy Department and not in my house.

None of this assumes that there is a simple relation between flat-out belief and degrees of confidence. In particular, it does not assume that to believe flat out that I have only one car I must assign this proposition a subjective probability of 1. If you were to offer me a bet in which I pay one dollar if I own only one car but receive one million dollars if it turns out that I own a second car, I might well accept this bet; for I judge that there is better than a one-in-a-million chance that, unknown to me, I own a second car. (Perhaps my aunt has just died and left me her car in her will.) Still, though I would take such a bet if offered, I believe flat out that I own just one car. What makes my attitude toward my having just one car one of flat-out belief, and not merely the assignment of some probability somewhat less than 1, is, at least in part, its distinctive role in the background of my further planning—in particular its role in providing a screen of admissibility for my options.[12]

3.4.2 The Asymmetry Thesis

Let us look more closely at flat-out belief and consider how the planning theory should see the relation between intention and belief so understood. Two main ideas have emerged so far. The first is that intentions and plans normally support coordination in part by providing support for expectations that they will be successfully executed. My intention to go to the meeting helps support interpersonal coordination by providing support for your expectation that I will be there, an expectation that will play its role in your decision to come to the meeting. And my intention also supports my own expectation that I will be there, an expectation that allows me to plan my afternoon accordingly. Intentions and plans can provide this support for associated expectations because they are conduct-controlling pro-attitudes, ones that have a characteristic inertia, and ones that play a crucial role as inputs into and constraints on further practical reasoning.

The second main idea is that there is a defeasible demand that one's intentions be consistent with one's beliefs. Violation of this demand is, other things equal, a form of criticizable irrationality.

Note that these two ideas, taken together, still do not entail that an intention to A actually requires a belief that one will A.[13] And, indeed, there is reason to reject such a purported connection between intention and belief as overly strong. Two sorts of examples are relevant here. First, there seem to be cases in which there is intention in the face of agnosticism about whether one will even try when the time comes. I might intend now to stop at the bookstore on the way home while knowing of my tendency toward absentmindedness—especially once I get on my bike and go into "automatic pilot." If I were to reflect on the matter I would be agnostic about my stopping there, for I know I may well forget. It is not that I believe I will not stop; I just do not believe I will.

Second, there seem to be cases in which there is intention in the face of agnosticism about whether one will succeed when one tries. Perhaps I intend to carry out a rescue operation, one that requires a series of difficult steps. I am confident that at each stage I will try my best. But if I were to reflect on the matter, I would have my doubts about success. I do not have other plans or beliefs which are inconsistent with such success; I do not actually believe I will fail. But neither do I believe I will succeed.

Examples such as these do not *prove* that an intention to A does not require a belief one will A; it remains open to the defender of that view to insist that the intentions in such cases are conditional in some way, or otherwise qualified. But I do think such examples are worrisome enough that I would do well to develop my account of intentions and plans in a way that does not require the strong assumption that to intend to A I must believe I will A. And that is what I will try to do. I will suppose that a normal role of an intention to A is to support an expectation that one will A; and I will also suppose that there is, other things equal, an important kind of irrationality involved in intending to act in ways inconsistent with one's beliefs. But I will not suppose that each and every intention to A involves a belief that one will A.

This clarification in hand, notice an important difference between these two ways in which, on my view, intention is related to belief. An intention to A normally provides the agent with support for a belief that he will A. But there need be no irrationality in intending to A and yet still not believing one will. In contrast, there will normally be irrationality in intending to A and believing one will not A; for there is a defeasible demand that one's intentions be consistent with one's beliefs. Let us label cases of intending to A without believing one will cases of intention-belief *incompleteness*. We can express the difference I have in mind here by saying that intention-belief inconsistency is closer to criticizable irrationality than is intention-belief incompleteness. This is the *asymmetry thesis*.

One good reason for accepting the asymmetry thesis is that intention-belief inconsistency more directly undermines coherent planning than does intention-belief incompleteness. If I intend to go to the bookstore later in the day but am only doubtful that I will, I can make my plans for tomorrow appropriately more complex. I can plan to stop at the market tomorrow if I make it to the bookstore today, and plan to stop at the bookstore tomorrow if I don't stop there today. But if I actually believe I will not make it to the bookstore today, it seems I should be able to plan on the basis of this belief. After all, that is a main role belief plays in ordinary planning. So I will be in a position to plan to stop at the bookstore tomorrow. But then I will be planning to go to the bookstore twice even though I know I need only go there once.

Consider another example. Suppose there is a log blocking my driveway; and suppose I intend to move the log this morning but believe that since it is too heavy I will not move it. So I need to fill in the rest of my plan for the day accordingly. In filling in my plan for this afternoon I plan on the basis of my beliefs about this afternoon, including my belief that (despite my efforts) the log will still be there. So I add an intention to have the tree company move the log this afternoon. So my plan for the day includes my moving the log this morning and my having the tree company move it this afternoon. But it seems folly to plan to cause the log to be moved twice.

In both cases a problem is created by having an intention concerning the nearer future and a belief that this intention will fail. It is this belief that plays a direct role in the background for planning concerning the further future. But the intentions in which this further planning results are at odds with the initial intention concerning the nearer future, undermining the coordinating role of such planning. And this provides a significant pragmatic rationale for a strong prohibition on intention-belief inconsistency.

In contrast, even though an intention to *A* normally supports the belief that one will *A*, the mere absence of this belief in success will not generate such odd consequences. Suppose that I intend to move the log this morning but neither believe I will move it nor believe I won't. When I plan for this afternoon, I am not in a position to plan on the basis of the belief that I will have moved it this morning; but I am also not in a position to plan on the basis of a belief that I will have failed to move it. So I will likely form two conditional intentions: to go to work if I have moved it, and to have the tree company move it if I haven't. And that seems fine. In contrast, a belief that I will fail to move it leads to a much odder plan for the day: to move it, and then to have the tree company move it. And this provides support for the claim that intention-belief inconsistency is closer to irrationality than is intention-belief incompleteness.

There is, however, a further complexity. One might reply to the argument so far by claiming that it depends on an overly simple conception of the role of belief in practical reasoning and planning. The argument has assumed that if I believe that I will fail to move the log this morning, this belief can be a basis for further planning about this afternoon: in planning for this afternoon I can plan on the assumption that I will fail to move the log this morning. But it might be objected that this is not generally true. Rather, in the special case in which you both intend to *A* and believe you won't, your belief should not play the role in planning for the further future that beliefs normally play. If you intend to *A* but believe you will fail, your further intentions concerning what to do when you fail to *A* should only be *conditional* intentions so to act *if* you do fail. I should only intend to call in the tree company *if* I fail to move the log. Even though I believe I will fail to move the log, I should not go ahead and intend simply to call in the tree company. So the consequences of intention-belief inconsistency need be no worse than those of mere agnosticism about the success of an intention. In both cases we merely need to construct more complex plans concerning the further future.[14]

This raises a hard question about belief. If my attitude toward my not moving the log does not support planning on the assumption that I will not move it, is my attitude really one of *belief*? I am inclined to answer in the negative. To believe something is not merely to assign a high probability to its occurrence. I might assign a high probability to my failing to move the log without believing I will fail. On the planning theory an important difference between these two attitudes lies in their different roles in my further planning. If I merely think failure quite likely, I am not yet in a position to plan on the assumption of failure. Normally I will go ahead and construct conditional intentions both for success and for failure. In contrast, what seems distinctive about believing I will fail is that it puts me in a position to plan on the assumption of failure. (Of course, I may still want to have a contingency plan for what to do if my belief proves to be false.) But if this is correct, then we should retain the straightforward model of the role of belief in planning, and so reject the cited reply to our argument in favor of the asymmetry thesis.

Another concern that might be expressed here is that intention-belief inconsistency may not be so close to criticizable irrationality as I have been claiming. I can sometimes try to move the log, believe I will fail to move it, and still not be guilty of criticizable irrationality. After all, it is sometimes worthwhile to make an attempt despite one's pessimism. But for me to try to move the log is for me to act in order to move it. To act in order to move it is to act with the intention of moving it. And to act with the intention of moving it requires having the intention to move it. It follows that I may sometimes intend to move the log, believe I will fail, and yet still not be criticizably irrational. And this challenges my claim that such intention-belief inconsistency is normally irrational.[15]

My response is to reject the inference from my trying to move the log to my intending to move it. This may seem counterintuitive; in any case, it is a view that requires some defense. For now, however, I only want to flag this issue: I will return to it in Chapter 9. Until then I will take as given the asymmetry thesis and the prima facie demand for strong consistency of intention and belief.

3.4.3 Option Admissibility

I now want to add some further remarks about the way in which prior intentions and plans provide a filter of admissibility on options.[16] The basis for this role of prior intentions in further reasoning is the need for consistency in one's web of intentions and beliefs: other things equal, it should be possible for me to do all that I intend in a world in which my beliefs are true. We must, however, be careful not to assume an overly simple relation between this consistency constraint and the nature of this option filter. Not every option that is incompatible with what the agent already intends and believes is inadmissible.

Consider an example. I intend to turn on my computer and I believe that turning it on will heat up my room. I do not intend to heat up my room, however: heating it up is just something I expect to do by turning on the computer. I also believe that turning on the air conditioner would keep the room cool even when the computer is on; but as of now I have no intention to turn on the air conditioner.

Consider the option of turning on the air conditioner. If I were simply to add a new intention in favor of this option to my prior intentions and beliefs, I would introduce inconsistency. In a world in which I execute both my prior intention to turn on the computer and an intention to turn on the air conditioner, one of my prior beliefs will turn out to be false. This is because my prior beliefs include the belief that turning on the computer will heat up the room and also the belief that turning on the air conditioner will prevent the room from heating up. But this should not make the option of turning on the air conditioner inadmissible. It seems perfectly reasonable for me to give this option serious consideration and to do this without in any way reconsidering or bracketing my prior intention to turn on the computer.

In contrast, suppose I intend to use my computer to heat up my room. Again, a new intention to turn on the air conditioner would introduce intention-belief inconsistency. This is because I could not successfully execute both my prior intention and this new intention in a world in which my prior beliefs about the effects of each intended act are true. But in this case this threatened inconsistency does make the option of turning on the air conditioner inadmissible.

Turning on the air conditioner is incompatible with my prior intention and beliefs in both cases. Yet in only the second case is it inadmissible. Why is this? Consider how my web of intentions and beliefs would change in each case under pressures of strong consistency if I were to decide to turn on the air conditioner. In the first case this decision would force a change in my *beliefs*. I will no longer believe that if I use the computer I will heat up my room. And this change in belief would suffice to prevent the threatened inconsistency. No change in intention would be needed.

In the second case, however, no such reasonable change in belief is available. To avoid the threatened inconsistency, what is called for is a change in my prior intention to use the computer to heat the room. Of course, a change in my belief that the air conditioner would cool off the room is possible. But nothing about a decision to turn on the air conditioner would justify such a change of belief. If I did go on to change this belief, and the rationale for this change was only that it would preserve consistency in my web of intentions and beliefs, I would be guilty of wishful thinking.

This leads to the following understanding of the relation between the demand for strong consistency and the admissibility of new options. Consider a new option, O. Hold fixed the agent's prior intentions, but add to the agent's web of intentions and beliefs a new intention to O. Also add changes in belief that would be justified given that new intention, but without any other revision in the agent's prior intentions. The option O is admissible if these changes in the web of intentions and beliefs would introduce no new inconsistency in that web. What matters for admissibility of a new option are one's intentions *prior to* a decision concerning that option and the beliefs one would reasonably have *after* a decision in favor of that option.[17]

3.5 Internal versus External Points of View

Let us briefly review the discussion so far. The modest extension of the desire-belief model failed to do justice to the direct roles of intentions as inputs to practical reasoning. But the intention-based-reasons view both failed to recognize the special role of intentions and plans in practical reasoning and ran into a bootstrapping problem. We have improved upon the modest extension of the desire-belief model by noting how prior intentions and plans guide and focus deliberation: they pose problems and constrain solutions to those problems. In doing this we have been able to recognize the special nature of the contribution of prior intentions and plans to further practical reasoning: in contrast with the intention-based-reasons view we do not see intentions and plans as contributing just one reason for action among many.

But how do we avoid bootstrapping difficulties? Our account may seem to be subject to the same worries about unacceptable bootstrapping as those that plagued the intention-based-reasons view. Return to Mondale. As long as he continues to intend to attack Star Wars, his relevant and admissible options will include asking certain questions (for example, the three he actually considers asking), but will not include asking certain other questions (such as a question about Middle East policy). Though Mondale knows he *could* ask a question that bypassed Star Wars in favor of Middle East policies, such an option will be inadmissible, for its performance is known by Mondale to be incompatible with his intended attack on Star Wars. Suppose now that Mondale correctly judges that his asking his third question is better supported by his desire-belief reasons than are its relevant and admissible alternatives. It seems that Mondale should then suppose that this is what it is rational to do, all considered—that this is what he ought on balance to do. But this seems to allow Mondale's prior intention to attack Star Wars—an intention that was irrational when formed—to bootstrap into rationality his derivative intention to ask his third question. So we again seem to be in danger of sanctioning unacceptable bootstrapping.

My response to this challenge is rooted in three main ideas. The first I have already emphasized. An agent's prior intentions play a direct role in his further practical reasoning—a role I have been at pains to elucidate. But the rationale for having attitudes that play such a role is at bottom a pragmatic one, grounded in a concern with the satisfaction of (rational) desire. This leads naturally to the second idea. Mondale's judgment that he ought to ask his third question is made from the *internal perspective of his deliberation,* a perspective within which Mondale's prior plans play the roles I have been emphasizing. But we can also take an *external* perspective in assessing Mondale's asking his third question, a perspective within which we bracket the influence of Mondale's prior plans and from which we are able to note the superiority of Mondale's instead pursuing issues about Reagan's Middle East policies. From this external perspective, roughly, we assess intentional actions solely on the basis of a concern with the expected satisfaction of (rational) desire. Since this concern is foundational, relative to the roles played by prior intentions and plans, criticisms of Mondale's actions from this perspective will have force. In making such external assessments we will need to appeal to standards of practical rationality that are not intended for direct use in the agent's deliberation about what to do. But, and this is the third idea, such external standards will play an important role in a theory of practical rationality that takes intentions and plans seriously. I proceed to expand on these ideas.

Mondale's perspective on his decision to ask his third question is *plan-*

constrained: it is limited to options that get through the filter of admissibility provided by his plans. This is a pervasive and justifiable feature of practical reasoning for limited agents like us. Nevertheless, *we* can step outside of Mondale's perspective, bracket Mondale's prior intention to attack Star Wars, and ask what action would be rational in a *non-plan-constrained* way. From such an external, non-plan-constrained perspective we can examine Mondale's option of asking his third question. And we can determine that this option is, after all, inferior to his pursuing issues about Reagan's Middle East policies—inferior, that is, even relative to Mondale's own desires and beliefs about what he would achieve through each course of action. Of course, this Middle East option is inadmissible for Mondale, given his intention to attack Star Wars. But it is nevertheless an option Mondale believes he *could* perform, and its inadmissibility for Mondale need not stop *us* from considering it and noting its superiority to Mondale's asking his third question.

In reaching such an assessment we are approaching the question of what Mondale ought to do from an *external* perspective. From this perspective we try to determine what course of action is best supported by Mondale's own desire-belief reasons for action, once we bracket the influence of Mondale's prior intentions and plans. Of course, from the internal perspective of Mondale's deliberation, these prior intentions and plans guide deliberation and constrain options. But they do not provide reasons for action in the basic way in which relevant desires and beliefs do. When we step out of the internal perspective of deliberation, then, it is natural to bracket such intentions and plans and try to determine what ways of acting are best supported by Mondale's relevant desires and beliefs, unconstrained by prior intentions and plans. We limit ourselves to options Mondale believes he *could* perform: for we want an assessment of what it would be rational for him to do relative to *his* desires and beliefs. But we need not limit ourselves to those options that are *admissible*, given Mondale's prior intentions. Granted, in attempting to reach such a determination we may need to engage in reasoning more extensive than that in which it would be wise of Mondale to engage, given limits of time and other resources. But never mind. We are not asking whether it would be wise for Mondale so to reason, but rather what it would be rational for him to do, relative only to his relevant desires and beliefs and putting to one side his prior intentions and plans.

To be sure, a defender of the intention-based-reasons view could also observe that once we bracket Mondale's prior intentions, his asking a question about Middle East policies is rational relative to his relevant desire-belief reasons. But this observation would not have the same significance for the intention-based-reasons view as it does for my account.

This is because on the intention-based-reasons view we would see such bracketing as the removal of reasons for action that are, so to speak, on a par with the desire-belief reasons that remain. So we would merely be observing that asking a question about Middle East policies would be rational relative to some proper subset of the agent's reasons for action. And such an observation can be made concerning very many of the actions open to us. There is frequently something to be said for even the silliest alternatives. In contrast, on my account the expected satisfactions of (rational) desires provide reasons for action that are basic in a way in which the framework reasons provided by intentions are not. And that is the source of the significance of a failure to be rational relative just to relevant desire-belief reasons.

So we need to distinguish two points of view from which the rationality of intentional action may be assessed. There is, first, the *internal point of view of the deliberating agent*. It is from this point of view that the agent's prior intentions and plans play their role in providing standards of relevance and admissibility for options. This internal perspective is a *plan-constrained* perspective on rationality. There is, second, the *external point of view* within which the influence of the agent's prior intentions is bracketed, and we seek to determine which options, among those the agent believes he could perform, are best supported by the agent's relevant desire-belief reasons. This is a *non-plan-constrained* perspective on rationality. As the case of Mondale illustrates, there is a clear potential for divergence between the assessments from these internal and external perspectives. An option that is rational relative to the internal perspective of deliberation may fail to be rational relative to the cited external perspective. Mondale's asking his third question was rational relative to the internal perspective of his deliberation at the time of the debate; but from the external, non-plan-constrained perspective we can see the superiority of asking instead a question about Middle East policy.

The possibility of this divergence also sheds more light on Buridan cases. Suppose I arbitrarily decide to take route 101 rather than route 280, even though at the time of my decision these routes seem to me equally attractive. Once I make this decision, my taking route 101 will be rational from my internal perspective, whereas my taking route 280 will not be, for it will be inadmissible. But from the external perspective each option may well remain equally desirable—until I begin driving toward route 101 and away from route 280.[18]

What makes such divergence possible is the divergence between two different constraints on options. From the internal perspective what is crucial is an option's *admissibility* given prior plans. As we have seen, such admissibility is determined by considerations of consistency applied to the agent's web of intentions and beliefs. From the external perspective, in contrast, what is crucial is whether the agent believes he *can* so act—whether he believes he has it in his power so to act. And these two conditions are significantly different. I might believe I have it in my power to drive my only car to Tanner Library even though the option of so acting is inadmissible given my prior intention to leave my car for Susan. And Mondale believes he has it in his power to ask a question about Middle East policy though this option is inadmissible given his intention to attack Star Wars instead.

So our assessment of Mondale's decision in the debate to ask his third question (as well as of his eventual action of intentionally asking that question) may vary depending on the perspective from which we make it. If we take the internal, plan-constrained perspective of the deliberating agent we may find it rational, all considered; and yet we may still determine that it is, all considered, not rational from the external perspective of non-plan-constrained rationality. Now, the rationale for being planning creatures is, I have urged, ultimately grounded in the long-run contribution of the associated patterns of reasoning and action to our getting what we want. So it is natural to take quite seriously assessments grounded in the external perspective, with its sole emphasis on the agent's desire-belief reasons. This means that Mondale's asking his third question may fail to be rational in an important way, even though from his own present perspective it is rational, all considered. So our theory can provide for a form of negative assessment of such unacceptable bootstrapping.

We may put the point in terms of a distinction between two kinds of ought judgments. In his deliberation Mondale aims at reaching a judgment of what he ought, on balance, to do—where this ought judgment is to be made from the internal, plan-constrained perspective of his deliberation. Call this an *internal-ought* judgment. From the external point of view of non-plan-constrained rationality we seek an, on balance, *external-ought* judgment. Although both ought judgments are relativized to Mondale's attitudes, Mondale's prior intentions and plans play a direct role with respect to the former but not the latter. We should not suppose that either ought judgment is more objective than the other. Both concern a relation between a type of action and certain attitudes of the agent's. Nor should we suppose that one generally takes precedence over the other. Rather, each has its distinctive role to play in our complex practices of deliberation and rational assessment. Internal-ought judgments will be central to deliberation; while the availability of external-ought judgments is one part of our solution to problems about bootstrapping.

*   *   *

This anyway is the basic idea. But I need to clarify what is involved when we take the external, non-plan-constrained perspective. Three features characterize this perspective. First, our interest is in determining what course of action is recommended by the agent's relevant desire-belief reasons. Second, in making this determination we bracket the screen provided by the agent's relevant prior intentions. And, third, in making this determination we are to ignore the costs to us of the reasoning and calculation that are required.

When we bracket Mondale's prior intention to challenge Reagan on Star Wars, we put aside this intention for the purpose of determining what options are to be considered. Options incompatible with this intention need no longer be blocked from consideration. This does not mean that we put aside any *desire* of Mondale's (for example, his desire to limit the arms race) that he sees such a challenge as promoting. Such desires remain in force and continue to provide reasons for various courses of action. But we do newly allow options incompatible with this intention to be considered; we partially lift the screen of admissibility.

Now, prior intentions not only contribute to the screen of admissibility. They also indirectly affect the agent's desire-belief reasons. When we take the external perspective and bracket these prior intentions, should we bracket their influence on these desire-belief reasons as well?[19]

Distinguish three different ways in which Mondale's prior intention to attack Star Wars might affect his desire-belief reasons. First, this intention might provide grounds for beliefs about how he himself will act, for example, a belief that he will attack Star Wars. Second, the presence of the intention might itself affect the costs of his acting differently by adding certain costs associated with the very process of changing his mind; and Mondale may well know this. Third, Mondale may have a desire to stick to his guns, and as a result his prior intention gives him a desire-belief reason for attacking Star Wars.

When we bracket Mondale's prior intention, we will want to bracket its influence on his beliefs about what he will do. We do not want to be able to argue, from the external perspective, that since Mondale is going to attack Star Wars it would be foolish for him to try also to challenge Reagan's Middle East policies! In contrast, it seems to me that we will not want to bracket indirect impacts of the second and third sorts on Mondale's desire-belief reasons. If Mondale supposes there would be costs associated with the very process of changing his mind concerning whether to attack Star Wars, we will want to include such costs in our external comparison of attacking Star Wars and challenging Middle East policies. And if Mondale in fact has some desire to stick to his guns, we will want to factor that in as well.

This brings us to another complication. We may bracket prior intentions and plans to varying degrees. There are two dimensions along which the extent of such bracketing can vary. The first is rooted in the hierarchical structure of plans. A lower-level element in a plan may be merely a means or a preliminary step to some intended end in that plan; or it may be merely a specification of a more general intention that lies behind it.[20] When this is so, we can bracket the lower-level element without bracketing the intended end or more general course of action that lies behind it in the agent's plan. For example, we might bracket Mondale's intention to attack Star Wars without bracketing his general intention to focus on defense policies. In this way our bracketing may vary in its *depth*. Second, an intention to act in certain ways will frequently be part of a larger plan that concerns the yet further future. For example, Mondale's intention to attack Star Wars may be part of a plan that includes this attack and also an attack on fiscal policy in the next news conference. In bracketing the intention to attack Star Wars we may or may not go on to bracket the entire plan in which it is embedded, including the intention to attack fiscal policy in the next news conference. So our bracketing may vary in its *length*.

When we take the external perspective of non-plan-constrained rationality, how deep and how long should our bracketing be? It would seem that the bracketing should be complete, that we should put aside all prior intentions and plans. But we need not do this all at once. When we take the external perspective, we may begin by bracketing only the prior intentions specifically at issue, for example: Mondale's intention to attack Star Wars. Making appropriate adjustments in the agent's beliefs, we proceed to determine what he should do, relative to his desires and beliefs. We then modestly increase the depth and length of our bracketing, without moving immediately to total bracketing. For example, we include in our bracketing Mondale's general intention to focus on defense policy, and his specific intention to focus on fiscal policy at the next debate. And we proceed again to determine what he should do. And so on. At each stage we make only modest increments in the extent of bracketing. At a certain point we may well have reasonable confidence that no further increases in the depth or length of bracketing would change our verdict. Once we reach such a point, we can stop and say that our verdict at this stage determines what would be, all considered, rational to do from our external perspective.

In Mondale's case it seems plausible to suppppose that as we increase the depth and length of our bracketing, the superiority of posing the question that challenges Reagan's Middle East policies, rather than a question that challenges Star Wars, will be a stable result. Assuming that this is so, we can say that posing the question concerning Middle East policies is superior from the external perspective of non-plan-constrained rationality. And this may be so even if Mondale's posing his third question concerning Star Wars is, on balance, rational from the internal, plan-constrained perspective of his deliberation.

chapter 4

Agent Rationality:
Toward a General Theory

IN Chapter 3 I was concerned with the impact of intentions on internal and external assessments of the rationality of intentional actions. But we not only assess the rationality of intentional actions; we also assess the rationality of *agents*. We assess, from an external perspective, the rationality *of* an agent *for* her intentional activity. We praise or criticize agents as more or less rational in acting as they do. Mondale's intentional *action* of asking his third question was, we may suppose, rational from one perspective, not rational from another. But we can also ask whether or not it was rational *of Mondale* to ask this question.

We have approached intention by way of clusters of dispositions and functional roles, clusters that partly constitute volitional and reasoning-centered commitment. But to understand commitment it is not enough just to identify such clusters. We need also to identify their relevance to judgments of the rationality of actions and agents. We have explored the different roles intentions play in internal and external assessments of the rationality of intentional actions. We now need to reflect on their roles in the assessment of agents.

The discussion to follow of issues about agent rationality will play three related roles. First, as I have just noted, it will play an important role in the overall account of the notion of commitment, a notion central to my theory of intention. Second, it will enable me to complete my discussion of issues raised by the threat of bootstrapping. Third, and finally, it will help me to highlight an important aspect of the conception of rational agency being developed here. On this conception a theory of practical rationality is not merely a theory of rational calculation. Rather, other processes and habits play important roles in rational agency, and their assessment in judgments of agent rationality is an important component of a normative account of practical rationality.

As a first step we need to look a bit more closely at the very idea of assessing the rationality of an agent for her intentions, actions, or even her nonactions.

4.1 Agent Rationality

Judgments of agent rationality are made from a standpoint external to the standpoint of deliberation. This does not mean that such assessments cannot be made by the agent about herself. It is just that the concern of the internal perspective of deliberation about what to do is with the rationality of various proposed courses of action, and not directly with the rationality of the agent in so acting. In particular, when the agent attempts to assess her own rationality for intending or acting in certain ways, there is no reason for her prior intentions and plans to play the special role that they do in her deliberation about what to do.

In assessing the rationality of an agent for some intention or intentional action our concern is to determine the extent to which the agent has come up to relevant standards of rational agency. A failure on the agent's part to come up to such standards makes that agent guilty of a form of criticizable irrationality. In reaching such assessments our concern is with the actual processes that lead to the intention or action and with the underlying habits, dispositions, and patterns of thinking and reasoning which are manifested in those processes. Our concern is with the extent to which these processes—and the underlying habits, dispositions, and patterns they manifest—come up to appropriate standards of rationality.[1] One main function of such standards will be in the context of education, broadly construed. We will use such standards as guides for the development of basic habits of thought and action, in our children and in ourselves. The theory of agent rationality is a part of the theory of education.

Since in making such judgments of agent rationality we are assessing underlying habits and dispositions, these judgments bear a resemblance to judgments of moral praiseworthiness or blameworthiness for some action or intention. This is because such judgments of praiseworthiness or blameworthiness are also typically based on assessments of the traits that lie behind and explain the action or intention. One important difference, however, is this. It is natural to suppose that a person is blameworthy for a failure to live up to some standard only if she at some point had it in her power to change herself so that she would live up to that standard. But on this assumption a failure of agent rationality need not bring with it culpability for that failure. When we criticize an agent for failing to live up to our standard of agent rationality, we need not suppose that she presently has it in her power to change herself so as newly to conform to that standard; nor need we suppose that she ever in the past had it in her power to change herself so as now to live up to that standard. Indeed, we need not even suppose that if she *could* now so change herself she *should*. Embarking on such changes has costs of its own (just consider the fees of psychiatrists these days). And the judgment that it is worth trying to make such changes goes beyond the critical assessment of the agent as not rational in doing something, given the failure of some relevant habit to satisfy appropriate standards. Judgments of agent rationality are in this way analogous to legal judgments of strict liability.[2] We hold agents up to a certain standard, independently of supposing that they have it in their power voluntarily and rationally to ensure conformity with that standard.

What sorts of standards are we to apply in making such judgments of agent rationality? Perhaps there are habits and patterns of thinking and reasoning that we find intrinsically rational, independent of any assessment of their impact when internalized by limited agents like us. But here I am going to take, instead, a broadly pragmatic approach to such matters. I am going to assume that we are to assess such habits and patterns in terms of the long-range consequences of their internalization by limited agents like us. Such a broadly pragmatic approach does seem to me to be the more plausible approach to such matters. But at the least my discussion can be taken to show what follows when we take this—at the least, plausible—approach.

I am also going to assume that the end relative to which we are to make such consequentialist assessments is the agent's long-term interest in getting what she wants. Here, however, the reader should recall my caveat, in Chapter 2, concerning the limitations of my discussion. I continue to put to one side possible criticisms of an agent's basic desires. You could say, if you wanted, that judgments of agent rationality are relative to the agent's long-term interest in satisfying her rational desires, or her long-term interest in leading an objectively good life, or something similar. Indeed, given the role of judgments of agent rationality in education, and the obvious social dimension of education, such changes may seem even more pressing here. But a serious consideration of these issues is simply beyond the scope of this book. So I am just going to put them aside for now. Whichever version you accept of the ends relative to which judgments of agent rationality are to be made, I think issues similar to those I will be discussing will arise, and the main outlines of the theory I sketch will be plausible.

In any case, the relativity to the agent's particular ends will tend to drop out of many such judgments. This is because over a wide range of desires rather similar habits and patterns of thought and action will tend to be useful, given general facts about our circumstances and capacities. At least this will be true within the framework of a particular cultural setting; and I will suppose that when we are making such judgments we are holding such matters fixed. This is why it is natural to think of such habits and patterns of thought and action as analogous to universal means or "primary goods": they are useful given a wide range of desires, over the long run.[3]

When we make judgments of agent rationality, then, we apply certain general standards of reasonableness. We require (or so, anyway, I am here assuming) that the agent's relevant habits, dispositions, and ways of arriving at decisions and actions come up to certain levels of effectiveness in their expected impact on that agent's long-term interest in getting what she wants. The relevant expectations here are not the agent's, but rather the expectations of those making the judgement of agent rationality.[4] In making such judgments we are to assess the relevant habits, and so on, in the light of our best theory of how such habits contribute to long-term desire-satisfaction.[5] A second point is that we do not, it seems to me, demand that such habits be *optimally* effective in their expected long-term impact on the agent's getting what she wants. As long as this expected impact exceeds an appropriate threshold, we can allow that there is room for some improvement and yet still judge the agent to be rational in the sense that she is not subject to criticism for the actions or intentions in which such habits issue.[6]

So much by way of general remarks about the external assessment of the rationality of an agent.

4.2 The Intention-Action Principle

I now turn to developing an account of agent rationality that comports with our model of the roles of intentions and plans in rational agency. I will proceed as follows. In this and the next section of this chapter I sketch a general approach to assessing the rationality of an agent in intentionally acting in certain ways. This approach involves two stages, and I describe principles for both of these stages. I then go on, in Chapter 5, to discuss an important question raised by these principles, namely: when is it rational of an agent to reconsider (or not reconsider) a prior intention? This discussion in hand I return, in Chapter 6, to the principles of agent rationality presented in Chapter 4 (this chapter). The principle provided here for the first of the two stages of the account of agent rationality—a principle I call the *intention-action principle*—I continue to accept throughout this book. But the principles described in this chapter for the second stage of the account of agent rationality turn out to have a nonhistorical character that requires revision. This leads me in Chapter 6 to an alternative approach to the second stage, an approach that makes my overall theory a *historical* theory of agent rationality. This historical theory in hand I return, in Chapter 7, to the idea of commitment.

To proceed. How should we think, within a planning framework, of the rationality of an agent in doing something intentionally?

Given an intentional action we can normally work our way back first to an intention which guides the action, and then to the deliberation and habits responsible for that intention. An intention which guides an action will be an intention concerning the time of the action. Of course, a guiding intention will concern more than the present moment: actions are not instantaneous, but extend over time and require continued monitoring and guidance.[7] But a guiding intention will be an intention to act in a certain way *beginning now*. This is a *present-directed* intention.[8] But frequently the deliberation that lies behind such an intention will have occurred at a time prior to the time of the action, issuing in an intention that was then *future-directed*.

This suggests a two-stage approach to the assessment of the rationality of an agent in acting. We first explain when it is rational of an agent intentionally to act in a certain way in terms of the rationality of the agent for relevant guiding intentions. Then we go on to say when it is rational of an agent to intend to do something.

Begin by considering the first stage—the stage in which we assess the rationality of an agent for intentionally *A*-ing in the light of her rationality for having relevant intentions. To simplify matters let us assume that when an agent intentionally *A*'s she also intends to *A*, and this intention guides her activity in *A*-ing.[9] So our question is, what is the relation between the rationality of an agent for intentionally *A*-ing and her rationality for intending to *A*?

Intentions are normally conduct *controllers:* in the normal course of events, if a rational agent intends to *A* now, she will at least try to *A*. So if we cannot criticize a person for intending to *A*, it seems we should not be able to criticize her for *A*-ing. A rational agent's control over her actions goes by way of her intentions. She does not separately control her present-directed intentions and her intentional actions. So there would seem to be no point in supposing that the agent escapes criticism for her present-directed intention to *A*, and yet still is subject to criticism for having failed to satisfy relevant standards in intentionally *A*-ing.

This suggests that the natural principle for our first stage is the following:

Intention-action principle

    If it is rational of S to have a present-directed intention to A, and S successfully executes this intention and thereby intentionally A's, then it is rational of S to A.[10]

It is important to keep in mind that this intention-action principle concerns the rationality of agents, not the rationality of actions. So the principle allows for the possibility that it is rational of S to intend now to A, that S successfully executes this intention and thereby intentionally A's, and yet that the action of A-ing is not recommended from the external perspective. Relatedly, the intention-action principle does not say that an intention to A provides a reason for A-ing that enters, together with relevant desire-belief reasons, into external assessments of the rationality of A-ing. As we have seen, our account needs to reject this suggestion in order to avoid sanctioning unacceptable bootstrapping. But we can still recognize the relevance of S's intention to A, when it is rational of S so to intend, to the rationality *of S* in A-ing. And this is what the intention-action principle does.

The central idea behind the intention-action principle, then, is that the present-directed intention to A and the resulting action of intentionally A-ing are too tightly connected for us to praise the agent as rational for the former and yet not praise her as rational for the latter. This is because the intention and action are not separately controlled by the agent, but rather the agent's control of her action goes by way of her intention.

The intention-action principle seems to me an extremely plausible approach to such matters. But there are complications. Gregory Kavka and others have discussed cases in which an intention to A is expected to have certain valued or disvalued effects independently of its actually being executed.[11] One might worry that such cases pose a challenge to our intention-action principle. It may seem that in some such cases there may be desire-belief reasons for an intention to A that are not reasons for the action of A-ing, and that this may drive a wedge between the rationality of an agent for intending to A and her rationality for intentionally A-ing. My procedure, however, will be to put such worries aside for now, and to develop a larger framework for assessing the rationality of agents for their intentions and actions. This framework in hand, I will return to such cases at the end of Chapter 6.

4.3 Rationality of an Agent in Intending

What about the second stage? To apply the intention-action principle we just need to know when it is rational of S to have a present-directed intention to *A*. But it will be useful to pursue the more general question: under what conditions is it rational of *S* to intend at t_1 to *A* at t_2 (where t_2 is not earlier than t_1)? A first step toward answering this question is to distinguish three kinds of intention.

4.3.1 Three Kinds of Intention

Implicit in our previous discussion is a distinction between two cases in which I intend at t_1 to *A* at t_2. Sometimes I have such an intention because I have just formed it on the basis of deliberation about whether to *A* at t_2. My intention in this case is a *deliberative* intention. In contrast, I might have formed this intention not on the basis of present deliberation but rather at some earlier time, t_0, and have retained it from t_0 to t_1 without reconsidering it. In this case my intention is *nondeliberative*.

Two clarifications. First, I may sometimes reason from a prior intention to a derivative intention in favor of a necessary means or preliminary step. Since my derivative intention favors a *necessary* means (or preliminary step) I will not have compared it in my reasoning to alternative admissible means. So my reasoning will not have been a case of deliberation in the full-blown sense that requires that I weigh pros and cons for and against conflicting options. Still, my derivative intention is sufficiently similar to an intention arrived at through such full-blown deliberation that it is natural to include it within the category of deliberative intention; and that is what I will do.

Second, in labeling an intention nondeliberative I do not mean to say that it has not been temporally updated. An intention at t_1 to *A* at t_2 may have been temporally updated from its initial formation at t_0 and still be nondeliberative. Suppose I decide on Monday to leave for Boston on Tuesday. On Tuesday I continue so to intend. But I also notice that it is now Tuesday, and so I come to have an intention I would express by saying, "I intend to leave for Boston today." Soon I come to have a present-directed intention I would express by saying, "I intend to leave for Boston now." Such temporal updating does not by itself make my intention deliberative: my present-directed intention to leave for Boston now is a nondeliberative intention.[12]

To this initial pair of categories let me now add a third. I might have a general policy to act in certain sorts of ways in certain kinds of circumstances. I might then note that at some time—in the present or the future—I am (will be) in such a circumstance and thereby be led to intend to act accordingly then. That is, I might have a general policy to *A* in circumstances of type *C*, and I might note at t_1 that I am (will be) in a *C*-type circumstance at t_2, and thereby arrive at an intention to *A* at t_2. In such a case my intention to *A* at t_2 is a *policy-based* intention.

Some examples: My general policy is to turn down a second drink when I have to drive home; I see the host of the party approach me with a second drink; applying my policy I form the intention to turn him down when he gets to me. My general policy is to allow myself to chair only one committee at a time. I am told that Clara is on the phone. While walking to the phone I surmise that she will ask me to chair a second committee and, applying my policy, form the intention to turn her down. My intentions to turn down the host and Clara are, when I form them, policy-based.

So we have three kinds of intention: deliberative, nondeliberative, and policy-based.[13] I do not claim that this list is exhaustive: there will be cases of intention that will not fit neatly into any of these categories (for example, certain kinds of spontaneously formed intentions). But these three cases are particularly central to the conception of temporally extended agency and agent rationality I want to sketch; and in assessing the rationality of an agent for intending to act in a certain way we will need to consider each of these cases separately. For present purposes I will focus on the deliberative and nondeliberative cases. Later, in Chapter 6, I will return to the policy-based case.

4.3.2 The Ahistorical Theory

Consider first the nondeliberative case. Under what conditions is it rational of S at t_1 nondeliberatively to intend to A at t_2?[14] It seems clear that it must at least be rational of S at t_1 not to reconsider that intention then. After all, we are supposing that S does not at t_1 reconsider this intention; and if this failure to reconsider is not rational of S, then it seems that S should not escape criticism for continuing so to intend.

This means that we need a theory of when it is rational of an agent not to reconsider some prior intention. I will turn to this matter in Chapter 5. For now, I want to ask a different question. Suppose we know when it is rational of an agent at t_1 not to reconsider some prior intention then. Is the rationality of such nonreconsideration itself sufficient for the rationality of the agent in nondeliberatively so intending then? That is, in the nondeliberative case does the fact that it is rational of S at t_1 not to reconsider his intention guarantee that it is rational of S at t_1 so to intend?

In Chapter 6 I will be arguing that the answer to this question should be "No." But first it will be useful to see what a theory would look like which answered in the affirmative. The rationale for such an affirmative answer (which I will later call into question) is this: If S in fact does not reconsider this intention, and if this nonreconsideration is rational of S, it seems odd to criticize S for continuing so to intend. After all, for S to

change this intention he would have to reconsider it; yet (we are supposing) it is rational for S not to engage in such reconsideration. This
leads to the following principle:

Nondeliberative rationality of an agent in intending

Suppose that prior to t_1 S has come to have the intention to A
at t_2. And suppose that S continues so to intend until t_1, and does
not reconsider this intention at t_1. Then it is rational of S so to
intend at t_1 if and only if it is rational of S at t_1 not to reconsider
that intention then.

Turn now to the case of deliberative intention: intention formed on
the basis of present deliberation. We have seen that such deliberation
takes the agent from a structured input to that intention. This structured
input consists of (a) a background of prior plans and flat-out beliefs and
(b) desire-belief reasons for and against relevant and admissible options.
So we may think of the rationality of the agent in deliberatively intending
to A as a function of the extent to which he lives up to relevant standards
with respect to both (a) and (b), and also with respect to reaching the
conclusion he reaches given this input structure. That is, we may ask a
series of questions: Was it rational of S to deliberate against that background? Was it rational of S so to believe and desire? Given those plans,
beliefs, and desires, was it rational of S to reach as a conclusion the
intention he in fact reached? And we may suppose that our answers to
these questions will determine how we should assess the rationality of S
for deliberatively so intending.

Now, in order to focus on the distinctive issues raised by intentions
and plans I have been putting to one side fundamental issues about the
rational assessment of the agent for having his particular desires and
beliefs; and I will continue to do so here. So for present purposes we can
think of the rationality of an agent in deliberatively intending to A as a
function of two things. First, he needs to have lived up to relevant standards with respect to the fixed background of prior plans. Second, he
needs to have reached a reasonable conclusion in his deliberation, held
against this background. This suggests the following principle:

Deliberative rationality of an agent in intending

If on the basis of deliberation at t_1 S forms the intention to A
at t_2, then it is rational of S at t_1 to intend to A at t_2 if and only
if:

(1) for those intentions of S's that play a direct role as a background of S's deliberation, it is rational of S at t_1 not to reconsider
those intentions then; and

(2) *S* reasonably supposes that *A* is at least as well supported by his reasons for action as its relevant, admissible alternatives.

Some brief remarks about condition (2). First, such a condition does not guarantee that *S* supposes that *A* is at least as well supported by his desire-belief reasons as all its *believed* alternatives. This is because some of these believed alternatives (that is, alternatives the agent believes he *could* perform) may be inadmissible given *S*'s background plans. Second, the assessment that *S* reasonably holds a certain view about option *A* is, in effect, an assessment of agent rationality. It is a judgment that it is reasonable *of S* so to judge. Sometimes this will be a fairly straightforward matter, for *S*'s desire-belief reasons may just clearly favor *A* over its relevant and admissible alternatives. But sometimes the matter will be extremely complicated. This is because such a judgment in favor of *A* is typically a product of a process of weighing conflicting desire-belief considerations, and such weighing is frequently not a straightforward matter of calculation or deductive inference. In particular, many times the agent's imagination will play complex and important roles in such weighing. The agent will attempt to weigh conflicting reasons by rehearsing in imagination just what would be involved in acting on one or the other of those reasons. In such cases an assessment of the rationality of *S* in reaching his conclusion in favor of *A* will need to assess the rationality of *S* in employing such procedures of "dramatic rehearsal (in imagination)" in his deliberation.[15] There are complex issues here that go beyond the scope of this book. But I take it that even without pursuing these issues we have enough of an understanding of condition (2) to proceed.

Turning to condition (1), note how this condition meshes with our earlier principle of nondeliberative rationality. Given this earlier principle, satisfaction of condition (1) will guarantee that it is rational of *S* to have those nondeliberative intentions which play a direct role in the background of the deliberation.

So we have a two-stage account of agent rationality. The intention-action principle is our first stage. The cited principles of nondeliberative and deliberative rationality of an agent in intending are in the second stage. These two second-stage principles are *a*historical principles. On these principles the assessment at t_1 of the rationality of the agent for intending at t_1 to *A* at t_2 does not depend on the history of that intention prior to t_1. It depends just on facts about the agent at t_1. As I have indicated, I will be challenging this idea later in Chapter 6. But first we need to consider when it is rational of an agent not to reconsider a prior intention.

chapter 5

Reconsideration and Rationality

Was it rational of Mondale to stick with his background of prior plans, rather than abandon or reconsider his prior intention to attack Star Wars? Prior intentions tend to persist and to resist reconsideration. But this is not just a causal tendency of such states of mind. It is not just that prior intentions resist reconsideration in the way in which diamonds resist being scratched. Rather, along with this tendency of prior intentions go associated norms of practical rationality—norms that concern the rationality of the reconsideration or nonreconsideration of prior intentions. The question about Mondale's retention and nonreconsideration of his intention to attack Star Wars is a special case of this general question about the norms associated with the inertia of intention.[1]

The first step is to reflect further on what is involved in reconsidering or not reconsidering some prior intention.

5.1 Reconsideration

5.1.1 Three Varieties of Reconsideration (or Nonreconsideration)

Let us begin by distinguishing three varieties of reconsideration (or nonreconsideration).[2] Reconsideration normally involves deliberation. But it does not follow that reconsideration is normally *based on* deliberation. Indeed, it seems clear that it is not. One typically does not deliberate about whether to reconsider, but just goes ahead and reconsiders (or does not reconsider). What accounts for the presence or absence of the reconsideration will most times not be present deliberation but rather certain underlying habits, skills, and dispositions. In such cases the (non)reconsideration is, I shall say, *nonreflective.*

There are occasions, however, in which an agent does reconsider—or refrains from reconsidering—on the basis of present deliberation about whether to reconsider. Perhaps I am worried about the wisdom of my plan to finish my book this year, but am also wary of the emotional costs of reopening the issue and of the danger of becoming so self-absorbed that I get little done. So I deliberate about whether to reconsider my prior plan to finish the book. Given our limits and the obvious costs of such second-order deliberation such cases will be rare. It will frequently be true that if I am going to deliberate at all, I might just as well jump right in and reconsider my prior plan. Still, such cases do occur. These are cases of *deliberative* (non)reconsideration.

Cases of deliberative and nonreflective (non)reconsideration need to be distinguished from *policy-based* (non)reconsideration. In the latter case I do—in contrast with nonreflective cases—stop explicitly to think about whether to reconsider a certain prior plan. I do not, however, seriously weigh desire-belief reasons for and against reconsideration; so my case is not one of deliberative (non)reconsideration. Rather, I just appeal to a *general policy* of mine about when to reconsider such plans and when not to bother; and I proceed on the basis of this policy. If I proceed, say, not to reconsider because of a reconsideration-stopping appeal to such a policy, my case is one of *policy-based* nonreconsideration.

Both reconsideration and nonreconsideration may come in each of these three varieties. But there is also an asymmetry we should note between reconsideration and nonreconsideration. Even the nonreflective reconsideration of a prior intention will itself be an intentional action. But the same is not true about nonreconsideration. Nonreflective nonreconsideration is typically not itself an intentional action of refraining from reconsidering. Rather, nonreflective nonreconsideration of a prior intention typically consists merely in the *absence* of reconsideration of that intention, an absence to be explained by appeal to relevant general habits and dispositions.

Consider an example of John Fischer's. Earlier this year I carefully considered whether to get earthquake insurance and decided not to. Most of the time I simply do not seriously reconsider this intention of mine; I treat the matter as settled. My nonreconsideration is nonreflective, and it amounts only to the absence of reconsideration rather than an action of intentionally refraining from reconsidering. This is the typical case, and it is the case that is basic to my theory. Still, I do occasionally receive solicitations in the mail for such insurance, and sometimes I stop briefly to think about whether to look at them in a careful way. But then I quickly appeal to my policy of only reconsidering such matters yearly unless there is some basic change. In such cases my nonreconsideration

is policy-based but not deliberative. Finally, faced with one such solici-
tation I might actually deliberate about whether I should seriously reopen
the issue. If I decide on the basis of such second-order deliberation that
it would be best not to reconsider my prior decision against insurance,
my nonreconsideration is deliberative.

5.1.2 Aspects of Reconsideration

I now need to consider in some more detail just what is involved in
reconsidering a prior intention. To reconsider a prior intention to A is
not just to entertain the possibility of a change in that intention. It is
seriously to reopen the question of whether to A, so that this is now a
matter that needs to be settled anew. One withdraws the intention from
the background against which one deliberates. One no longer appeals to
that intention in one's practical reasoning. This does not mean that one
puts aside one's desire-belief reasons in favor of A-ing. But it does mean
that options incompatible with that intention (given one's relevant beliefs)
may newly become admissible. Typically this involves explicitly rethink-
ing whether to A. Sometimes, however, one seriously considers some
other option one takes to be incompatible with one's A-ing, and does
this in a way that *implicitly* reopens the question of whether to A.[3] For
example, Mondale might begin seriously to deliberate about the merits
of attacking Reagan's Middle East policies while being fully aware that
so acting would be incompatible with his attacking Star Wars. In such
deliberation Mondale would be implicitly reconsidering his intention to
attack Star Wars. When I speak of reconsideration, I shall include such
implicit reconsideration as well as the more explicit case.

Reconsideration of one's prior intention to A involves seriously reopening the question of whether to A. One puts one's prior intention to
one side and, at least temporally, does not, strictly speaking, intend to
A. This distinguishes reconsideration from other processes with which it
might be confused. Let me mention two. First, we sometimes stop long
enough to think about a prior intention in a way that does not involve
being open to *changing* it, but does allow us to notice new reasons for
so intending and to incorporate them into our reasons for so intending.
Suppose that in the debate Reagan says something silly about Star Wars
even before Mondale can attack on that issue. Mondale might notice this
and think: "Now it is even clearer that I should attack his Star Wars
plan." Mondale never seriously *reopens* the question of whether to attack
Star Wars; but he does *reaffirm* his intention to attack in a way that
incorporates new considerations into his reasons for so intending. He
considers again, without (strictly speaking) reconsidering.

Second, suppose Mondale actually stops in the debate and briefly considers whether to reconsider his intention to attack Star Wars. And suppose that, on reflection, he concludes that the costs of reconsideration would be too high and decides not to reconsider this plan of his. Though Mondale considers reconsidering his prior intention, he does not (strictly speaking) reconsider it. He does not seriously reopen the question of whether to attack Star Wars.[4]

In both these cases Mondale does not, strictly speaking, reconsider his prior intention to attack Star Wars. But it is also not true that there is *merely* an absence of reconsideration on Mondale's part. Rather, in reaffirming his prior intention or in deliberating about whether to reconsider and deciding not to, Mondale incorporates new considerations into his reasons for intending to attack Star Wars. In the first case his intention is now partly based on a reason that cites Reagan's most recent remark; in the second case it is now partly based on a reason that cites the inadvisability of bothering to reconsider. So there can be processes that are *reason-changing* even though they are not, strictly speaking, processes of reconsideration. There are cases of reason-changing nonreconsideration of a prior intention; and these cases should be distinguished from the ordinary case of nonreconsideration that is *reason-preserving*.[5] Nonreconsideration that is deliberative will not be reason-preserving; for when one refrains from reconsideration on the basis of present deliberation about whether to reconsider, this adds the inadvisability of reconsideration to one's reasons for intending. Nonreconsideration that is nonreflective will typically be reason-preserving. But even nonreflective nonreconsideration can sometimes be reason-changing: just consider the case of reaffirmation noted above.

To proceed. As I have noted, some of an agent's beliefs about the future will depend in a critical way on his intentions. My belief that I will be at Tanner Library this afternoon is based on my knowledge that I intend to go there. If I reconsider this intention, I must bracket the support it provides for this belief and others. I must take care not to keep assuming I will be at Tanner, even while reconsidering my intention to go there. (Matters are different, of course, if I have other grounds for this belief—perhaps I know I will be kidnapped and taken there if I do not go on my own.) Keeping track of the ways in which one's beliefs depend on intentions being reconsidered may become a fairly complex matter, especially as one reconsiders more extensive elements in one's prior plans. But this should not be taken to show that one may rationally proceed without adjusting one's beliefs as one reconsiders. Rather, it shows just how complicated—and so, costly—reconsideration of prior intentions can be.

Finally, reconsideration can be more or less extensive. Like the bracketing discussed in Chapter 3, one's reconsideration may extend more or less deeply into the hierarchy of one's plans; and it may also reach more or less extensively into one's further plans for the future. I may reconsider my intention to go to Tanner this afternoon, while holding fixed my intention to go to some library today. And Mondale might reconsider his intention to ask his third question, while holding fixed his intention to attack Star Wars. In both cases the reconsideration is relatively shallow. Finally, Mondale might reconsider his intention to attack Star Wars in this debate together with his intention to focus on fiscal policy in the next press conference. The scope of such reconsideration is greater than that of mere reconsideration of the intention to attack Star Wars.

So reconsideration can be more or less extensive, it has the effect of partially lifting the filter of admissibility on options, and it involves, among other things, various costs associated with the adjustment of one's beliefs.

5.2 Rationality of an Agent in Reconsidering (or Not Reconsidering)

We are now ready to turn to the main business at hand: When is it rational of an agent to reconsider (or not reconsider) a prior intention? What our preliminary discussion helps us see is that we need to narrow the question further. If the (non)reconsideration is itself deliberative, it will be a deliberative intentional action. So we can apply the treatment of deliberative agent rationality we began to develop in Chapter 4 and will develop further in Chapter 6. If the (non)reconsideration is itself policy-based, it will be a policy-based intentional action. So we can apply the treatment—to be developed in Chapter 6—of the rationality of an agent for her policy-based intentional conduct. What we need to focus on here is the exceedingly common case of *nonreflective* (non)reconsideration. This is the case that is central to my account of the rationality of an agent for (non)reconsideration.

5.2.1 *The Nonreflective Case*

When is such nonreflective (non)reconsideration of a prior intention rational of the agent? I propose a *two-tier* approach, an approach analogous in structure to certain versions of rule-utilitarianism. Nonreflective (non)reconsideration of a prior intention is the upshot of relevant general habits and propensities. These will involve, for example, tendencies to take notice of certain sorts of problems but not of others—to treat certain aspects of the environment as salient. Holding fixed the agent's other capacities,[6] we may, in a rough-and-ready way, assess the expected impact of such general habits on the agent's long-term prospects of getting what she wants. When this expected impact exceeds some appropriate threshold, we may say that these habits concerning reconsideration are reasonable of the agent to have. We may then say that the nonreflective (non)reconsideration of a prior intention was rational of S if it was the manifestation of general habits of reconsideration that were reasonable of S to have.

To elaborate, it will be useful to introduce the notion of the *stability* of a plan, a notion that coincides roughly with the commonsense notion of the firmness of an intention. An agent's habits and dispositions concerning the reconsideration or nonreconsideration of a prior intention or plan determine the stability of that intention or plan. Such dispositions may vary in a wide variety of ways. My disposition to refrain from reconsidering my prior plan may be rather minimal: I might be inclined to reconsider it given only a slight divergence between the way I find the world when I come to act and the way I expected it to be when I first settled on my plan. Or my disposition may involve substantial rigidity, as when I would only reconsider it in the face of some extreme divergence from my expectations—an earthquake, for example.

A plan might be stable in some respects and not in others. Perhaps my discovery that there is a special lecture today at Berkeley would not trigger my reconsideration of my plan to go to Tanner Library, whereas my discovery that this manuscript is due a month later than I had thought would. In contrast, things might be the other way round for an analogous plan of yours. My plan might be unstable in a respect in which yours is stable, and vice versa.

The stability of a plan is generally a long-term feature of that plan: I do not constantly adjust the stability of my plans. To do that would undermine the point of having plans, for I would then be constantly reconsidering their merits. Further, I do not normally decide how stable my plan is to be. Generally I do not, having settled on a plan, begin to reason yet again about how stable my plan should be (though in special cases I might). Rather, the stability of my plan is largely determined by general, underlying dispositions of mine.

The stability of my plans will generally not be an isolated feature of those plans but will be linked to other features of my psychology. For example, if I am the sort of person who is constantly on the alert for dangers in my environment, my plans are likely to have a kind of instability they would not have if I were a person too engrossed in my projects to be very sensitive to such dangers.[7] I might be more likely than most to reconsider my plan to go to Tanner Library upon hearing of a smog alert in the area. Frequently the extent of stability of my plans will be connected with underlying tendencies to *attend to* certain sorts of things and not others—to see certain features of my environment as *salient*. I may be more likely to take notice of certain sorts of hazards than you, and this fact may well be tied to a certain kind of instability that my plans have and yours do not.[8]

So the stability of a plan is a complex phenomenon susceptible of complex forms of assessment. We may want to say that a plan is, for instance, too stable in some respects and not stable enough in others. But the crucial point for present concerns is that this complex stability is grounded in various general habits and propensities, habits and propensities whose reasonableness we may assess in a broadly consequentialist way. The nonreflective (non)reconsideration of a certain prior intention is rational of S if it is the manifestation of general habits of reconsideration that are reasonable of S to have.

Recall Ryle's distinction between knowing *that* and knowing *how*.[9] One of the things one may know (more or less well) how to do is to reason.[10] What we have seen is that the stability of my plans is part and parcel of my overall skill at practical reasoning. To know how to reason is in part to know *when* to reason (or not reason) about what.

In reaching an assessment of the rationality of an agent for her nonreflective (non)reconsideration of a prior plan it is our expectations, not the agent's, that are crucial. But it is the agent's (rational) desires, not ours, that are similarly crucial. Note further that in assessing such underlying habits and propensities it is not only their impact on the agent's *actions* that matter. Though this impact will, of course, be central, there are also other ways in which the habits underlying the stability of an agent's plans will have a relevant impact. Suppose, for example, that I have a high sensitivity to certain kinds of environmental hazards, a sensitivity associated with certain kinds of plan instability. These kinds of instability may in fact conduce to a kind of useful preventive activity. But they may also lead to a kind of apprehensive and fearful consciousness that will undermine my long-term interest. And that impact is also relevant to our assessment of such a sensitivity.

What more can be said about the conditions under which habits of (non)reconsideration are reasonable? There are two rather general points to be made here. First, given our limits and the important role of plans in reliably extending the influence of present deliberation to future action we may expect that reasonable habits of (non)reconsideration will involve a tendency not to reconsider a prior plan except when faced with some problem for that plan.[11]

But what should be seen by an agent as a problem for her prior plan? Here we need to distinguish a problem *for* a plan from a problem *posed by* a plan. As I emphasized in Chapter 3, partial plans typically pose problems about means and preliminary steps. But the presence of such problems need not pose a challenge to the prior plan—they need not be problems *for* the plan. (Of course, if one found oneself unable to discover adequate means to one's planned end, that would be a problem for one's prior plan.) Problems for a prior plan will normally involve at least one of the following elements: some relevant divergence between the world as one finds it and the world as one expected it to be when settling on the plan; some relevant change in one's desires or values; or some relevant change in some of one's other intentions. Concerning problems of the first sort we can go on to distinguish between problems raised by unexpected obstacles in the way of one's planned course of action and problems raised by unexpected opportunities that arise as alternatives to one's planned course of action.[12] Further refinements are doubtless possible, though I will not pursue them here. The main point is that reasonable habits of (non)reconsideration will involve a presumption against reconsideration and in favor of increased stability. Relatedly, there will also be a kind of social pressure in the same direction: toward habits of nonreconsideration that support increased stability of plans. This is because the stability of my plans is one of the things that makes me a reliable partner in various schemes of interpersonal coordination.[13]

This brings me to the second point about reasonable habits of reconsideration. Sometimes the stakes are quite high, and there is an opportunity for calm and careful reconsideration of one's prior plan. It seems plausible to suppose that it is in the long-run interests of an agent occasionally to reconsider what he is up to, given such opportunities for reflection and given that the stakes are high, as long as the resources used in the process of such reconsideration are themselves modest. The unexamined life may still be worth living; but the occasionally reexamined life seems likely to be superior, even for limited creatures like us. Alongside the presumption in favor of increased stability of one's plans, then, we should place a presumption in favor of occasional reconsideration, given sufficiently high stakes and an appropriate opportunity. Reasonable habits of nonreconsideration should comport with both these presumptions.

Of course, these presumptions will apply differently to different sorts of plans and circumstances. A plan aimed at coordinating one's activities for today, and one's activities today with one's friend's, is likely to fall squarely within the presumption in favor of stability and nonreconsideration. A long-term plan to become a concert pianist is more likely to fall within the presumption of occasional reconsideration—as long as circumstances are apt and do not impose undue costs on the very process of further reflection. Reasonable habits of (non)reconsideration should reflect these differences.

A further point is that it does not follow from the fact that certain habits of reconsideration are superior to those I have that it would be rational of me to try to change myself so as to develop those habits. Whether it would be rational of me to *act* in such a way will depend also on the costs of bringing about the change, and these may be high. It is possible, then, that my habits of reconsideration are not reasonable of me to have, and yet it would be rational of me not to try to change them in a basic way.

So we have a two-tier account of the rationality of an agent for her nonreflective (non)reconsideration of a prior intention. On this account we first ask, in a consequentialist spirit, what underlying habits of (non)reconsideration are reasonable. Then we ask whether, in the particular case, the nonreflective (non)reconsideration manifests reasonable habits. It is rational of the agent, in that particular case, to reconsider (or not reconsider) just in case she thereby manifests reasonable habits of (non)reconsideration. This two-tier principle is not, of course, intended for use by the agent in deliberating about whether to reconsider; such deliberation is absent from the cases to which this principle is to be applied. This principle is for the external assessment of an agent, not a principle to be used internally, in the agent's deliberations about what to do. It is a principle of practical rationality whose role is not directly to guide the action of the agent, but rather to be applied from an external perspective in assessing the rationality of the agent.[14]

Note that this two-tiered account of nonreflective (non)reconsideration does not see my prior intention as providing a reason against its own reconsideration, a reason I can appeal to in deliberation about whether to reconsider that intention. If I actually stop and deliberate about whether to reconsider my prior intention, I can make an indirect appeal to that intention as evidence for the wisdom of nonreconsideration. I can also concern myself with the effects of such reconsideration on the stability of other plans. For example, I can ask whether such reconsideration is likely to promote undesirable habits of instability. But it is no part of the present theory that I can directly cite my prior intention as by itself a reason, over and above my relevant desire-belief reasons, against its own reconsideration. And this seems a virtue of my two-tier theory. If I were able to appeal to my intention directly as a reason against reconsidering itself, it seems that I would be able to justify a kind of unacceptable stubbornness. But my two-tier theory does not endorse such stubbornness, for it does not suppose that my intention by itself provides such a reason against its own reconsideration. Instead, the two-tier theory provides an external principle for the assessment of agents who nonreflectively refrain from reconsideration.

A standard worry about rule-utilitarianism is that the two forms of reasoning it sanctions seem potentially in conflict.[15] It sanctions utilitarian reasoning concerning rules but not concerning particular acts. But given its commitment to the former it may seem unclear how it can block such reasoning in the latter case, the case in which we are assessing particular acts. Such a worry does not arise for the present account of nonreflective (non)reconsideration. This is so because this is only an account of the rationality of an agent for (non)reconsideration that is *not* based on present deliberation. This account does *not* say that an agent who really does deliberate about whether to reconsider should not reason directly about the consequences of such reconsideration; for this account simply does not address such a case of *deliberative* (non)reconsideration. In the sort of case the present account does address there is no need to block direct consequentialist reasoning by the agent concerning his particular case of (non)reconsideration; for in the cases in question there is no deliberation at all about whether to reconsider.

Consider a potential objection. Suppose certain of my habits of reconsideration are overly rigid, and so not reasonable of me to have. In a particular case they lead me nonreflectively to refrain from reconsidering a prior intention. On the account just mooted this nonreconsideration is not rational of me. But what if, in this case, habits it would have been reasonable of me to have had would also have led to nonreconsideration? Why is that not enough to make my nonreconsideration rational of me?

The answer is that it is the rationality of me, the agent, that is in question here, not the advisability of nonreconsideration. Perhaps in such a case nonreconsideration would be advisable: perhaps it would be recommended from our external perspective; perhaps it would be expected of a person whose relevant habits are reasonable. But when we ask whether my actual nonreconsideration was rational of me, what matters is not how I might have been led not to reconsider, but how I was so led.

A second problem is raised by the possibility that the expectable consequences of various habits of reconsideration can be quite idiosyncratic. Suppose the Devil tells you that he will make you very sick whenever you reconsider an earlier decision. Are we to say that extremely rigid habits of nonreconsideration are reasonable for you, though not for ordinary folks?

There are two different positions open to us here. On the one hand, we could just grant that habits it is reasonable of me to have may not be reasonable for you to have, and that significant differences in our circumstances may induce analogous differences concerning reasonable habits of reconsideration. On the other hand, we could assess habits of reconsideration with respect to background assumptions about what is normal for beings like us. This would allow for certain individual differences—for example, differences in general abilities to reason quickly in emergency situations—but would rule out such extreme cases as the one just mooted. Taking this second tack we could say that the Devil has made it rational for you to try to develop unreasonable habits of reconsideration.

Whichever tack we take, we will want to allow an agent to take account of his habits of reconsideration in his policies of adopting future-directed plans. If you know that you are an extremely rigid person, one unlikely to reconsider a prior intention, you will have reason to be particularly careful before you make up your mind in advance. But this still leaves open the question of which of these two approaches we should take.

I think that reflection on the role that judgments of agent rationality play in our lives argues for a version of the second approach. As noted above, judgments of agent rationality are central to our concern with education. In reflecting on what habits, tendencies, and processes of intention formation and retention are reasonable of an agent, our concern is, in large part, with the question of what habits (and so on) to encourage and develop in ourselves and others over the long run. We want standards that are widely applicable, at least within the general constraints of our culture and our general capacities and limits. So we want standards that are shaped by a concern with normal cases, given general cultural and psychological constraints.

This suggests that we take some version of the second approach to cases like that just described. If you inculcate in yourself extremely rigid habits in order to avoid the Devil's threatened infliction of sickness, you may well be acting rationally. But you are nevertheless causing yourself to have habits that are not themselves reasonable. The appearance of paradox here disappears once we keep clearly in mind that function of the latter assessment of your habits of reconsideration: it is to assess the extent to which these habits come up to a standard appropriate for guiding the education and development of agents like us over the long run.

5.2.2 A Puzzle about the Deliberative Case

I have been discussing a two-tier approach to the rationality of an agent for her nonreflective (non)reconsideration of a prior intention. As I noted, these nonreflective cases are central to my theory and require their own treatment. In contrast, cases of deliberative and policy-based (non)reconsideration can be seen as special cases of the general treatments of deliberative and policy-based intentional conduct to be provided later. The case of deliberative (non)reconsideration, however, does raise a special puzzle, one I should like to discuss briefly before going on.

Suppose that Mondale believes that if he does reconsider his intention to attack Star Wars he will end up doing something else instead. This is a belief Mondale might have even while supposing that such reconsideration would not be worth its costs. But if Mondale does have this belief, the following will be true: it will not be consistent with his beliefs that he successfully execute *both* an intention to attack Star Wars *and* an intention to reconsider that very intention. So the option of reconsidering his prior intention to attack Star Wars will, it seems, be *inadmissible* as long as Mondale has that very intention. From this it seems to follow, on my theory, that as long as Mondale intends to attack Star Wars he is not in a position to deliberate about whether to reconsider that intention. And that seems odd.

The solution is to recall the notion of *implicit* reconsideration. Suppose that in the debate Mondale begins to deliberate about the merits of attacking Reagan's Middle East policies. Given Mondale's beliefs this may well amount to implicit reconsideration of his intention to attack Star Wars; for Mondale knows full well that he cannot attack both policies. Assuming that this implicit reconsideration is itself nonreflective, we can use the two-tier approach in assessing the rationality of Mondale for so reconsidering.

The situation is similar in the (unusual) case in which Mondale deliberates about the merits of reconsidering his intention to attack Star Wars while believing that if he does reconsider he will not in the end attack Star Wars. In deliberating about whether to reconsider this intention he is explicitly raising the question of whether to reconsider. But, given his beliefs, we may assume that he is also implicitly reopening the question of whether to attack Star Wars. So in deliberating about whether to reconsider this intention he thereby already implicitly reconsiders it. It is not that my theory precludes such deliberation. Rather, the theory shows us that when the agent has such a belief about the consequences of reconsideration, the mere act of deliberating about reconsidering the prior intention itself may well amount to an implicit reconsideration of that intention. And if we assume that this implicit reconsideration is itself nonreflective, it will be subject to the two-tier theory.

5.3 Application to the Example

Let us see how the discussions in these past two chapters of plan stability and agent rationality apply to Mondale's case.

5.3.1 Reasonable versus Ideal Stability

I asked the question: was it rational of Mondale not to reconsider his prior intention to attack Star Wars? Now, Mondale's nonreconsideration of his prior intention was, we may assume, sufficiently nonreflective for us to apply the two-tier theory. So the first step is to locate those habits of reconsideration that Mondale manifests in failing to reconsider his prior intention. We then ask whether the expected long-term impact of these habits on Mondale's getting what he wants exceeds an appropriate threshold. If it does, then they are habits that it is reasonable of Mondale to have; and his failure to reconsider is rational of him. If the expected impact of these habits does not exceed this threshold, then it is not rational of Mondale not to reconsider.

Recall that we are supposing that Mondale's asking his third question is on balance rational from his internal perspective but not on balance rational from our external, non-plan-constrained perspective. Given this latter, externally assessed failure of rationality could it nevertheless have been rational of Mondale not to have reconsidered his prior intention?

Yes, it could. To see this clearly it is useful to introduce a distinction between the reasonable and ideal stability of a plan. The stability of an intention or plan is *reasonable* if the associated habits of reconsideration are reasonable of the agent to have—if the expected impact of these habits on the agent's long-term interest in getting what she (rationally) wants exceeds an appropriate threshold. The two-tier theory tells us that if the stability of a prior intention or plan is reasonable, then, in the normal case, its nonreflective (non)reconsideration is rational of the agent.

To get at the notion of ideal stability we need to ask when reconsideration of Mondale's prior intention would be recommended from our external, non-plan-constrained perspective as superior to just going ahead and nondeliberatively executing that intention. It would not, we may assume, be recommended if such reconsideration would be expected to lead to no change of mind; for then the costs of reconsideration would be wasted.[16] Nor would it be recommended if the expected benefits from a change of mind would be outweighed by the expected costs of reconsideration—for example, the loss of time for Mondale and the impact of hesitancy on viewers. Reconsideration would only be recommended if the expected benefits of a change in intention would outweigh the costs of reconsideration. Let us say that the stability of Mondale's prior intention is *ideal* just in case Mondale is disposed to reconsider it in all, and only in, situations of this last kind—if he is disposed to reconsider it precisely when such reconsideration would be recommended from our external, non-plan-constrained perspective.

It seems clear that reasonable and ideal stability will typically diverge, and will do so for three reasons. The first is that reasonable stability is assessed relative to the expectations of the external assessor, whereas ideal stability is assessed relative to the expectations of the agent. To the extent that these expectations diverge we can expect corresponding divergence in assessments of reasonable and ideal stability. In any case, even given similarity in the relevant expectations of the agent and the external assessor, there remain two other sources of divergence between reasonable and ideal stability. The first is that, given our limits, it is not plausible that our dispositions could be so finely tuned as to ensure ideal stability. The second is that habits and dispositions concerning reconsideration will have expected consequences that are not expected consequences of the reconsideration (or nonreconsideration) of some prior intention. For example, others' knowledge of Mondale's rather rigid habits might make him more attractive to them as a partner in coordinating schemes. (This would be a special case of the general phenomenon already noted: a general social pressure toward increased stability of one's plans, given their role in social coordination.) But their knowledge, and the associated benefits for Mondale, may be in part a consequence of things other than Mondale's reconsideration or nonreconsideration of prior plans. So even the level of stability that is *maximally* advantageous for Mondale may diverge from ideal stability. This is because ideal stability is defined solely in terms of the pros and cons of reconsideration, whereas—as we have just noted—the pros and cons relevant to a consequentialist assessment of the stability of a plan go beyond this.

So it is possible that the stability of Mondale's prior intention to attack Star Wars is reasonable and that Mondale nonreflectively refrains from reconsideration, even though reconsideration of this intention is recommended from our external non-plan-constrained perspective. In such a case it would be rational of Mondale not to reconsider even though reconsideration is externally advisable.

5.3.2 Combining the Theories

Let us now combine these two theoretical structures: the two-tier approach to nonreflective (non)reconsideration and the accounts of deliberative and nondeliberative agent rationality sketched in Chapter 4. Let us see how, taken together, these structures treat Mondale during the debate.[17]

Mondale nondeliberatively intends to attack Star Wars and does not reconsider this intention. Rather, he reasons from this intention to an intention to ask his third question as a means to attacking Star Wars. This latter intention—the intention to ask the third question—is one Mondale now holds deliberatively. Finally, Mondale proceeds to execute both intentions: he proceeds to attack Star Wars by asking this question.

To assess Mondale for his intention to attack Star Wars we apply the principle of nondeliberative rationality. This requires us to determine whether it is now rational of Mondale not to reconsider this intention. In the normal case in which this nonreconsideration is nonreflective we can apply the two-tier theory. To assess Mondale for his intention to ask his third question we apply the principle of deliberative rationality. This requires us, again, to determine whether it was rational of Mondale not to reconsider his prior intention to attack Star Wars. And it also requires us to determine whether it was reasonable of Mondale to conclude that his third question was at least as well supported by his reasons for action as alternative, admissible means (for example, asking the first question). Finally, on the intention-action principle, Mondale's intentional actions of attacking Star Wars and asking his third question are rational of him to perform if these intentions are rational of him to have. In light of my earlier discussion of the possible divergence between reasonable and ideal stability it is clear that on the theories presently under consideration it might be rational of Mondale to have both these intentions, and so rational of him intentionally to perform both of these actions, even though these actions would not be recommended from the external, non-plan-constrained perspective.

In the case of Mondale and the debate that I have so far been discussing I have been assuming that it was irrational of Mondale initially to decide to attack Star Wars. This is what first raised the specter of bootstrapping problems. To explore the theories under consideration a bit further let us turn briefly to a second version of Mondale's case. In this second version we suppose that it was, in fact, rational of Mondale initially to decide to attack Star Wars. But when the debate comes, Reagan acts in ways that are rather unexpected, and as a result Mondale's confidence in his prior decision is somewhat shaken. But it is not shaken enough to force him to reconsider. Instead, Mondale goes ahead in his means-end reasoning concerning how to pursue this attack and decides to ask his third question.

Suppose that the stability of Mondale's prior intention to attack Star Wars is reasonable but not ideal. In the debate Mondale nonreflectively refrains from reconsidering this intention, and this is rational of him. But let us suppose that, given Reagan's unexpected behavior, reconsideration of Mondale's prior intention would in fact be recommended from the external perspective, even taking account of the costs of reconsideration. This is a possibility raised by the potential divergence between reasonable and ideal stability. Applying the principle of nondeliberative rationality, we can infer from the rationality of Mondale in (nonreflectively) not reconsidering his intention to attack Star Wars that it is now (nondeliberatively) rational of Mondale so to intend. Applying the principle of deliberative rationality we may conclude that it is (deliberatively) rational of Mondale to intend to ask his third question. And by applying the intention-action principle, we may reach analogous conclusions about Mondale's intentional actions of attacking Star Wars and asking his third question. Just as in the original Mondale case, in this second version of Mondale's case it may be rational of Mondale so to intend and so to act even though these actions would not be recommended from the external perspective.

These results for both Mondale cases have some plausibility. But now it is time to see the weaknesses of the account of agent rationality as so far developed.

chapter 6

Agent Rationality:
The Historical Theory

MY PLANNING theory as so far developed contains the following elements: a model of the role of partial plans in practical reasoning; an account of internal and external assessments of the rationality of intentional action; a two-tier approach to the assessment of an agent for nonreflective (non)reconsideration of a prior plan; a two-stage approach to the rationality of an agent in intentionally acting in certain ways; the intention-action principle as the first stage of this approach; and a pair of principles for the second stage. All but this last pair of principles seem to me acceptable components of a conception of rational agency that takes intentions and partial plans seriously. This last component, however—the pair of principles for the second stage of the account of agent rationality—is, I think, in serious tension with the picture of human agents as limited, rational planners that lies behind much of my discussion. Or so, anyway, I now want to argue.

6.1 The Historical Approach to Nondeliberative Rationality

6.1.1 General Considerations

Begin by returning to my initial stab at a principle of nondeliberative rationality:

> *Nondeliberative rationality of an agent in intending*
>   Suppose that prior to t_1 S has come to have the intention to A at t_2. And suppose that S continues so to intend until t_1, and does not reconsider this intention at t_1. Then it is rational of S so to intend at t_1 if and only if it is rational of S at t_1 not to reconsider that intention then.

As noted, this is an *ahistorical* principle. When we apply the principle to S at t_1, the prior history of the intention drops out of consideration. In particular, two sorts of historical facts are treated as irrelevant. First, it does not matter whether, when S earlier, at t_0, formed this intention, it was then rational of him so to intend. Even if it was *ir*rational of S at t_0 so to intend, it will be rational of S at t_1 so to intend as long as it is rational of S at t_1 not to reconsider that intention then. Second, it does not matter whether there was some period of time between t_0 and t_1 during which it was not rational of S not to reconsider his intention to A at t_2. All that matters is that it be rational of S *at* t_1 not to reconsider.

I believe that it is a mistake to ignore such historical considerations. Take the second point first. Recall the second Mondale case: the case in which Mondale's original decision to attack Star Wars was rational of him to make but in which Reagan later acted in unexpected ways. Let us now add a further feature to this case and call the resulting case the *third* Mondale case. Let us suppose that a day before the debate but after the original decision Mondale had received reliable advice from his aides that Reagan was likely to act in the way in which he in fact did act. Given this information and the available time, it might have been irrational of Mondale to fail, throughout the day before the debate, to reconsider his attack plan. Even so, if Mondale has not reconsidered before the debate starts, it might now—during the debate—be rational of him not to reconsider. A general tendency not to reconsider important plans at the very last moment, except in very special cases, will have many advantages in the long run. On the ahistorical principle, then, before it comes time to attack Star Wars it will become rational of Mondale to intend to attack. Just by postponing reconsideration long enough Mondale makes it rational of himself to intend to attack. And this seems to make it too easy for him to get off the hook of criticizable irrationality.

This problem suggests that we expand the time during which it must be rational of the agent not to reconsider his intention. That is, we add to the ahistorical principle of nondeliberative rationality a historical condition that must be satisfied for it to be rational of S at t_1 to intend to A at t_2, namely: it must have been rational of S not to have reconsidered this intention throughout some appropriate period of time, a period of time beginning sometime after the original formation of the intention and including t_1.

But although this is a step in the right direction, I do not think it will suffice. The problem derives from the first sort of historical fact that the ahistorical theory ignores. These are facts about the rationality of the agent in initially reaching the intention in question. Here we need to return to a version of the first Mondale case. Recall that in this case Mondale's initial decision to attack Star Wars is so influenced by wishful thinking that it is not rational of Mondale to make it. Now let us suppose that the decision is reached a short time before the debate. Let us further suppose that once having reached this decision it is rational of Mondale not to reconsider; for the debate is to begin quite soon. So even on the suggested revision of the ahistorical theory, when the time for the attack arrives it will be rational of Mondale to intend to attack. Yet, again, this still seems to let Mondale too easily off the hook. Despite his rationality in not reconsidering, his irrationality in originally deciding to attack seems to infect his rationality during the debate in intending to attack.

Granted, in such a case we do not want to criticize Mondale for not reconsidering his intention during the debate. But it does not follow from this that Mondale is not subject to criticism for so intending, given the history of that intention. We have here a bootstrapping problem for agent rationality, one analogous to the earlier bootstrapping problem for the rationality of action. Given the benefits of general tendencies toward stable plans, intentions that it is irrational of the agent to form threaten too easily to become intentions it is later rational of the agent to have. To block this problem it seems that an adequate historical approach must reach all the way back to the earlier deliberation and decision which accounts for Mondale's intention.

The ahistorical principle treats the assessment of an agent for non-deliberatively intending at t_1 to A as an assessment of a time-slice of that agent at t_1. It ignores facts both about her original formation of this intention and about her rationality in retaining it from then until t_1. But such a time-slice picture seems inappropriate given the point—central to this discussion—that we are planning agents for whom the connection between reasoning and action tends to be spread out over time, and facilitated by the formation of prior, partial plans. As John Rawls remarks, standards of assessment should be suited to the nature of the thing being assessed.[1] In the present case a time-slice standard seems at odds with the model of temporally extended rational agency that has emerged from our reflections on intentions and plans. The time-slice standard seems wrongly to ignore historical facts about both the formation and the retention of the agent's intention. In its place we want an account that sees an agent's rationality at t_1 for intending to A as a function of the extent to which the relevant processes that lead to her so intending come up to standards appropriate for limited, rational, and temporally extended agents like us.

Consider the entire process beginning with Mondale's initial deliberations about whether to attack Star Wars and ending with his intention to ask his third question. We may distinguish three stages of this process: an initial piece of deliberation issuing in an intention to attack Star Wars; a period of nonreconsideration of the initial intention; and a further piece of means-end reasoning issuing in the intention to ask the third question. We may call this entire process a piece of *extended deliberation*. Much of the deliberation that lies behind our intentions is extended deliberation. Otherwise we would be time-slice agents—agents who are always starting from scratch in their deliberation. Mondale's case is an example of this general phenomenon: his intention to ask his third question is based on such extended deliberation. It is by way of this extended deliberation that this intention is based on his desire-belief reasons for attacking Star Wars, reasons that entered his deliberation earlier, when he first decided to attack Star Wars. So it is natural to suppose that—contrary to the ahistorical theory—when we come to assess Mondale for so intending, our assessment should be shaped by our assessment of him *for this extended deliberation*. As T. M. Scanlon once put it in conversation, this is how we ensure that the reasons and deliberation that really are responsible for this intention are included within the scope of our assessment.

We need, then, a *historical* theory of nondeliberative agent rationality. Such a theory should accord an appropriate role in our judgments of agent rationality both to the rationality of the agent in initially forming a prior intention, and to her rationality in retaining that intention through nonreconsideration. The problem is that once we take such historical considerations seriously we are in danger of being overwhelmed by the enormous complexity and variety of the histories lying behind our various intentions. In an attempt to say something relatively clear, in a way that does not run completely roughshod over such complexities, I will proceed as follows. I will first try to provide a historical principle for a sort of case of nondeliberative intention that seems to me susceptible of a relatively straightforward treatment. I will call this case the *basic case* for the theory. I will then try to determine how such historical considerations should influence our principle of deliberative rationality. Historical treatments of nondeliberative and deliberative cases in hand, I will then turn, as I once promised, to the case of policy-based intention. Only then will I return to the nondeliberative case and consider a pair of variations on the basic case, with an eye to determining what a historical theory that takes intentions and our limits seriously should say about such variations. I will conclude this chapter with a discussion of a puzzle left over from Chapter 4.

6.1.2 A Historical Principle for the Basic Case

The basic case for my treatment of the rationality of an agent for her nondeliberative intentions has the following features:

(1) Prior to t_0 the agent, S does not intend to A at t_2.

(2) At t_0 S deliberates about whether to A at t_2 and, on the basis of this deliberation, forms an intention to A at t_2.

(3) From t_0 through to t_1 S does not reconsider this intention, and this nonreconsideration is nonreflective and reason-preserving.[2]

(4) As a result of (2) and (3), at t_1 S intends to A at t_2.

Now, we are looking for a theory that sees the rationality of an agent for her intentions as dependent on the extent to which the relevant processes that lead to those intentions come up to appropriate standards. In the basic case it seems quite plausible to suppose that the relevant process is the *extended deliberation* that begins at t_0 and continues through to t_1. This makes it natural to endorse something like the following historical principle of agent rationality:

> *Historical principle of nondeliberative rationality for the basic case*
> In the basic case it is rational of S at t_1 to intend to A at t_2 just in case:
>
> (a) it was rational of S at t_0 to form this intention; and
> (b) it was rational of S from t_0 to t_1 not to reconsider this intention.

On this principle for the basic case—and in contrast with the ahistorical theory—rational nonreconsideration in the present does not by itself guarantee the present nondeliberative rationality of an agent in intending. Rather, rational nonreconsideration functions as a kind of *rational link* to prior deliberation. Rational nonreconsideration allows the earlier rationality of the agent in forming the intention to be *transmitted* to a later time; it allows the agent now to inherit this earlier rationality. But if there was no such rationality in forming the intention at t_0, there is nothing to transmit or inherit.[3]

On this historical theory it remains true that it may be rational of an agent nondeliberatively to intend to A even though the recommendation from the external, non-plan-constrained perspective would be to reconsider that intention and decide differently. For this to be true, however, it is not enough that it now be rational of the agent not to reconsider this intention. Rather, it must have been rational of the agent initially to have formed that intention, and also rational of her throughout not to have reconsidered. Still, an agent's earlier rationality in deliberatively deciding at t_0 to A at t_2 can sometimes be transmitted to her at t_1 even if, taking an external perspective at t_1, we would recommend a different intention. To see this, return to the second Mondale case. This is the case in which Mondale's initial decision to attack Star Wars is rational of him to make; Reagan's behavior during the debate is rather unexpected; but Mondale nevertheless does not reconsider his initial decision. And let us assume that we have here an instance of the basic case—that Mondale's nonreconsideration is nonreflective and reason-preserving. On our historical principle for the basic case, as long as it was initially rational of Mondale to intend to attack Star Wars and it was rational of him throughout not to reconsider, it will be rational of him during the debate so to intend. The rationality of Mondale in initially reaching his intention to attack Star Wars is transmitted to Mondale at the time of the debate. This may be true even though it is also true that if Mondale had reconsidered his prior intention in the face of unexpected behavior on Reagan's part, it would not have been rational of Mondale to continue so to intend, and even though such reconsideration would be recommended from the external perspective.

For any instance of the basic case we may ask two questions: Was it rational of the agent at t_0 initially to have formed the intention to A at t_2? And was it rational of the agent nonreflectively to have refrained from reconsidering that intention from t_0 to t_1? Assuming a yes–no answer to each question we have, then, four possible cases. The historical principle tells us that only in one of these is it rational of the agent at t_1 to intend to A at t_2, namely, in the case for which both questions are answered affirmatively. On this historical approach my rationality (in the basic case) in now nondeliberatively intending to A depends on certain *past* desire-belief reasons, certain *past* processes of deliberation, and the *past and present* absence of reconsideration, each of which is in part responsible for this intention.

Consider now two versions of the basic case that may seem to pose problems for the historical principle. In the first it was rational of me initially to form the intention to A, but then it was not rational of me throughout t_0 to t_1 nonreflectively to refrain from reconsidering that intention. Nevertheless, it is also true that if I had reconsidered I would have rationally stuck to my guns and retained my prior intention.[4] The historical principle insists that it is not rational of me at t_1 so to intend. Is this plausible?

I think it is, as long as we recognize two points. First, in such a case the historical principle does not say it is *ir*rational of me to intend to A. It only says it is *not* rational of me so to intend. As we will see even more clearly when we consider certain variations in the basic case, we are sometimes obliged to reach fairly complex judgments of agent rationality rather than single, all-in judgments. Though in the present version of the basic case I do not fully come up to the relevant standard of rationality, we may also want to reject an all-out assessment of me as irrational. Instead, we may want to say that I was rational in some respects, not rational in others. Second, in such a case the externally assessed rationality of the action may differ from the rationality of the agent. Since my failure to reconsider my intention is not rational of me, it is not rational of me so to intend. Assessments of the rationality of agents are sensitive to how in fact the agent comes to have the intentions he has, not to how he might have come to have them. But though it is not rational *of me* so to intend, it still may be true that my intention and action would themselves be recommended as rational, on balance, from the external, non-plan-constrained perspective; for my intention and action may well be recommended by the balance of my relevant reasons for action.[5]

The second problem case involves what John Etchemendy once called "the snowball effect." My decision at t_0 to A at t_2, though not rational of me then, may still lead me to take steps such that by t_1 it would be rational of me to decide to A on the basis of deliberation then. Suppose my decision at t_0 to attend concert A rather than concert B, although irrational of me to make, still leads me to drive in the direction of the former and away from the latter. By t_1 it may be true that if I were to deliberate again about what concert to go to I would opt for concert A. If, however, I in fact never do reconsider my initial decision (and my nonreconsideration is nonreflective and reason-preserving), the historical principle will still insist that it is not rational of me at t_1 to intend to go to concert A. It will insist on this even if it is rational of me not to reconsider. Is this plausible?

I think it is; but again we must recognize the two points noted above. First, the historical principle need not say it is *ir*rational of me to intend at t_1 to go to concert A. The relevant processes underlying my intention to go to concert A—namely, the extended deliberation from t_0 to t_1— fail to come up to a standard appropriate for a limited rational agent like me. So it is not rational of me at t_1 so to intend. But it may also not be simply irrational of me so to intend. Rather, an appropriate assessment of me for so intending may have to be complex in a way that recognizes my rationality for not reconsidering my intention at t_1. Second, the principle allows for a difference between agent and action rationality. The fact that I would still have intended at t_1 to go to concert A, even if I had reconsidered at t_1, does not vindicate me for intending at t_1 to go to concert A when in fact I do not reconsider. Nevertheless, my action at

t_1 of heading toward concert A may be what would be recommended as rational from the appropriate external point of view.

One way to see the virtue of this view is to consider that moment at which I come to be so far away from concert B that heading toward concert A newly becomes rational from the external perspective.[6] Do you really want to say that at that moment it also becomes rational *of me* to intend to go to concert A even though I do not actually use this information newly to support this intention? The historical principle predicts—correctly, it seems to me—that you do not.[7]

Consider now one final complication for the historical principle.[8] You might ask whether it was rational of Mondale to ask his third question *considering only what has transpired since the beginning of the debate.* This limitation of concern might be made explicit in your inquiry, or it might only be implicit, but clear given the context of the discussion. Once concern is limited in this way the historical principle may, of course, be inappropriate; for the historical principle may treat as relevant events that occurred prior to the postulated cutoff point (the beginning of the debate). But the fact that we can limit our concern in this way does not show that we should reject the historical principle as an account of judgments of agent rationality that are not in such a way artificially limited or circumscribed.

My conclusion is that my historical principle deals appropriately with the basic case of nondeliberative intention. It is a plausible way of capturing, for the basic case, the idea that the rationality of the agent for her intention depends on the extent to which the relevant aspects of the history of that intention come up to appropriate standards.

Throughout this discussion, though, I have been assuming that we know when it is rational of an agent to intend to A on the basis of present deliberation about whether so to act. I have been assuming we have some notion of the rationality of an agent for her *deliberative* intentions. Now it is time to substitute some hard cash for this promissory note.

6.2 The Historical Approach to Deliberative Rationality

Judgments of the rationality of an agent for an intention formed on the basis of present deliberation play a dual role in my historical planning theory. First, they provide assessments of the agent at the time of the deliberation for intentions formed on the basis of that deliberation. Second, they provide an anchor[9] for assessments of the rationality of the agent for later, nondeliberative intentions. This means that the account we offer of the rationality of an agent for her deliberative intentions will have extensive repercussions. What, then, should the historical planning theory say about this matter?

Recall the principle accepted by the ahistorical account:

> *Deliberative rationality of an agent in intending*
> If on the basis of deliberation at t_1 S forms the intention to A at t_2, then it is rational of S at t_1 to intend to A at t_2 if and only if:
>> (1) for those intentions of S's that play a direct role as a background of S's deliberation, it is rational of S at t_1 not to reconsider those intentions then; and
>> (2) S reasonably supposes that A is at least as well supported by his reasons for action as its relevant, admissible alternatives.

Consider condition (1). Note that on the *a*historical principle of *non*-deliberative rationality, satisfaction of condition (1) guarantees that it is rational of S at t_1 to have those nondeliberative intentions that are in the relevant background. But on the *historical* approach to nondeliberative rationality this is no longer so. In particular, if it was originally *ir*rational of S at t_0 to form the intention to A, then (according to the historical approach) it may not be rational of S at t_1 to intend to A, even if at t_1 it is rational of S not to reconsider. So we need to ask whether the historical approach obliges us to make some change in condition (1) of the principle of deliberative rationality.

Suppose that I reason from an intention formed earlier concerning some end to a new intention concerning means or preliminary steps. My initial intention is one I now hold nondeliberatively. To keep things manageable let us suppose that the extended deliberation lying behind this nondeliberative intention is an instance of the basic case: I initially formed the intention on the basis of deliberation, and from that time on have retained it through reason-preserving, nonreflective nonreconsideration. Suppose further that my nonreconsideration of my initial intention is rational of me at the time of action. Still, other facts about the history of this initial intention—facts about its initial formation or its nonreconsideration prior to the time of action—make it *not* rational of me so to intend. Does this failure of rationality in intending the end infect the assessment of me in intending the means (or preliminary steps)?

For example, suppose I deliberate about whether to avoid a certain embarrassment by lying to you when you call me later in the day. Suppose I give in to temptation and decide—irrationally—to tell the lie. A while later the phone rings and, given the press of time, it is now rational of me nonreflectively to refrain from reconsidering whether to tell the lie. Still, I need to deliberate quickly concerning preliminary steps: how can

I ensure that the relevant subject comes up? Suppose I decide to ensure this by asking a certain question. Perhaps this decision is rational given my prior intention to tell the lie, an intention it is rational of me now not to reconsider. Still, it is not rational of me to intend to tell the lie, given the history of this intention. Is it nevertheless rational of me to intend to take the preliminary step of asking the question?

Considerations similar to those offered in support of the historical approach to nondeliberative rationality seem forceful here as well. On the ahistorical approach, just by waiting long enough I can make it rational of me both to tell the lie and to take the needed preliminary steps. And in both cases this seems too easily to block criticism of me. We want, rather, to treat the extended deliberation that lies behind my intention in favor of lying as relevant to the assessment of me for deliberatively intending the preliminary steps to the lie. In this way we ensure that the deliberation and the reasons that are in fact responsible for my intention to ask the question are treated as relevant to the assessment of me for that intention. This extended deliberation will include both the initial formation of my intention concerning the end and its nonreflective retention up to the time of the formation of the intention concerning preliminary steps. The natural way to do this is simply to strengthen condition (1) along the following lines:

> *Historical principle of deliberative rationality*
> If S at t_1 forms the intention to A at t_2 on the basis of deliberation at t_1, then it is rational of S at t_1 to intend to A at t_2 if and only if:
> (1′) for those intentions of S's that play a direct role as a background of S's deliberation, it is rational of S at t_1 *so to intend*; and
> (2) S reasonably supposes that A is at least as well supported by his reasons for action as its relevant, admissible alternatives.

In interpreting condition (1′) we are to use the historical approach to the rationality of an agent in nondeliberatively intending. When historical considerations affect S's rationality in having those background intentions that play a direct role in his reasoning, they will also affect the rationality of S for having the intention reached as a conclusion of that reasoning. This is the impact on my account of agent rationality of the fact that many intentions and actions have a hybrid character: they may be based on present deliberation, but that deliberation may itself take as fixed certain prior intentions and plans. On this historical principle, then, it is not rational of me to intend to ask the question as a preliminary step to the lie it is not rational of me to intend.

Remarks similar to those made concerning the historical approach to nondeliberative rationality are in order here as well. First, the present historical principle need not insist that it is, all considered, *ir*rational of me to intend to ask the question (as a preliminary step to telling the lie). It just must insist that it is *not* rational of me to intend to ask the question. It can grant that although it is not rational of me to intend to tell the lie, it is rational of me not to reconsider that intention. We can also note that given my intention to tell the lie, my asking the question is rational from my internal, plan-constrained perspective. And in some such cases we may want to resist any all-in assessment of agent rationality for the intention to ask the question.

Second, divergences between, on the one hand, assessments of the deliberative rationality of an agent for intending to act in a certain way and, on the other hand, external assessments of that intention or action, are possible in both directions. First, although it is not rational of me in the present case to intend to ask the question (as a step to telling the lie), this action might still be recommended from an appropriate external standpoint. Second, in the second Mondale case[10] it might be rational of Mondale deliberatively to intend to ask his third question (as a means to attacking Star Wars) even though this action would not be recommended from the external standpoint.

So we have a historical theory of agent rationality for both deliberative and nondeliberative cases.

6.3 Another Look at Bootstrapping

We have gone beyond the ahistorical theory in making the rationality of an agent in reaching earlier intentions directly relevant to her rationality in her later intentions and actions. We have noted two main ways in which this can happen. First, the rationality of S at t_1 for nondeliberatively intending to A may be influenced by her rationality at t_0 in initially forming that intention. Second, the rationality of S at t_1 for deliberatively intending to B will be influenced by her rationality at t_1 in nondeliberatively intending to C, where this intention to C plays a direct role in the background of the deliberation leading to this intention to B. And her rationality at t_1 for nondeliberatively intending to C may itself be shaped by her rationality at t_0 in initially deciding to C.

What are the consequences of this theory for the original case of bootstrapping introduced in Chapter 2? In this case Mondale's initial decision to attack Star Wars in the debate is irrational. Let us continue to suppose that this is an instance of the basic case: after reaching his decision Mondale nonreflectively refrains from reconsidering, and his nonreconsideration is reason-preserving. In the debate Mondale proceeds to ask his third question as his way of attacking Star Wars.

Mondale's intentional *action* of asking his third question may be assessed from both internal and external perspectives. And these assessments may well diverge: this intentional action may well be rational from Mondale's internal perspective and yet fail to be rational from our external perspective. When we ask about the rationality of *Mondale* for so acting, we turn to the historical theory. We first determine—using the two-tier approach—whether it was rational of Mondale throughout not to reconsider his prior intention to attack Star Wars. Let us suppose for now that it was. Even so, on the historical theory it will not be rational of Mondale, at the time of the debate, to intend to attack Star Wars, given the history of this intention. So even if Mondale's action of asking his third question is itself rational when assessed from Mondale's internal perspective, and even if it was throughout rational of Mondale not to reconsider the crucial prior intention to attack Star Wars, it may still be true that it is not rational of Mondale to ask his third question, given the history of his intention to attack Star Wars. Though we can recognize the virtues of asking the third question, as seen from the internal perspective of Mondale's deliberation, we can still offer serious criticisms both of this action and of Mondale for so acting. We need not fully endorse such bootstrapping; and that is what we wanted.

6.4 Personal Policies and Policy-Based Rationality

We have so far been focusing on future-directed intentions to act in a certain way on a certain relatively specific occasion. Such intentions are the bread and butter of coordinating plans, and it is by way of such plans that, I have urged, we can get a good theoretical handle on intention. But intentions can also be general and concern potentially recurring circumstances in the agent's life. Such general intentions constitute what I shall call *personal policies*. I want now to consider how the theoretical apparatus we have been developing can be extended to such personal policies.[11]

Examples of personal policies abound in our lives. A list of personal policies of a person in our culture might well include: Buckle up seat belts when driving in a car. No more than one drink when you have to drive home. Never agree to chair more than one committee at a time. Refuse second desserts. Don't let lists get longer than about seven items. Check brakes every 6000 miles. Check house insurance yearly. Change furnace filters every two months. Read some German prose every night before going to bed.[12] Don't make important decisions at the end of a long and stressful day. In each case the policy concerns not just a single future situation, but a kind of circumstance that is expected to recur in the life of the agent. And in each case the agent might well have a general intention so to act in the cited circumstances.[13]

Why bother with such general policies? Why don't we just buckle our seat belts when we come to them? At least part of the answer follows the lines of my discussion of relatively specific intentions. First, the formation of general policies helps extend the influence of deliberation: it is a partial solution to the problems posed by our limited resources for calculation and deliberation at the time of action. Second, general policies facilitate coordination. My general intention to read German every night shapes my daily plans in ways that help me achieve a complex of ends, only one of which is proficiency in German.

In addition to this two-part rationale there may be yet a further rationale for bothering with general policies. It may sometimes be easier to appreciate expectable consequences (both good and bad) of general ways of acting in recurrent circumstances than to appreciate the expectable consequences of a single case.[14] If this is so, then deliberation about general policies, rather than about more specific cases, may at times be a better "guide to life." But such deliberation requires, as a background, the capacity to have the complex of dispositions characteristic of intentions—both general and relatively specific.

General policies come in many varieties. Some will be *periodic* in the sense that their occasions for execution are guaranteed by the mere passage of a specific interval of time. This is true of intentions to change filters every two months, or to check insurance policies yearly. In contrast, some general policies will be *circumstance-triggered*. This is true, for example, of an intention to buckle up when you drive: its occasion of execution is not guaranteed by the mere passage of time but requires that certain specific circumstances obtain. Sometimes the triggering circumstances will be up to the agent, sometimes not. Whether I drive a car at all is up to me; but whether I am asked to chair yet another committee is not.

In each case a general policy exhibits a characteristic kind of *defeasibility*. When I intend to buckle up when I drive, or to change furnace filters every two months, I do not intend so to act *no matter what*. I am not committed to buckling up in certain emergency situations, or to changing filters in an earthquake. We might try building all these qualifications into the specification of what is intended, but the task seems hopeless as long as we avoid trivial specifications like "unless the circumstances make so acting inappropriate." Instead, we should just recognize that there is an inevitable defeasibility in almost all such general policies: there can be circumstances in which one will appropriately block the application of the general policy to the particular case even though one will still retain that general policy. In an emergency I do not give up my general policy of buckling up, but I might still block its application to my particular case and not bother with my seat belt.

This means that for general policies we need to make a distinction between *reconsidering* or *abandoning* the general intention, on the one hand, and *blocking* its application to a particular case, on the other. Faced with new information about seat belts I might reconsider my personal policy concerning their use. But in an emergency situation I do not reconsider or abandon my policy; I only block its application to the particular case.

A similar distinction does not arise in the case of an intention concerning a single, relatively specific occasion. Mondale intends to attack Reagan's Star Wars policy in the debate. For Mondale in the debate to block the application of this intention to his circumstances is for him to abandon that intention. There is no intermediate possibility of blocking its application to this situation but retaining the intention nevertheless; for the intention is precisely about this very situation. But once we consider more general intentions concerning potentially recurring circumstances in the agent's life, there emerges a distinction between abandoning the intention and blocking its application to the particular case.

As in the case of relatively specific intentions, there are strong pragmatic grounds for including general policies within the scope of the demands for consistency and coherence. My general intention to read German nightly poses problems about means—problems whose solution may well lead me to a bookstore. And it constrains my other intentions—both general and relatively specific—by way of considerations of consistency. I am not, for example, in a position also to adopt a general policy of playing basketball nightly, knowing, as I do, that such activities exhaust me and leave me unable to concentrate on reading German. Unless my general intention to read German nightly played these roles in my ongoing planning and action, it would be ill-suited to promote coordination or usefully to extend the influence of deliberation.

Along with general policies go *policy-based* intentions. I have a general policy of changing filters every two months. This morning, on the basis of this policy, I form the intention to change the filters this afternoon. And this relatively specific intention will now function as part of a larger, coordinating plan for my day: it will pose problems about means and constrain my other options. My intention this morning to change filters this afternoon is a *policy-based* intention. This policy-based intention is not merely a nondeliberative intention; for it is not simply a case of retaining an intention previously formed. But neither is my policy-based intention usefully treated as a deliberative intention. Since it is not based on a present attempt by me to weigh pros and cons for and against conflicting options, it is clearly not based on full-blown deliberation. But it also differs from an intention in favor of necessary means, an intention presently derived from a prior intention in favor of a specific end. The difference here is that if I were to balk at intending the necessary means I would have to abandon the intention in favor of the end. But this is not quite so when I apply a general policy to a particular case: the defeasibility of general policies makes it possible to block the application of the policy to the particular case without abandoning the policy.[15] So we do best to seek a separate treatment, within the historical framework, of such cases of policy-based intention.

Let us focus on the following extension of the basic case:

> (1) At t_0 S deliberates about what policy to adopt concerning a certain range of activities. On the basis of this deliberation S forms a general intention to A when C (for example, to buckle up when driving a car).
> (2) From t_0 to t_1 S retains this general intention through non-reflective, reason-preserving nonreconsideration.
> (3) At t_1 S recognizes that he will be (is) in circumstance C at t_2 (where t_2 is the same as or later than t_1).
> (4) On the basis of his general intention and this recognition S forms the intention at t_1 to A at t_2.

Call this the *policy-based extension of the basic case*. My question concerning this case is as follows: Under what conditions is it rational of S at t_1 to have this policy-based intention to A at t_2? The historical approach suggests that it will be rational of S so to intend only if: (a) it was rational of S at t_0 initially to decide, on the basis of deliberation, on the cited general policy; and (b) it was rational of S not to reconsider this policy from t_0 to t_1. But these two conditions do not suffice. They do guarantee, on the historical approach to nondeliberative rationality, that it is rational of S at t_1 to have his *general* intention at t_1. But we still need to ask about the relation between S's rationality at t_1 for this general intention and his rationality for the *specific, policy-based* intention at t_1 to A at t_2.

One approach is to see the relation between general policy and specific intention as analogous to the relation between guiding intention and intentional action.[16] On the intention-action principle, if it is rational of S to intend to A now, and that is why he intentionally A's now, then it is rational of S so to act. On the suggested analogy we would suppose that if it is rational of S to have the general intention at t_1 to A when C, and if S recognizes that it will be (is) C at t_2 and so comes to intend at t_1 to A at t_2, then it is rational of him at t_1 specifically to intend to A at t_2.

But this approach seems wrong. General policies, I have noted, are defeasible: it may sometimes be rational to have the general policy but irrational not to block its application to the particular case. In rushing my wife to the hospital it may be foolish of me to worry about buckling up. But this does not mean that I should abandon my general policy of buckling up. Rather, I should just block its application to my particular case. To complete the historical approach to policy-based intentions we need to ask about the rationality of blocking or not blocking the application of a prior, general policy to a particular case.

Here the natural analogy is with nonreconsideration. The nonreflective absence of reconsideration of a prior intention is, I have urged, the "default" case. And we may assess the rationality of an agent for such nonreconsideration by way of a two-tier approach: we assess the reasonableness of the relevant, underlying habits and then apply this assessment to the particular case of nonreconsideration. Similarly, the absence of blocking of the application of a general policy to a particular case is plausibly seen as the "default." And an analogous two-tier approach to the assessment of such nonblocking seems appropriate.

Suppose S has a general policy to A when C, recognizes that it is (will be) C, and so comes to have a relatively specific intention to A. And suppose that the absence of blocking on S's part is itself not based on further deliberation, but is explainable by appeal to relevant general habits similar to those involved in nonreflective nonreconsideration. If these habits are reasonable (in my consequentialist sense) of S to have, then it is rational of S not to block his general policy in this case.

Such a two-tier approach in hand, we can extend the theory of agent rationality as follows:

Historical principle of policy-based rationality
  In the policy-based extension of the basic case it is rational of S at t_1 to have the policy-based intention to A at t_2 if and only if:
  (a) it was rational of S at t_0 to form the general intention to A when C; and
  (b) it was rational of S from t_0 to t_1 not to reconsider this general intention; and
  (c) it was rational of S not to block the application of his general intention to this particular case.

6.5 Variations on the Basic Case

I return now, as promised, to nondeliberative intention and the basic case. I want to consider how the theory should respond when we change certain aspects of this basic case. In particular I will consider two different variations on the way in which the initial decision to A later is linked to the later present-directed intention to A. I do not of course claim that the variations I will consider are the only possible variations or complications: my account will remain partial. But I hope that my treatment of these different cases will help map out some of the main ideas needed to develop the theory further.

Before proceeding let me anticipate a general theme that will emerge.[17] I have attempted so far to couch my principles for agent rationality primarily in terms of an *all-in* judgment that it is rational of an agent to intend or act in a certain way. As we complicate matters, however, such all-in judgments become increasingly unavailable. We must increasingly settle for judgments that say only that in this respect it was rational of S to A, in this other respect it was not. This complexity has already been anticipated in my discussion of the snowball effect. But the point will emerge even more clearly as we vary the basic case.

When we can no longer arrive at such all-in judgments of agent rationality, the principles I have been developing play the role of mapping out the various dimensions relevant to judgments of agent rationality. Sometimes judgments along these different dimensions converge sufficiently for an all-in judgment to be in order. But when they do not, the theory is still useful in indicating what these dimensions are and how we are to assess rationality along each of them.

6.5.1 The First Variation: Recommitment

A central feature of the basic case is that after forming a future-directed intention on the basis of deliberation, the agent retains that intention over time by way of nonreflective, reason-preserving nonreconsideration. This nonreconsideration can transmit to a later time the agent's earlier rationality in originally forming the intention; and if the agent's initial formation of the intention was not rational of him, then it will not be rational of him later so to intend, as long as his intention is preserved in this way. In contrast, if after initially forming his intention the agent later proceeds to change his mind and give up this intention, then his earlier rationality (or irrationality) will no longer influence later judgments of his rationality. But what if, rather than giving up his initial intention, the agent later stops and seriously reconsiders it but, in his new circumstances, decides to stick to his guns and "recommits" himself to so acting? How should such reconsideration and recommitment affect judgments of his rationality for so intending at the time of reconsideration and thereafter?

To keep the discussion manageable I am going to limit it a bit. In discussing the basic case I was much concerned with cases in which the earlier rationality of the agent in forming an intention to act was a candidate for transfer to the agent at a later time. In discussing this first variation I am going instead to limit my concern to cases in which the initial formation of the intention was *ir*rational of the agent. And I am going to be asking whether later reconsideration and recommitment can *block* the impact of this earlier irrationality.

Limiting discussion in this way helps to highlight one of the questions raised by this variation. I have said, roughly, that the rationality of an agent for his intention depends on the rationality of the relevant processes leading to that intention. In the basic case the relevant process is the extended deliberation that leads to the intention. But in the present variation it is not clear just what the relevant process includes. In particular, it is not clear just how far back it goes. Does it go all the way back to the initial formation of the intention, or does it go only as far back as the later reconsideration and recommitment?

Suppose that initially, at t_0, I deliberate about whether to A at t_3 and decide in favor of so acting. And suppose that this is irrational of me. But suppose that I stop at t_1 and seriously reconsider whether to A at t_3. Though it was initially irrational of me to decide at t_0 to A at t_3, circumstances are different at t_1. Perhaps this is an example of the snowball effect: my actions from t_0 to t_1 have changed the circumstances in ways that newly favor my A-ing at t_3. Suppose that the upshot of my reconsideration is that I decide to stick with my plan, and recommit myself to A-ing at t_3. And given the new circumstances, it is now rational of me so to decide. Later, at t_2, I continue so to intend as a result of nonreflective, reason-preserving nonreconsideration from t_1 to t_2. When you come to assess my rationality for so intending at t_2, must you look all the way back to my initial formation of the intention at t_0, or only back to my later reconsideration and recommitment at t_1?

Return to the example of the two concerts. Suppose that at t_0 I decide to attend concert A at t_3 rather than concert B. This decision is initially irrational. But later, at t_1, after I have traveled far in the direction of concert A, I stop and reconsider my intention. Recognizing how much closer I now am to concert A than to concert B I decide to stick with my earlier intention. I recommit myself to going to concert A. And this time around, given the change in circumstances, it is rational of me deliberatively so to intend. At a still later time, t_2, I continue, as a result of nonreflective, reason-preserving nonreconsideration from t_1 to t_2, nondeliberatively to intend to go to concert A. Is my rationality at t_2 in intending to go to concert A linked to my initial formation of the intention at t_0, or only to my later reconsideration and recommitment. at t_1?

I think that at least in some such cases we need look only as far back as my later reconsideration and recommitment. Otherwise my account would have the flavor of an unacceptable doctrine of original sin. Surely we can sometimes escape from our earlier irrationalities without giving up our plans; sometimes bygones *are* bygones. The natural way of escaping from earlier irrationality is to stop and seriously reconsider what we are up to. If this reconsideration results in a recommitment to a course of action—a recommitment that is now, in our present circumstances, rational of us—then this should be sufficient to break the link with our past irrationality.

So it seems that, at least sometimes, my later reconsideration and recommitment blocks the link from my intention at t_2 to its initial formation at t_0. In effect, my later reconsideration counts as a new start: as a result of it I newly ground my intention to go to concert A on this later deliberation about whether to go. In such a case it is my rationality in this later recommitment at t_1 that is crucial to my rationality at t_2. In such a case, reconsideration of my prior intention "negatives" the rational link with the initial formation of that intention, and it sets up a new anchor for later assessments of agent rationality.[18]

Why is this? Why should serious reconsideration and recommitment negative the link with the past? The answer seems to be that when I seriously reconsider my prior intention to A, I bracket this intention: during the course of the reconsideration I no longer, strictly speaking, intend to A. One sign of this is that I am treating as admissible certain options believed by me to be incompatible with my A-ing. So when I recommit myself to A-ing, there is a historical discontinuity: my intention to A is not just my earlier intention retained through time. It has the same status as a new intention to refrain from A-ing, should that instead be the result of my reconsideration.

This is not to say that reconsideration of, and recommitment to, a prior intention *always* negatives the link to past irrationality. The problem is that reconsideration can be cursory and perfunctory. It seems to me that as the reconsideration becomes increasingly minimal we are (and should be) less inclined completely to allow the earlier history of intention formation to drop out. To block earlier irrationality the agent must be seriously prepared, in his reconsideration, to give up his prior intention if that is what is recommended by his new reflection. When the reconsideration is cursory and perfunctory, this commitment to change (if needed) may not be there. And without such a commitment we do not have the clear-cut historical discontinuity needed fully to negative the link to the past.

The historical principle for the basic case allows for a single, all-in assessment of the rationality of the agent for nondeliberatively intending to A. But sometimes relatively perfunctory reconsideration (and the resulting recommitment) is sufficient to have some impact on the assessment of the present rationality of the agent for his intention, but is insufficient fully to negative the link with the past. In such cases we may not be able to reach an all-in assessment of agent rationality. In some of these cases we will simply have to rest content with two conflicting assessments: it was irrational of the agent initially so to decide, but rational of him later to recommit himself to his intention. We are not forced to reach a further, all-in assessment of agent rationality; and in some such cases we may not be able to.

Nevertheless, if the reconsideration is full-blown and serious, if the agent really is seriously open to a change of plans, and if he nevertheless decides to stick with his prior plan, then it does seem to me that the resulting recommitment should negative the link to the past. In particular, if the new recommitment is rational of the agent, it provides a rational anchor for later assessments of agent rationality, one that blocks the link to the earlier irrationality of the agent.

All this leaves open the question of whether it was rational of the agent so to reconsider. Suppose that at t_1 I am nonreflectively reconsidering my initial intention to go to concert A. And suppose that, given that I am reconsidering, it is rational of me to recommit myself to so acting. But suppose also that the habits and propensities manifested in my reconsideration are ones it is not reasonable of me to have, so that it is not rational of me to reconsider. Perhaps these habits involve a tendency toward having plans that are too unstable. Or perhaps my motivation in reconsidering was merely to get myself off the hook of my earlier irrationality,[19] and this motivation generally leads me to have overly unstable plans. In such a case it might be rational of me after t_1 to intend to go to concert A even though at t_1 it was not rational of me to reconsider that intention, and even though, had I not reconsidered, it would not have been rational of me after t_1 so to intend.

This may seem paradoxical, but I do not think it is. What it does show is that my earlier irrationality in deciding to go to concert A may make later irrationality inevitable: for either I later irrationally reconsider, or I later continue irrationally so to intend. But such a result, far from being paradoxical, seems to me just what we should expect.

6.5.2 The Second Variation: Reason-Changing Nonreconsideration

In the basic case the agent retains his intention through nonreflective, reason-preserving nonreconsideration. In the first variation on the basic case the agent later reconsiders and recommits himself to his initial intention. I now turn to a different variation in the link between initial formation and eventual execution of an intention. In this variation the agent does not reconsider, strictly speaking, his initial intention. But neither does he merely retain it through reason-preserving, nonreflective nonreconsideration. Rather, he retains it through a reason-*changing* process.

Reconsideration of a prior intention to *A* involves seriously reopening the question of whether so to act. As noted in Chapter 5, however, one may *reaffirm* one's prior intention in a way that does not involve being open to changing it, but does succeed in incorporating new considerations into one's reasons for so intending. Recall my action of heading toward concert A after having previously decided—albeit, not rationally—in favor of concert A over concert B. Suppose that as I approach concert A I stop briefly to note how close I am to that concert and how far I am from concert B. Although I do not seriously reopen the question of whether to go to concert A, I do note to myself that now concert A is certainly the better concert for me to go to; for I am now much closer to that concert than to concert B. This reaffirmation of my intention to go to concert A does not seriously reopen the question of whether to go, but it nevertheless results in a change in my reasons for so intending.[20] As a result of this reaffirmation I newly incorporate into my reasons for so intending my knowledge that I am close to concert A.

Cases of deliberative nonreconsideration provide another kind of case in which there is a reason-changing process that is still not one of reconsideration. Normally one just nonreflectively refrains from reconsidering one's prior intention; one does not first deliberate about whether to reconsider and then decide not to, on the basis of this second-order deliberation. Still, there do seem to be cases of deliberating about whether to reconsider and then deciding not to. In such cases the agent need not, strictly speaking, reconsider his prior intention.[21] Though he seriously raises the question of whether to reopen the question of whether to act as he now intends, he may not, strictly speaking, actually reopen the question of whether so to act. Nevertheless, his second-order reflection is a reason-changing process.

Recall my decision not to get earthquake insurance. Suppose this decision was initially irrational of me to make. But suppose that sometime after this decision I stop and deliberate about whether to reconsider this decision. And suppose that I rationally decide not to: the emotional turmoil and complex calculations involved in reconsideration would just not be worth it. So I continue to intend not to get earthquake insurance. Yet my intention is now based, in part, on a new reason: the excessive costs of reconsideration. My second-order deliberation, although not resulting in reconsideration, was nevertheless a reason-changing process.

There is a complication here.[22] Second-order deliberation about whether to reconsider a prior intention can shade off into actual—even if somewhat attenuated—reconsideration of that intention. One tries to see whether reconsideration would be worth it by doing a bit of (perhaps rather attenuated) reconsidering and seeing how it goes. If this reconsideration proceeds far enough (but still leaves one with one's original intention), it will remove the case from my second variation: we will now have a case of the first variation, and now our question will be whether this reconsideration is sufficient to negative the link with the past and give us a new anchor. In contrast, the cases of interest for discussion of the second variation are those in which the deliberation remains sufficiently at the metalevel so that it does not count as reconsideration of the prior intention. (Of course, there will be borderline cases.)

So we have two kinds of reason-changing processes that may accompany the retention of a prior intention, and that need not involve reconsideration, strictly speaking: reason-changing reaffirmation in which one does not seriously reopen the question of whether so to act; and second-order deliberation about whether to reconsider, which results in a decision not to. If S retains his intention from t_0 to t_1 through such a reason-changing process, then even if S does not reconsider his intention, his case diverges from the basic case, and the historical principle does not yet tell us how to assess S's rationality at t_1. What should we say about such cases?

This second variation raises a question similar to that raised by the first variation, namely, just how far back should we go in picking out the historical processes relevant to our assessment of the agent's rationality for his present intention? Should such reason-changing processes block the link with the earlier formation of the intention, even though these processes are not, strictly speaking, ones of reconsideration? Just as with the first variation, this question is clearest for those cases in which the initial formation of the intention was irrational of the agent. So let us focus on such cases.

Two fairly simple views suggest themselves here. On the one hand, we might just suppose that the occurrence of such reason-changing processes, in the absence of reconsideration, should not at all block the link with the earlier, irrational intention formation. The rationale for this would be that even in reason-changing nonreconsideration I still do not seriously reopen the question of whether to act as I initially intend. In merely reaffirming my prior intention to go to concert A I did not take seriously the possibility that, even now, the reasons of distance were not sufficient to compensate for the reasons for going to concert B instead. And in merely engaging in second-order deliberation about whether to reconsider my prior intention not to get insurance, I do not get to a point at which I have actually reopened, in a serious way, the question of whether to get it. Yet it is plausible to suppose that it is this phenomenon of seriously reopening the question of whether so to act, with its associated openness to change in one's intentions in the light of present reasons, that is crucial. That is, it is plausible to suppose that it is this feature of reconsideration that allows it to negative the link with the past. Unless I seriously reopen this question, there is not the sort of historical discontinuity between present and past intention needed to establish a new anchor.

On the other hand—and this is the second view that suggests itself here—we might suppose that such reason-changing processes, though not ones of reconsideration, strictly speaking, are nevertheless sufficient to negative the link with the past and establish a new anchor. On this view, once the agent incorporates new reasons into the reasons for his intention, we are forced newly to assess his rationality for so intending. We are forced to ask whether the reaffirmed intention in favor of so acting is, taking into account the new reasons, reasonable of the agent to reach. If it is, then it is now rational of him so to intend, and we can now anchor future judgments of nondeliberative rationality in this judgment of agent rationality. For example, suppose that after my second-order deliberation about whether to reconsider my intention not to buy insurance it is reasonable of me to judge that going ahead with this intention is best, partly because of the costs of reconsideration. If this is so, then we have a new anchor, and we have negatived the connection to the previously irrational decision not to buy such insurance. It is not necessary, in order to establish this new anchor, for there to have been full-blown reconsideration.

The first of these views collapses such cases of reason-changing non-reconsideration in the direction of the reason-preserving nonreconsideration of the basic case. The second of these views collapses such cases in the direction of the full-blown reconsideration and recommitment of the first variation. And neither view seems quite right. On the one hand, suppose I really do reasonably judge that now my heading toward concert A is superior to going to concert B, thereby reaffirming my prior intention to go to concert A. This fact does seem somehow relevant to an assessment of my rationality now in intending to go to concert A, even though I do not seriously reopen the issue of whether to go to that concert. On the other hand, it also seems that my failure seriously to reopen the issue of whether so to act still forces us somehow to take into account my earlier irrationality in reaching my prior intention to go to that concert. In the absence of the sort of historical discontinuity characteristic of full-blown reconsideration, the failures in my earlier deliberation and decision seem to remain to some extent relevant to an assessment of me for my intention now to go.

The solution is to grant that in such cases of reason-changing non-reconsideration an assessment of the agent's rationality for so intending should be a function of both aspects of the history of the intention: its initial formation and the later reason-changing process. The effect of this will many times be to lead us to give up the hope, in cases such as these, of reaching a single, all-in assessment of the rationality of the agent in intending. In many of these cases we will have to rest content with two conflicting assessments: it was irrational of the agent initially so to decide, but rational of her later to make such a reason-changing judgment in favor of her intention. And to these conflicting assessments we may also need to add the further assessment that it was (say) rational of the agent then not to reconsider seriously her prior intention. As noted earlier, we are not forced to reach a further, all-in assessment of the rationality of the agent for her intention; and in many such cases we may not be able to.

When the agent reaches her intention on the basis of present delib-eration about what to do, we can sometimes reach an all-in assessment of her rationality then in so intending.[23] And when the agent now non-deliberatively intends to *A*, and this intention has been retained through nonreflective, reason-preserving nonreconsideration from earlier delib-eration, we can sometimes reach an all-in assessment of the agent's ra-tionality in so intending—the historical principle of nondeliberative rationality tells us how to do this for the basic case. Finally, when there has been serious and full-blown reconsideration after an initial formation of an intention, we can just treat the reconsideration and its associated deliberation as a new anchor, one that negatives the link to the further past. This then puts us in the position of assessing the rationality of the agent for deliberatively intending so to act; and here, we have seen, we can sometimes reach an all-in assessment. But when the link from past deliberation to present intention involves reason-changing processes that are not ones of full-blown reconsideration, I see no clear, general principle for reaching a single, all-in assessment. Two distinct processes remain significantly relevant to our assessment: the agent's initial formation of her intention, and the later reason-changing process. When our assessments of these processes point in opposite directions, there seems to be no guaranteed way of combining these assessments into an all-in judgment. In many such cases we will just have to rest content with assessments that take this form: in this respect it is rational of her so to intend, in this other respect not.

Having introduced this complication into the treatment of nondeliberative rationality, we must be prepared to recognize that it will also infect the treatment of deliberative rationality as well. This treatment of deliberative rationality will also need to respond to the distinction between reason-preserving and reason-changing nonreconsideration in ways that parallel the treatment of nondeliberative rationality. Recall the example of my intending to lie to you when you call me on the telephone, and my proceeding to deliberate—once the phone rings—about preliminary steps to this lie. When the phone rings, I do not stop to reconsider my intention to tell the lie. But now let us suppose that I do stop long enough to *reaffirm* this intention, and to note that now it has the further support provided by the press of time and the costs of reconsideration. My reaffirmation is a case of reason-*changing* nonreconsideration. And let us suppose that this judgment that I make in reaffirming my initial intention to lie is a judgment that it is reasonable of me to make. In such a case you may not be in a position to reach an all-in assessment of me for so intending then. This is the conclusion we have just reached in discussing the second variation. Lacking such an all-in assessment, the historical principle of deliberative rationality precludes an all-in judgment that it is rational of me to intend to ask the question (as a preliminary step to telling the lie). This leaves you in the position of needing to make an assessment of me for intending to ask the question whose complexity reflects the complexity of the assessment of me for intending to tell the lie.

Let us take stock. We have been able to develop a fairly clear historical approach to the rationality of an agent in deliberatively intending, to the rationality of an agent in nondeliberatively intending in the basic case, and to the rationality of an agent in holding a policy-based intention in the policy-based extension of the basic case. To this we have added the plausible view that full-blown reconsideration and recommitment together negative the link with the past and set up a new anchor. The treatment of cases involving reason-changing nonreconsideration has been less clear-cut—though it did help reinforce the important lesson that a single, all-in assessment of agent rationality is not always available. But this seems to be the level of precision of which the subject matter admits. Even with these limitations, however, I think we have a plausible framework for thinking about agent rationality, a framework that comports with our underlying model of the role of intentions and partial plans in the ongoing thinking and reasoning of limited rational agents like us.

6.6 Kavka's Puzzle

It is time to address one last worry about my approach to agent rationality. It seems to be possible for an agent to have desire-belief reasons in favor of an intention to *A* that are not desire-belief reasons in favor of *A*-ing. This apparent possibility may seem to threaten the approach I have taken, for it may seem to threaten the tight connection—expressed in the intention-action principle—between the rationality of an agent for intending to *A* and her rationality for intentionally *A*-ing. In the concluding section of this chapter I want to explore this issue.[24]

I will focus on an example recently discussed by Gregory Kavka in his article "The Toxin Puzzle."[25] Suppose that on Monday you are offered a million dollars if on Tuesday you intend to drink a certain toxin on Wednesday. It is common knowledge that drinking this toxin will make you very sick for a day but will not have a lasting effect. If you do so intend on Tuesday, the million dollars will be irreversibly transferred to your bank account; this will happen whether or not you actually go ahead and drink the toxin on Wednesday. Now, in such a case it seems you have a very strong desire-belief reason to *intend* on Tuesday to drink the toxin on Wednesday, for this intention will get you the million dollars. But this reason for the intention to drink the toxin does not provide a reason for the intended action of drinking the toxin on Wednesday. Indeed, come Wednesday it seems you will have no very good desire-belief reason for drinking the toxin. You have a strong desire-belief reason for intending on Tuesday to drink the toxin on Wednesday, and no corresponding desire-belief reason for drinking it on Wednesday. And it may seem that such a divergence between reasons for intention and reasons for intended action challenges the approach to agent rationality I have been sketching.

Exactly how might such cases challenge our theory? The intention-action principle ties the rationality of an agent for intending to *A* quite tightly to her rationality for intentionally *A*-ing. And this tight connection may seem to be challenged by such examples. But we must be careful here. In the example the intention at issue is a *future*-directed intention. Yet the intention-action principle concerns the connection between *present*-directed intention and intentional action. So, as so far stated, the example does not yet challenge that principle in a straightforward way.

I think that the most powerful way of developing the example as an objection to my theory is as follows. Given the strength of your reasons for intending on Tuesday to drink the toxin on Wednesday, it may well be rational of you deliberatively so to intend on Tuesday. But your intention on Tuesday to drink the toxin on Wednesday is an intention to drink the toxin under certain expected conditions. Come Wednesday, these are exactly the conditions that you know to obtain. There is no relevant divergence from your expectations on Tuesday about what will happen on Wednesday. But if there is no such divergence from your relevant expectations, it will be rational of you not to reconsider the intention on Wednesday. So on the theory it may well be rational of you on Wednesday intentionally to drink the toxin, since it was rational of you on Tuesday deliberatively to intend to drink it on Wednesday and it is rational of you on Wednesday not to reconsider that intention. And that seems wrong. After all, by Wednesday there is nothing to be gained by drinking the toxin and much suffering to be endured if you do drink it; and you know all this.

So we have the following quartet of premises:

> (1) It is rational of you on Tuesday deliberatively to intend to drink the toxin on Wednesday, given your strong desire-belief reasons on Tuesday for so intending then.
>
> (2) If it is rational of you on Tuesday deliberatively to intend to drink the toxin on Wednesday, and if you find the relevant conditions on Wednesday to be just as on Tuesday you expected them to be, then it is rational of you on Wednesday not to reconsider that intention then.
>
> (3) Conditions as you find them on Wednesday are just as on Tuesday you expected them to be, and that is why on Wednesday you do not reconsider your prior intention to drink the toxin.
>
> (4) Both the historical principle of nondeliberative rationality for the basic case and the intention-action principle are correct.

From (1) through (3) we can infer that it is rational of you on Wednesday not to reconsider your prior intention to drink the toxin. Since your nondeliberative intention on Wednesday is (we may assume) an instance of the basic case, we can apply the historical principle of nondeliberative rationality. This tells us that it is rational of you on Wednesday to intend to drink the toxin then. The intention-action principle then tells us that it is rational of you intentionally to drink the toxin. So from (1) through (4) we can infer:

(5) It will be rational of you on Wednesday intentionally to drink the toxin.

Since this conclusion seems seriously wrong and the argument seems valid, one of the premises must be rejected. But premises (1) and (2) seem acceptable, and premise (3) is just a factual assumption. So we must reject premise (4) and with it my theory of agent rationality. Or so, anyway, it is being urged.

My reply is that we should instead challenge the first two premises of the argument. Consider premise (1). This premise assumes that your reasons on Tuesday for intending to drink the toxin on Wednesday will make it rational of you so to intend on the basis of deliberation. But in deliberation about the future we deliberate about what to *do* then, not what to intend now,[26] though of course a decision about what to do later leads to an intention now so to act later. Granted, our reason for bothering to deliberate and decide now about what to do later will typically be grounded in the expected benefits of settling the matter in advance; in particular, it will typically be grounded in the expected contribution such a future-directed decision would make to coordination and to expanding the influence of deliberation on conduct. This has been a main theme of this book. Nevertheless, what we deliberate *about*, when we deliberate about the future, is what to do then. This means that in such deliberation about the future the desire-belief reasons we are to consider are reasons for various ways we might *act* later. It follows that your special million-dollar reason for intending now to drink the toxin later will not get into the deliberation about whether to drink it later. Where this reason will naturally appear will be in your present-directed deliberation (if such there be) about whether on Tuesday somehow to cause yourself to have an intention to drink on Wednesday. That is, the million-dollar reason is a reason for a present action of causing yourself so to intend; this reason is relevant to deliberation about whether so to act now, not to deliberation about whether to drink the toxin later.

Suppose, then, that you do have available on Tuesday some way of causing yourself so to intend. Note that this will not be simply ordinary deliberation. The deliberation that would ordinarily give you an intention on Tuesday to drink on Wednesday would be deliberation about whether to drink on Wednesday, and such deliberation, though of course possible, will not have the desired result; for the million-dollar reason will not have force in that deliberation, whereas the reason of sickness will. But perhaps you can now cause yourself to intend to drink later by using a form of self-hypnosis, or something similar. If you can do this, it may well be rational of you intentionally so to act; for you thereby get yourself a million dollars. But now the question is whether we can infer from

> (a) It is rational of you intentionally to cause yourself in such a way to intend on Tuesday to drink on Wednesday.

to

> (b) It is rational of you so to intend on Tuesday.

Note that my theory so far has not addressed this issue: the principles developed so far do not tell us how to answer the question just posed. So it is open to the theory to block the present objection just by rejecting the inference from (a) to (b)—by insisting that it can be rational of you intentionally to cause yourself to have an intention it will not be rational of you to have.

For the sake of argument, however, let us suppose that it *is* rational of you to intend on Tuesday to drink the toxin on Wednesday. Let us accept, for now, a version of premise (1)—one that is modified so as not to assume that the intention is formed on the basis of deliberation about whether to drink, but that still maintains that it is rational of you on Tuesday to intend to drink on Wednesday. That is, let us assume for now that

> (1') It will be rational of you on Tuesday to intend to drink the toxin on Wednesday, given your strong desire-belief reasons on Tuesday for having this intention then.

In light of this change to (1') we will also want to change (2) so that its antecedent does not assume that the intention was acquired on the basis of deliberation:

> (2') If you acquire on Tuesday the intention to drink the toxin on Wednesday, if on Tuesday this intention is rational of you to have, and if you find the conditions on Wednesday to be just as on Tuesday you expected them to be, then it is rational of you on Wednesday not to reconsider that intention then.

We now face a different problem in reaching the supposed conclusion, (5). The problem is that in changing to (1') and (2') we have given up the assumption that our case is an instance of the basic case. So we are no longer in a position directly to apply the historical principle of nondeliberative rationality for the basic case; for that principle applies only to cases in which the initial formation of the intention is based on deliberation. To be sure, from (1'), (2'), and (3) we can still infer that it will be rational of you on Wednesday not to reconsider your prior intention to drink the toxin. But we are no longer in a position to infer directly that it will be rational of you on Wednesday to intend to drink the toxin and to drink it intentionally.

Still, it may seem that my theory should embrace a natural extension of the historical principle of nondeliberative rationality, one that does not require that the initial formation of the intention was based on deliberation. On this extension it is rational of S at t_1 nondeliberatively to intend to A at t_2 if S initially came to have this intention at t_0 (prior to t_1), if it was rational of S so to intend at t_0, and if it was rational of S from t_0 to t_1 nonreflectively not to reconsider this intention.[27] Given this extension of the historical principle of nondeliberative rationality we may reason from (1'), (2'), (3), and (4)—suitably extended—to (5).

We cannot be confident about this proposed extension of the historical principle until we have explored more fully the question of when it is rational of an agent to have an intention that is initially the result of non-deliberation-based processes. And this is a matter I will not try to settle here. But, again for the sake of argument, let us suppose here that some such extension is acceptable, and therefore that we really are threatened with the conclusion, (5). This suggests that we look more closely at premise (2').

Something very much like premise (2') is suggested by David Gauthier: "I do not deny that it may be rational to adopt an intention but not act on it. But when this is so, conditions must change from those envisaged in adopting the intention. What I do deny is that it can be rational to adopt an intention and then rational to abandon it should the very conditions envisaged in adopting it come to pass."[28]

The claim suggested here is that if it was rational of you at t_1 to adopt the intention to A at t_2, and if at t_2 the conditions are just as you envisaged they would be in adopting this intention at t_1, then it is rational of you not to abandon this intention at t_2. And this is very close to the claim made in premise (2').

My response is to distinguish two senses in which one may "adopt" an intention. On the first reading of "adopt," what Gauthier suggests is very likely true, but does not establish premise (2'). On the second reading of "adopt," the one which would support premise (2'), what he says is very likely false.

On the first reading we suppose that to "adopt" the intention to drink the toxin is to form it *on the basis of deliberation about whether so to act*. And it is quite plausible that if it was rational of you to form the intention at t_1 to A at t_2 on the basis of deliberation at t_1 about whether to A at t_2, and "the very conditions envisaged" in making this decision come to pass at t_2 (and you know this at t_2), then it would still be rational for you at t_2 to decide to A on the basis of similar deliberation then.[29] So, when "adopt" is read in this way, what Gauthier suggests seems plausible enough. But it does not support premise (2') of the argument against my theory. This is because premise (2') supposes that the fact that things go as expected guarantees that it is rational of you not to reconsider the prior intention to A, even if your rationality for initially intending to A is *not* a case of *deliberative* rationality.

For Gauthier's claim to support premise (2') we must interpret "adopt" as including *non*-deliberation-based acquisition of an intention, including the case in which you cause yourself so to intend by way of self-hypnosis or the like. And when we do that, Gauthier's claim seems dubious. Even if it was rational of you to acquire a new intention by way of such non-deliberation-based processes, and even if circumstances develop as expected, it might still be incumbent on you to reconsider if the opportunity arises. There is no guarantee that in acquiring an intention by way of such non-deliberation-based processes you acquire an intention that would match a decision based on deliberation; there is no such guarantee even if it was rational of you so to acquire your intention. Even if it is rational of you on Tuesday to acquire and to have the intention to drink toxin on Wednesday, when Wednesday arrives you will have ample opportunity to reconsider and to deliberate about whether to drink. It will be obvious to you then that you have nothing to gain and much to lose from drinking the toxin. And it does not seem very plausible that reasonable habits of reconsideration—habits whose expected long-term impact on the agent's interest in getting what she wants exceeds an appropriate threshold—would inhibit reconsideration in such cases.[30] So premise (2'), as well as Gauthier's claim interpreted in the spirit of premise (2'), does not seem very plausible.

My conclusion, then, is that we should at the least reject premise (2'). So my theory is not committed to conclusion (5). Instead of leading to an unacceptable conclusion, my general approach to agent rationality seems, rather, to be in a good position to unravel some of the issues raised by Kavka's puzzle.

chapter 7

Commitment Revisited

IT IS time to return to commitment. Future-directed intention, I have urged, involves a characteristic commitment to future action. This commitment is in part a matter of the roles which such intentions actually do play in our lives, and in part a matter of the roles that, rationally speaking, such intentions should play: commitment has both descriptive and normative aspects. Let us see what light is shed on these twin aspects of commitment by the ideas presented in the previous chapters.

Recall the pressures in the direction of skepticism about the very idea of a commitment to future action. I suggested in Chapter 1 that we can express these pressures in the form of a trilemma. Consider my intention today to go to Boston tomorrow. This intention cannot involve a commitment to the later action in the sense that my present state itself controls my later conduct; for that would be action at a distance. But this intention also should not involve a commitment to the later action in the sense that it is an unchangeable, irrevocable attitude in favor of so acting; for such irrevocability would clearly be irrational. So this intention will involve a commitment to the later action only in the sense that I will so act later if (but only if) it is later rational so to act. But then why should I bother today to form the intention about tomorrow? Why should I not just cross my bridges when I come to them? On the first horn, future-directed intentions are metaphysically objectionable; on the second horn, they are rationally objectionable; and on this third horn, they just seem a waste of time.

We now have the conceptual resources needed to respond to this trilemma and to provide a treatment of commitment that avoids all three horns. Future-directed intentions are typically elements in larger, partial plans. These plans play a crucial role in coordination and in extending the influence of deliberation over time, thereby helping us avoid becoming time-slice agents. As elements in such partial plans, future-directed intentions play important roles as inputs to further reasoning aimed at filling in or modifying these plans, as well as in the more direct motivation of action when the time comes. And the normal functioning of such intentions and plans also involves aspects of rational agency that go beyond actual reasoning or calculation—in particular, underlying habits of retention and (non)reconsideration of prior plans. Rather than exerting a ghostly mode of influence on later action, an intention now to A later shapes later action by way of characteristic processes of reasoning and intention retention and (non)reconsideration. These processes do not require that the prior intention be irrevocable; but they still provide for a substantive and crucial role for such intentions in the normal functioning of limited rational agents like us. So we escape all three horns of the trilemma.

This model of the role of intentions and plans in limited rational agency provides an account of both the descriptive and the normative aspects of commitment. Begin with the descriptive aspect. This consists in the roles future-directed intentions play in connecting—by way of partial plans—prior deliberation and later conduct. As I noted in Chapter 2, there are two dimensions of commitment: volitional and reasoning-centered. Each of these dimensions of commitment has a descriptive aspect.

The descriptive aspect of the volitional dimension of commitment consists in the characteristic role of present-directed intention in controlling (and not merely potentially influencing) present conduct. If I intend to A now, my intention will normally lead me at least to try to A. Borrowing a term from Chisholm we may say that an intention to A now normally issues in my *endeavoring* now to A.[1] Future-directed intention involves volitional commitment because of its relation to present-directed intention: if my future-directed intention manages to survive until the time of action, and I see that this time has arrived and nothing interferes, it will control my action then. Present-directed intentions have a special relation to action, and future-directed intentions are the sort of state that will have this special relation if they survive until the time of action is seen to have arrived.

The descriptive aspect of the reasoning-centered dimension of commitment, in contrast, consists in the characteristic roles of future-directed intentions in the interim between their acquisition and their execution. These roles include both their characteristic persistence and their part in guiding further practical reasoning, reasoning that issues in derivative intentions. Future-directed intentions resist (to some extent) revision and reconsideration. And future-directed intentions involve dispositions to reason in appropriate ways: to reason about means, preliminary steps, or just more specific courses of action; and to constrain one's intentions in the direction of consistency.

The descriptive aspect of the commitment characteristic of intention consists, then, in these dispositions and roles. The normative aspect of commitment consists in the norms and standards of rationality associated with these roles. Let us briefly review some of the main conclusions we have reached about these norms and standards.

Begin by distinguishing two kinds of norms. Some norms are *internal norms,* norms to be used directly in the agent's own practical reasoning about what to do. In contrast, some norms are *external norms,* norms whose primary use is not in the agent's own practical reasoning about what to do, but rather in reaching some external assessment of the agent, her habits, her reasoning, or her intentional actions.[2] Our investigations have uncovered norms of both sorts associated with the dispositions and roles characteristic of intention.

First, there are internal norms associated with the role of prior intentions in guiding further practical reasoning and planning. Central to these are the demands for means-end coherence and strong consistency, demands that are themselves rooted in a more fundamental concern with (rational) desire-satisfaction. It is because of these demands that prior intentions play a direct role in further practical reasoning. It is because of these demands that prior intentions pose problems and constrain admissible options for such reasoning, thereby providing framework reasons: reasons whose role is to help determine the relevance and admissibility of options.

Second, we have articulated an important complex of external norms, norms to be used in making external assessments of the agent. There is the two-tier approach to the assessment of the rationality of the agent for her nonreflective (non)reconsideration of a prior intention. There is the intention-action principle, a principle which specifies the crucial way in which the rationality of an agent for her present-directed intention can shape her rationality for her ensuing intentional action. And there is the trio of historical principles concerning the rationality of an agent for her intentions, principles that cover deliberative, nondeliberative, and policy-based cases. All of these norms are themselves grounded in a basic concern with (rational) desire-satisfaction together with an appreciation both of our limits and of the associated fact that we are not time-slice agents.

So we have a complex account of the commitment characteristic of future-directed intention. This commitment has both descriptive and normative aspects. It is tied both to the role of present-directed intention in controlling present action and to the roles of future-directed intention in the interim between intention-acquisition and intention-execution. By unpacking this complex of dispositions and norms we demystify commitment without allowing it to collapse into mere desire and expectation. We explain it without supposing that it involves a ghostly mode of influence of future conduct by present decisions, without requiring that a commitment to action be irrevocable, and without making it a mystery why we ever bother to form intentions for the future.

Now, some philosophical work in the theory of action reveals a tendency to see intention as either a special kind of evaluation or a special kind of belief. Donald Davidson's later work on intention is an example of the former sort of view; Stuart Hampshire and H. L. A. Hart's is an example of the latter.[3] On the view of intention sketched here intention is a state characterized by a complex of functional roles and associated norms. These roles and their associated norms constitute the special commitment characteristic of intention. Such roles involve, of course, systematic relations with attitudes of evaluation and belief. But on the present theory we need not try to assimilate intention to either kind of attitude. We can just say that an intention to act is a complex form of commitment to action, a commitment revealed in reasoning as well as in action. To say this we must take seriously dispositions to reason in certain ways, and the functional roles of attitudes both in reasoning and in other processes that are part of the psychological background against which practical reasoning takes place. And this highlights once again the importance of practical reasoning and planning to our understanding of intention.

chapter 8

Two Faces of Intention

I HAVE been sketching a planning conception of intention. On this conception a central fact about us is that we are planning creatures. We frequently settle in advance on plans for the future. These plans help guide our later conduct and coordinate our activities over time, in ways in which our ordinary desires and beliefs do not. Intentions are typically elements in such coordinating plans: as such, intentions are distinctive states of mind, not to be reduced to clusters of desires and beliefs.

Now it is time to return to the relation between intention and intentional action. Recall the observation with which I began this book. We do things intentionally, and we intend to do things. Our commonsense psychology uses the notion of intention to characterize both our actions and our mental states: I might intentionally start my car, and I might intend to start it. My intention to start it clearly does not guarantee that I do. But beyond that it is not obvious how these two phenomena are related. A central problem for a theory of intention is to provide a plausible account of this relation.

One thing seems clear: it is part of our commonsense psychological framework that these phenomena are not completely *un*related. In classifying both our actions and our states of mind in terms of some root notion of intention, commonsense psychology clearly assumes that there is some important commonality. Our problem is to say what this commonality is, by spelling out the relation between intentional action and intending (or, having an intention) to act.

8.1 The Simple View

How should the planning theory of intention view this relation? I may intend to start my car today: this is a future-directed intention. But I may also intend to start my car beginning now: this is a present-directed intention. Such a present-directed intention does not guarantee that I actually start my car. But if I do start my car intentionally, then it seems plausible to suppose I have such a present-directed intention to start it. After all, while starting the car I surely intend to do *something*. Given that what I do intentionally is to start it, it seems that what I intend will include starting it.

This suggests a general solution to our problem: for me intentionally to A I must intend to A; my mental states at the time of action must be such that A is among those things I intend. I will call this the *Simple View*. The Simple View does not say that there must be a separate *event* of intending to A for each intentional A-ing. But it does require that one's mental *states* at the time one intentionally A's include an intention to A.[1]

Let me clarify this further. Suppose I intentionally start my car. On the Simple View it follows that

(1) I intend to start my car.

The point I want to note here is that I can have the intention reported in (1) whether or not I actually do start my car. The form of (1) is *not*

(2) aRb

where *b* is replaced by a singular term denoting an actual, particular action of my starting my car.[2]

The Simple View is a special case of a more general conception, the *Single Phenomenon View*. On this more general view, intentional action and the state of intention both involve a certain common state, and it is the relation of an action to this state that makes that action intentional. The Simple View adds to this more general conception the requirement that this state is just an intention so to act.

The Simple View has its virtues. It recognizes the distinctiveness of intentions, and provides a straightforward and initially plausible account of the relation between such intentions and intentional action. It is a view toward which common sense initially leans, as well as a view implicit in many discussions of intention in moral philosophy.[3] Nevertheless, although I will be accepting a version of the more general Single Phenomenon View, I find the Simple View unacceptable. Our conception of the state of intention is that of a single state tied to two very different sorts of phenomena. Intention is Janus-faced, tied both to coordinating plans and intentional action. The Simple View does not allow sufficient theoretical room for both these faces of intention.

In Sections 8.2 and 8.3 I explain why. In Sections 8.4 through 8.7 I sketch a route between the desire-belief model and the Simple View, a route that remains within the framework of the more general Single Phenomenon View. My proposal continues to see intentions as distinctive, and to see the intentionality of an action as dependent on its relation to such intentions. But it rejects the account of this relation provided by the Simple View. It holds, instead, that although to *A* intentionally I must intend to do something, I need not intend *to do A*. This leads to a distinction between *what* I intend and the *motivational potential* of my intention. I conclude this chapter by arguing that this distinction has a further important virtue. It allows our concern with the ascription of responsibility to shape our classification of actions as intentional without thereby distorting our classifications of mental states in ways which undermine critical regularities.

8.2 The Argument against the Simple View

My argument against the Simple View is rooted in my conception of intentions as elements in larger, coordinating plans, and the resulting demands for strong consistency. Recall that to be well suited as elements of such coordinating plans my intentions need to be (other things equal) strongly consistent, relative to my beliefs. It should be possible (other things equal) for me successfully to execute all my intentions in a world in which my beliefs are true. But once we take this demand for consistency seriously, the Simple View is subject to challenge.

The challenge can be presented in terms of a series of three examples.[4] In the first case I am playing a video game in which I am to guide a "missile" into a certain target. I am quite skilled at such things, but it is a difficult game and I am doubtful of success. Still, I aim at the target and try to hit it. As it happens, I succeed in just the way I was trying. My success was not merely a matter of luck; it depended heavily on my considerable skill at such games. Further, hitting the target was what I wanted to do; I was not just aiming at the target as a way of ensuring that the "missile" would go several inches to the right.[5]

Do I hit the target intentionally? It seems that I do. I want to hit it and so am trying to hit it. My attempt is guided by my perception of the target. I hit the target in the way I was trying, and in a way that depends on my relevant skills. And it is my perception that I have hit it that terminates my attempt. So even though I am doubtful of success while I am trying, if I do succeed in hitting the target I hit it intentionally. On the Simple View, then, I must intend to hit the target. And this is, for all we have said, an acceptable result.[6] Even though I am doubtful that

I will hit the target, the intention to hit it need not violate the demand for strong consistency.

Suppose now that a second game is added, a game which also involves guiding a "missile" to a certain target. Since I am ambidextrous and can play one game with each hand, I decide to play both games simultaneously. As before, the games are difficult and I am doubtful of success at either of them. As it happens I miss target 2 but I do succeed in hitting target 1 in the way I was trying and in a way that depended on my relevant skills. Here again, it seems to me, I hit target 1 intentionally. The mere fact that I was also trying unsuccessfully to hit target 2 does not prevent me from intentionally hitting target 1.

The Simple View must say, then, that I intend to hit target 1. And this seems plausible. But what about my intentions concerning target 2? I was trying equally hard and with equal skill, as well as with equally weak confidence of success, to hit target 2. It seems clear from the symmetry of the case that if I intend to hit target 1 I also intend to hit target 2. Of course, in the example I do not hit target 2, whereas I do hit target 1. But, as already noted, this difference does not prevent me from intending to hit target 2.

So the defender of the Simple View must suppose that in this case I intend to hit each target. This sets the stage for my argument against this view, an argument which requires one more addition to my example.

Let us now suppose that the two games are known to me to be so linked that it is impossible to hit both targets. If I hit one of the targets, both games are over. If both targets are about to be hit simultaneously, the machines just shut down and I hit neither target. Both targets remain visible to me; so I can see which target I hit if I hit either one. And there is a reward for hitting either target. But I know that although I can hit each target, I cannot hit both targets. Still, I know it is difficult to hit either target, so I again decide to play both games simultaneously; I see the risk of shutting down the machines as outweighed by the increase in my chances of hitting a target. I proceed to try to hit target 1 and also to try to hit target 2. I give each game a try.

Suppose I do hit target 1 in just the way I was trying to hit it, and in a way which depends heavily on my considerable skill at such games. It seems, again, that I hit target 1 *intentionally*. So, on the Simple View, I must intend to hit target 1. Given the symmetry of the case I must also intend to hit target 2. But given my knowledge that I cannot hit both targets, these two intentions fail to be strongly consistent. Having them would involve me in a criticizable form of irrationality. Yet it seems clear that I need be guilty of no such irrationality: the strategy of giving each game a try seems perfectly reasonable. If I am guilty of no such irrationality, I do not have both of these intentions. Since my relevant intention in favor of hitting target 1 is the same as that in favor of hitting target 2, I have neither intention. So the Simple View is false. If it were true, I would be guilty of a form of criticizable irrationality; but I need be guilty of no such irrationality. The Simple View imposes too strong a link between intention and intentional action, a link that is insensitive to differences in the demands of practical reason.[7]

This argument against the Simple View appeals to constraints on intention that do not apply in the same way to intentional action. In this respect it is similar to an alternative argument that has been sketched in the literature, one that I will discuss briefly.

Suppose I intend now to go to the concert tonight. What must I believe about my future concert-going? As I noted in Chapter 3, some philosophers accept the strong thesis that I must now believe I will go.[8] Once we are given this strong belief requirement on future-directed intention, however, it is natural to suppose that present-directed intentions are subject to a similar belief condition. And this leads directly to an argument against the Simple View.[9]

This argument has two premises. The first is just this strong belief requirement. The second is the observation that a person can do something intentionally even though, at the time of action, he is in doubt about whether he is so acting. We have already seen an example of this: I might intentionally hit the target even while being doubtful of success. Donald Davidson offers another example.[10] A person might try hard to make ten carbon copies on a typewriter while being skeptical of success. Still, if this is what he wants to do, and if he does, in fact, make ten copies in the way he was trying and in a way that depends on his relevant skills, then it seems that he intentionally makes ten copies. Again, we have intentional action despite lack of belief.

So we have two premises: a strong belief requirement on intending to act, and the observation that one may *A* intentionally even while doubting that one is *A*-ing. These two premises entail that the Simple View is false. Given the strong belief requirement, when I act intentionally in a way in which I do not believe I am acting, I will not intend so to act.

Like my initial argument the present argument tries to cite a constraint on intention that does not similarly apply to intentional action. But whereas I cited the constraint that rational intentions are to be strongly consistent, given the agent's beliefs, the present argument cites a strong belief condition on intention. For reasons I indicated in Chapter 3, however, it seems to me that this strong belief condition is problematic in ways in which the demand for strong consistency is not. Though there is notorious disagreement on this matter, it seems to me plausible to suppose that sometimes intentions just do not satisfy such a strong belief condition. At the least the strong belief requirement is no more obvious than the Simple View itself. So a philosopher committed to the Simple View could plausibly resist the present argument by turning it on its end and seeing it as an objection to the strong belief requirement. One person's *modus ponens* is another's *modus tollens*.

In contrast, the demand for strong consistency of intentions is more difficult to avoid. First, instead of requiring an actual belief that I will A in order for me to intend to A, it demands only that (other things equal, and if my intentions are to be rational) I not have beliefs inconsistent with the belief that I will A. Second, this constraint is even compatible with the possibility of my intending to act in a certain way while believing I will not. It just requires us to say that, other things equal, I would then be guilty of a form of criticizable irrationality. Finally, it will be more difficult to turn the tables on my argument, rejecting the requirement of strong consistency in order to hold onto the Simple View. This is so because this consistency constraint seems to be firmly grounded in a basic feature of intentions: their role in coordinating plans.

Nevertheless, objections to my argument remain. I turn now to consider some of these.

8.3 Objections and Replies

My argument depends on two claims about the final video-games case in which the games are known to be linked and I succeed in hitting target 1:

> (a) If in this case I had present-directed intentions which failed to be strongly consistent, I would be criticizably irrational.
> (b) I hit target 1 intentionally.

Let us consider some ways in which a defender of the Simple View might try to challenge these claims.

Begin with (a). Such a defender might urge that, for all I have said, only *future*-directed intentions are subject to the strong consistency requirement. So, contrary to (a), I can intend to hit target 1 *now*, and similarly target 2, without being criticizably irrational.

This objection is inadequate for two reasons. First, the argument for the demand for strong consistency depends on the observation that intentions typically play a coordinating role as elements of larger plans. Now, although this role is clearer in the case of future-directed intentions, it is also important in connection with present-directed intentions. Suppose my intentions concerning the video games are embedded in a larger plan for the day. I begin the day with what are then future-directed intentions concerning the games. When the time comes, these become present-directed intentions. But they continue to be part of my coordinating plan, and so they continue to be subject to the demand for strong consistency.

Second, the very idea that present-directed intentions escape the consistency demands to which future-directed intentions are subject seems to me not very plausible. After all, they are equally intentions. We do not think belief works this way: we do not see beliefs about the present as subject to weaker demands of consistency than beliefs about the future.

A second objection to (a) grants that there is a general presumption against such inconsistency, but urges that this presumption can sometimes be overridden and, indeed, is overridden in the present case. I have strong pragmatic reasons for intending to hit each target, since that is how I best pursue the reward. Given these pragmatic reasons to have both intentions, the fact that they fail to be strongly consistent (given my beliefs) need not convict me of criticizable irrationality, contrary to (a).[11]

My response is to reject the contention that I must intend to hit each target in order best to pursue the reward. What I need to do is to *try* to hit each target. But this does not mean that I must *intend* to hit each target. Perhaps I must intend *something*—to shoot at each target, for example. But it seems that I can best pursue the reward without intending flat out to hit each target, and so without a failure of strong consistency.[12] Given a presumption against such a failure, that is what I should do. If I nevertheless do intend to hit each target, I am criticizably irrational. So (a) remains plausible.

What about (b), the claim that what I do intentionally is to *hit target 1*? Here the defender of the Simple View might urge that what I do intentionally is only to *hit one of the two targets*. So all that the Simple View requires is that I intend to hit one of the two targets. And that intention is not threatened by the demand for strong consistency.

In assessing this objection we must be careful to distinguish my case from other, superficially similar cases. For example, suppose there is a single target in front of you and you know it is either target 1 or target 2. But since the targets are labeled on the back, you do not know which target it is. Still, you do know that you get a reward for hitting target 1 or for hitting target 2. So you shoot at and hit the target in front of you, which turns out to be target 1.

Now, on one natural reading of 'trying', you were not trying specifically to hit target 1. You were only trying to hit whichever target it was that was in front of you. Further, on a natural reading of 'knowingly', you did not hit target 1 knowingly; for you did not know that it was target 1, rather than target 2, that you were hitting. Such observations make it plausible to say that although in hitting target 1 you intentionally hit one of the two targets, you did not intentionally hit target 1.

Again, suppose there are two targets close together, and one gun. You only have enough skill to aim in the vicinity of the pair of targets, trying to hit one or the other. And that is what you do. Suppose you hit target 1. Then it is plausible to say that in hitting target 1 you have intentionally hit one of the two targets without intentionally hitting target 1.

In both these cases, then, it might plausibly be insisted that you do not intentionally hit target 1. It is important to note, however, that my case is different from these. I am trying to hit each of two targets (though I am not trying to hit both). I am not just trying to hit a single target, which, for all I know, is one or the other of two different targets. Nor am I just aiming the same shot at both targets in the attempt to hit one or the other. Rather, each of the two targets separately guides my attempt to hit it. Further, I know that if I successfully hit target 1, my endeavor to hit it will be terminated by my knowledge that I have hit that very target. So my case differs from yet a third variation in which I know, rather, that the machine will only tell me if one of the targets is hit, without telling me which one.[13] In this third variation it may be plausible to insist that all I do intentionally is to hit one of the targets. But, again, my case is importantly different.

These contrasts with variant cases highlight features of my case which argue for the claim that I intentionally hit target 1. First, I want to hit target 1 and so am trying to do so. Second, my attempt to hit target 1 is guided specifically by my perception of that target, and not by my perception of other targets. Relevant adjustments in my behavior are dependent specifically on my perception of that target. Third, I actually hit target 1 in the way I was trying, and in a way that depends on my relevant skills. Fourth, it is my perception that I have hit target 1, and not merely my perception that I have hit a target, that terminates my attempt to hit it. Granted, if I had instead hit target 2, that also would have terminated my endeavor to hit target 1, given my knowledge of how the games are linked. Nevertheless, what actually does terminate my attempt to hit target 1 is my perception that I have hit that target. When all this is true, it seems to me too weak just to say that I have intentionally hit one of the targets. Rather, I have intentionally hit target 1.

Both crucial claims in my argument against the Simple View are, then, quite plausible. But this is not the end of the matter. We need also to know the larger theoretical advantages and disadvantages of giving up the Simple View. In the remainder of this chapter and in Chapter 9 I will pursue some of these larger issues. Insofar as the alternative framework I sketch is independently plausible, we have further support for the rejection of the Simple View.[14]

8.4 Intention and Motivational Potential

The Simple View supposes that there must be a tight fit between what is done intentionally and what is intended. I propose to give up this assumption and to distinguish between what is intended and the sorts of intentional activity in which an intention may issue. Making this distinction, we can say that when I *A* intentionally I intend *something*, but I may not specifically intend to *A*. Our notion of intentional action embodies a complex scheme for the classification of actions (or, perhaps, actions "under a description"). To understand the relation between intention and intentional action we must recognize that the factors that determine what is intended do not completely coincide with the factors that, on this scheme, determine what is done intentionally.

Recognizing this we can accept a version of the Single Phenomenon View, one which sees intention as the common element in both intentional action and the state of intention. Actions are intentional in part because of their relation to intentions. But the admissible relations are more complex than those envisaged by the Simple View.

In the theory of action one can be led into two different mistakes (among others). The first, built into the desire-belief model, is to suppose that intentional action involves no distinctive state of intention at all. The second, made by the Simple View, is to suppose that intentional action always involves an intention so to act—a supposition that does not do justice to the role of intentions in coordinating plans. I am proposing a way between these two. In acting intentionally there is something I intend to do; but this need not be what I do intentionally.

Supposing, then, that there are cases in which I intentionally *A* and yet do not intend to *A* but only intend to *B*, for some appropriate *B*, a full account of our scheme for classifying actions as intentional will need to sort out just when this can be so. Whatever its details, such an account will implicitly specify a four-place relation between intentions, desires, beliefs, and types of actions. It will say what types of actions may be performed intentionally in the course of executing a certain intention, given a certain background of desires and beliefs. This allows us to define a useful notion, that of the *motivational potential* of an intention. *A* is in the motivational potential of my intention to *B*, given my desires and beliefs, just in case it is possible for me intentionally to *A* in the course of executing my intention to *B*. If I actually intend to *A*, then *A* will be in the motivational potential of my intention. But we need not suppose that if *A* is in the motivational potential of an intention of mine, then I intend to *A*.

Consider the last video-games example. My intention includes my hitting target 1 in its motivational potential: it is possible, given my desires and beliefs, for me to hit target 1 intentionally in the course of executing my intention. Nevertheless, I do not intend flat out to hit target 1. Though hitting target 1 is in the motivational potential of my intention, it is not *what* I intend.

What then do I intend? There are several possibilities. I might intend to shoot at target 1 and also to shoot at target 2. I might intend to try to hit target 1, and also to try to hit target 2. I might intend to hit target 1 if I can, and similarly in the case of target 2. I might even just intend to hit one of the two targets; but we must be careful to distinguish this case from the cases discussed in Section 8.3 in which, though I intend to hit one of the two targets, my intention does not include hitting target 1 in its motivational potential. The important point is just that my intention may include hitting target 1 in its motivational potential without including it in what is intended.

That my intention includes hitting target 1 in its motivational potential, even though it is not an intention to hit target 1, does not by itself *explain* why it is true that I hit target 1 intentionally. This is clear from the definition of motivational potential. The notion of motivational potential is intended to *mark* the fact that my intention to *B* may issue in my intentionally *A*-ing, rather than to explain it. It is a *theoretical placeholder:* it allows us to retain theoretical room for a more complex account of the relation between intention and intentional action while leaving unsettled the details of such an account. Such an account would not itself use the notion of motivational potential but would, rather, replace it with detailed specifications of various sufficient conditions for intentional conduct.

Let me put the point this way. On the theory just sketched, if I *A* intentionally then I *A* in the course of executing some intention to *B*, and, given my desires and beliefs, this intention contains *A* in its motivational potential. This means that there will be some true statement(s) along the lines of

> If *S* intends to *B* and *S* *A*'s in the course of executing his intention to *B* and _____, then *S* *A*'s intentionally.

A full-blown theory of intentional action would tell us how such blanks should be filled in. For example, our discussion of the video-games example suggests that one such specification of sufficient conditions would be roughly along the following lines:

> *S* intentionally *A*'s if:
>
> (1) *S* wants to *A* and for that reason intends to try to *A*; and
>
> (2) *S A*'s in the course of executing his intention to try to *A*; and
>
> (3) *S A*'s in the way he was trying to *A*; and
>
> (4) conditions (2) and (3) depend, in an appropriate way, on *S*'s relevant skills.

Without working out the details, we can see that such a specification would use conditions like (3) and (4) to fill in the theoretical space opened up by the distinction between what is intended and what is in the motivational potential of an intention.

This new theoretical space allows us to formulate a more satisfactory alternative to the desire-belief model, on the one hand, and the Simple View, on the other. In contrast with the desire-belief model, we can grant that intentional action involves a distinctive pro-attitude—namely, intention—that is not reducible to the agent's desires and beliefs. But, in contrast with the Simple View, the intention that is involved in intentionally *A*-ing need not be an intention *to A*. By allowing this flexibility in what is intended we do better than the Simple View in providing for the consistency demands on intentions. We can allow, for example, that when I intentionally hit target 1 what I intend need not involve me in inconsistency.

One might object that this distinction, the distinction between what is intended and what is in the motivational potential of an intention, is illusory. As Anscombe remarks, "The primitive sign of wanting *is trying to get*."[15] But what is true about wanting seems even more clearly true about intention: the "primitive sign" of an intention to *A* is trying to *A*. In the face of this I have tried to drive a wedge between an intention whose execution may involve both trying to *A* and intentionally *A*-ing, and an intention to *A*. I have claimed that one might have the former intention and yet still not intend to *A*. But, one might object, how is that possible? Differences in what I intend should reveal themselves in differences in the roles played by my intentions. But the basic role that present-directed intentions play is in motivating and guiding present conduct. So it may seem unclear that there is a real difference between intending to *A* and having an intention whose role includes the motivation of intentionally *A*-ing.

The response to this worry is that intentions play other important roles, roles I have been emphasizing throughout this book. Differences in these roles can serve to discriminate between two intentions, both of which include *A* in their motivational potential but only one of which is an intention to *A*. Future-directed intentions are elements in coordinating plans and inputs into further practical reasoning. In terms of the role played in such plans and reasoning, an intention to *A* differs from other intentions which include *A* in their motivational potential. Among these differences are the constraints imposed on yet other intentions, given the demand for strong consistency. What I intend, when I have a future-directed intention, will be in part reflected in the ways in which my intention constrains my other intentions through this consistency demand. Thus, if my future-directed intentions concerning targets 1 and 2 do not convict me of criticizable inconsistency, then, given my beliefs, they are not intentions to hit target 1 and to hit target 2. This is so even though my intention concerning target 1 includes hitting it in its motivational potential, and similarly with my intention concerning target 2.

A similar point applies to present-directed intentions. What I intend when I have a present-directed intention will not be simply a matter of the sorts of intentional conduct in which my intention might issue. I can have a present-directed intention which includes hitting target 1 in its motivational potential even though I do not intend flat out to hit target 1. For my intention to be an intention *to hit target 1* it must constrain my other intentions accordingly, by way of the demand for strong consistency. And, as we have seen, my intentions concerning targets 1 and 2 may include hitting each target in their motivational potential without constraining each other in the ways characteristic of intentions to hit these targets.

8.5 Motivational Potential Extended

Desires, beliefs, and intentions are basic elements in the commonsense psychology underlying intentional action. Intentions are typically elements in plans. Intentional action generally involves an intention to act. The state of intention is the common element in both the states and the actions included within our conception of intention: the Single Phenomenon View is correct. The intention involved in intentional action need not, however, be an intention so to act. My intention may include *A* in its motivational potential even though I do not, strictly speaking, intend to *A*. The coherence of this last idea is ensured by the role intentions play in coordinating plans.

This approach depends on driving a wedge between what I intend and the motivational potential of my intention. Now, the wedge I have so far argued for has been rather thin: it has directly concerned only certain special cases in which the demand for strong consistency created problems for the Simple View. But once we have this wedge we can widen it in a way that promises to be useful.

Suppose I intend to run the marathon and believe that I will thereby wear down my sneakers. Now it seems to me that it does not follow that I intend to wear down my sneakers, and in a normal case I will not so intend. One sign of the absence of such an intention will be the fact that I am not at all disposed to engage in further reasoning aimed at settling on some means to wearing down my sneakers. In contrast, if I intended to get to the track by 9:00 A.M., as a means to running the race, I would be disposed to engage in reasoning aimed at figuring out how to do that.[16] My attitude toward wearing down my sneakers does not play the role in further means-end reasoning that an intention to wear them down would normally play.

Even so, if I proceed to run the marathon and actually do wear down my sneakers, then I might well do so intentionally. Perhaps this is clearest in a case including two further features.[17] First, I not only believe I will wear them down; I consciously note this while I am running. Second, wearing them down has some independent significance to me; perhaps they are a family heirloom. In a case containing these two further features I think we would classify my action as intentional. Yet it does not seem that these further features must change *what I intend* in running the race. Given my relevant beliefs and desires, in executing my intention to run the race I may intentionally wear down my sneakers; and this even though I do not intend to wear them down. So although *what* I intend does not include wearing down my sneakers, the motivational potential of my intention does.

Generalizing, we can expect a full theory of intentional action to generate true statements along the lines of:

> If S intentionally B's in the course of executing his intention to B, and S believes that his B-ing will result in X, and his B-ing does result in X and _____, then S intentionally brings about X.

For present purposes we can leave aside the subtle issue of just how the blank should be filled in (for example, must it add that S is aware that he is bringing about X and is not indifferent as to whether or not he does bring it about?). The important point is that these sufficient conditions will not include the requirement that S actually intend to bring about X. This means that motivational potential can be extended by our beliefs about the upshots of what we intend even when what we intend is not thereby extended.[18]

I will be returning to related issues about expected but nonintended upshots of intended actions in Chapter 10. For now I want to emphasize the complexities of our scheme for the classification of actions as intentional. The Simple View forces us to read these complexities back into the agent's intentions: it includes in what is intended everything done intentionally. My version of the Single Phenomenon View loosens the connection between what is intended and what is done intentionally: it sees what is intended as a fact about the agent's mind which need not reflect all the complexities of our scheme for classifying actions as intentional.[19] It does this by using the notion of motivational potential to provide a buffer between the considerations that influence the intentionality of action and those that influence what a person intends.[20]

8.6 Motivational Potential and the Distinctiveness of Intention

I now want to argue that this buffer helps support the central claim that intentions are distinctive states of mind. It does this by protecting regularities important to the defense of this claim.

The classificatory schemes involved in our commonsense framework play certain roles in our lives, and we can expect the details of such schemes to be shaped by those roles. An important role played by our scheme for classifying actions as intentional is that of identifying ways of acting for which an agent may be held responsible: our concern is not limited to the description and explanation of actions, but extends to the assessment of agents and to the appropriateness of reactive attitudes like indignation and resentment.[21] This is why it seems natural to classify as intentional my wearing down my sneakers. After all, as Sidgwick notes in defending his proposal to "include under the term 'intention' all the consequences of an act that are foreseen as certain or probable": "we cannot evade responsibility for any foreseen bad consequences of our acts by the plea that we felt no desire for them."[22]

Now, the case for seeing intentions as distinctive states of mind depends on locating them in an explanatory system connecting environment and behavior, and on identifying their distinctive role in this system. To do this there need to be underlying regularities connecting intentions with each other and with other states and processes. Further, these regularities must be significantly dependent on *what* is intended; a regular connection between, say, intentions formed during winter quarter and nervousness is not the sort of regularity we need. To the extent to which our scheme for determining what is intended is shaped by our concern, not only with explanation of action but with the assignment of responsibility, it will be harder to find such regularities. Such a concern would tend to lead to the ascription of intentions which do not play their normal roles in motivation and practical reasoning.

To see this, consider again my intention to get to the track by 9:00 A.M. as a means to running the race. This intention plays a pair of roles important to attempts at explanation. First, it triggers further means-end reasoning concerning how to get to the track by then. Second, when the time comes, it motivates activity guided by my beliefs (many of them perceptual) about where the track is.[23] In these respects it contrasts with my mere expectation that I will wear down my sneakers as a result of running. I am neither disposed to engage in reasoning aimed at settling on a means to wearing them down, nor do I guide my running of the race by keeping track of the state of my sneakers.[24]

There are, then, distinctive regularities connecting what is intended with further practical reasoning and with the beliefs that guide our activity. The Simple View undermines such regularities. By reading back from the intentionality of my wearing down my sneakers to an intention to wear them down, it ascribes to me an intention which is outside the web of these regularities; for my attitude toward wearing down my sneakers does not play the roles characteristic of an intention to do so. To support such regularities we need to allow our concern with responsibility to shape what is done intentionally without similarly shaping what is intended. We need to allow our concern with responsibility to lead us to classify my wearing down my sneakers as intentional without forcing us to say that I intend to wear them down. This is what the notion of motivational potential allows my theory to do.

Returning to my video-games example I can make a similar point. Here the relevant regularity is a general tendency toward equilibrium. Generally, when an agent notices that his intentions fail to be strongly consistent, he will make an attempt at revision, an attempt aimed at achieving consistency. But this regularity is undermined if we suppose that in cases such as the video-games example there are strongly inconsistent intentions and yet no tendency toward appropriate revision. The notion of motivational potential allows us to protect this regularity and yet still grant that I hit target 1 intentionally.

The point is not that our scheme for classifying actions as intentional is any less important than our scheme for characterizing states of mind as intentions. Nor am I claiming that the former is somehow gratuitous in a way in which the latter is not.[25] My point is rather that these schemes serve different interests and cut different ways. When we attempt to connect these schemes in an overly simple way—as the Simple View does—we do violence to this complexity.

8.7 Spontaneous Intentional Action

I now want briefly to consider one final objection to my version of the Single Phenomenon View. Suppose you unexpectedly throw a ball to me and I spontaneously reach up and catch it. On the one hand, it may seem that I catch it intentionally; after all, my behavior is under my control and is not mere reflex behavior, as when I blink at the oncoming ball. On the other hand, it may seem that, given how automatic and unreflective my action is, I may well not have any present-directed intention that I am executing in catching the ball. The worry here is not based on the false assumption that all present-directed intentions are preceded by corresponding, future-directed intentions. The worry, rather, is that once we see what a present-directed intention is (in part by reflecting on future-directed intentions and plans), it is unclear that such unreflective, spontaneous behavior must involve such a state. Perhaps our scheme for classifying actions as intentional, while treating as central actions involving intentions, is more inclusive than that.[26]

In response two points need to be made. First, many such spontaneous actions might best be characterized as actions that, although they are under the agent's voluntary control and are purposive, still are not intentional (even though they are not unintentional). Second, it may be in some cases that in catching the ball I am executing some long-standing personal policy—for example, a policy of protecting myself from flying objects. I do not have a present-directed intention specifically to catch this very ball, but my action still involves an intention, namely: my general intention to protect myself in such circumstances.[27]

The first point allows us to block at least some potential counterexamples; for such cases of purposive and voluntary—but still not intentional—behavior do not fall under my version of the Single Phenomenon View. The second point suggests that the intention involved in spontaneous intentional action need not itself be present-directed, but may rather be a long-standing general intention, one that applies to the present case.[28] Taken together these points go at least part of the way toward answering the present objection. But matters here are complex, and I am unsure whether such a defense can work for all cases. Perhaps there will remain cases of spontaneous intentional action that fall outside my version of the Single Phenomenon View. Still, it does seem that the present theory will apply to the vast majority of the cases of intentional activity of planning agents like us. And that is good enough for my purposes.

8.8 Janus-faced Intention

Let me sum up. Intention is Janus-faced, tied both to intentional action and coordinating plans. In this chapter I have sketched a version of the Single Phenomenon View that provides room for both of these faces of intention and for an appropriate link between them. In doing this I have tried to avoid the oversimplifications of the Simple View. I have also tried to leave room for the different effects which our concern with the ascription of responsibility has on the different classificatory schemes included within our conception of intention. And, finally, I have tried to do this in a way that recognizes, exploits, and supports the distinctiveness of an agent's intentions and plans.

Throughout this discussion I have focused on the use of the adverb "intentionally" to characterize action. But we also characterize actions by speaking of an intention *with which* the agent acted. Once we recognize the two faces of intention, how should we think of the phenomenon of acting *with* an intention? This is the question I will turn to in the next chapter.

chapter 9

Acting with an Intention

9.1 Three Notions of Acting with an Intention

The first step is to make some distinctions. Consider:

> (1) I open the curtains with the intention of washing the windows.

In such a case I see my action as part of a larger plan, one that includes my later action of washing the windows. My intention to wash the windows is part of what J. L. Austin suggestively describes as "a miner's lamp on [my] forehead which illuminates always just so far ahead as [I] go along."[1] We may call this a case of acting with a *further* intention. Such a case should be contrasted with:

> (2) I open the curtains with the intention of getting more light.

In this case my action is not seen by me as part of a plan that includes a distinct, later action of getting more light. Rather, I see my current action as, in the circumstances, sufficient to achieve my end of more light. I open the curtains with the intention of *thereby* getting more light. We may call this simply a case of acting with an intention, reserving the expression 'acting with a further intention' for cases of the first sort.

In many cases we act both with an intention (*simpliciter*) and with a further intention. This is a consequence of the pervasive role of future-directed intentions and plans in our lives. Many times while acting with an intention we are also executing part of a larger plan, and putting ourselves in a position to execute further elements of that plan later. So we are also acting with a further intention. I may open the curtains both with the intention of getting more light and with the further intention of washing the windows.

What is the relation between acting with an intention and intending?

I think it is clear that when I open the curtains with the *further* intention of washing the windows, I intend to wash them. But what about acting with the intention (*simpliciter*) of getting more light? Does it follow that I intend to get more light?

I think we need to distinguish two readings of (2). On the *strong* reading, (2) does indeed entail that I intend to get more light, perhaps as part of a larger plan of action. On the *weak* reading, (2) only entails that I act *in order to* get more light; it does not entail (though it does not preclude) that, strictly speaking, I *intend* to get more light.[2]

To see why we need both readings recall the final video-games example from Chapter 8. In this example I shoot at target 1, and I do so in order to hit that target. Hitting that target is my aim in shooting at it: it is what I am trying to do. As Chisholm would put it,[3] I *endeavor* to hit that target. For me to endeavor to hit the target is, in part, for me to guide my conduct accordingly. In a normal case this means that, other things equal, I will be prepared to make adjustments in what I am doing in response to indications of my success or failure in hitting it. I will be prepared to adjust the direction in which I am shooting in response to indications of the movement of the target and in ways believed by me to promote that goal.

Given that I endeavor to hit target 1, do I shoot *with the intention* of hitting it? There seems to be one sense of the expression 'with the intention' according to which I *do* shoot with the intention of hitting target 1. This is the sense of acting with the intention of *A*-ing that is equivalent to endeavoring to *A*.[4] Now, one lesson of the video-games example is that, in this endeavoring sense, I may act with the intention of *A*-ing and yet not intend to *A*. After all, I endeavor to hit target 1; yet, as we have seen, there is good reason to deny that I intend to hit target 1. This endeavoring sense of acting with an intention is the weak reading of that notion.

In contrast, there is also a reading of (2) which amounts to the claim that I act on the basis of what is, strictly speaking, an intention to get more light. Perhaps I earlier decided to get more light, engaged in some means-end reasoning, and then decided in favor of opening the curtains (rather than turning on the light). I then opened the curtains in part on the basis of my intention to get more light. I act with the intention of getting more light, in the strong sense of 'with the intention'.

I act with the intention, in the weak sense, of getting more light, as long as I act in order to achieve the purpose or goal of getting more light—as long as my aim in so acting includes getting more light. I act with the intention, in the strong sense, of getting more light only if I intend (strictly speaking) to get more light and that is why I am so acting.

The video-games example shows us that the former does not guarantee the latter. Rather, acting with an intention in the strong sense is a special case of endeavoring to achieve a certain goal.

Of course, present-directed intention is intimately related to endeavoring. Normally, if I intend to A now and am not prevented, then I will at least endeavor to A. Nevertheless, one may endeavor to A without, strictly speaking, intending to A. The issue, of course, is not the *words* 'intention' and 'endeavoring', but the web of regularities and norms in which the various phenomena are embedded. This web is different for intentions of the sort that enter into plans, on the one hand, and the phenomenon of endeavoring, on the other. We do well to build a recognition of these differences into our theory by keeping a clear distinction between endeavoring and intending—between the weak and the strong notions of 'acting with an intention'.

So we have three notions of acting with an intention: I may act with a further intention, or I may act with an intention *simpliciter*; and in the second case we need to distinguish weak from strong readings.[5] Let us now put these distinctions to some use.

9.2 Reflection on Some Recent Literature

The distinction between intending and endeavoring is useful in understanding some of the recent literature on intention. Let me give some examples.

There is a tradition in the philosophy of action that identifies present-directed intention with volition.[6] Now, 'volition' is something of a term of art. But I think it is fair to say that the paradigm for understanding volition is the phenomenon of attempting or endeavoring to do something or to bring about something. When one identifies present-directed intention with volition, one implicitly assumes that if I now attempt or endeavor to A I now intend to A. But this is to conflate weak and strong notions of 'with an intention'. If I endeavor to hit target 1—and so "will" to hit that target (or will that I hit it)—I do act with the intention, in the *weak* sense, to hit it. But I still may not intend, strictly speaking, to hit it. So it is a mistake to identify present-directed intention with volition.

A similar point is implicit in Grice's British Academy lecture.[7] Grice introduces a general notion of *willing*, a notion which has the feature that I will that I A whenever I either intentionally A or intend to A later. In the present-directed case, I will that I A now (in Grice's sense) just in case I endeavor now to A. Grice then goes on to claim that my intention to A is my willing to A together with my belief that, as a result, I will

A. Taken together with the observation that I can intentionally *A* while not believing I am *A*-ing,[8] this entails that willing that I *A* (and so endeavoring to *A*) does not ensure intending to *A*. Of course, having rejected the idea that an intention to *A* requires a belief that one will *A*, we are not in a position to adopt Grice's positive account of intention as, roughly, willing plus belief. But we can still agree (for reasons different from Grice's) with the negative claim, implicit in the account, that willing (and so endeavoring) does not ensure intention.

George Wilson's monograph, *The Intentionality of Human Action,*[9] raises a related issue. Wilson argues that when I intentionally bring about some goal, *G*, there is some behavior of mine, *b*, such that I intend *of b* that it bring about *G*. Wilson calls this an "act-relational intention," and distinguishes it from a "future action" intention. On Wilson's account future-action intentions are always general: they are, roughly, intentions to perform some action of a certain kind in the future. In contrast, an act-relational intention is always directed at a particular piece of present behavior.

What should Wilson say about the video-games case? It seems he should suppose that I intend of one piece of behavior that it cause target 1 to be hit, and also intend of another piece of behavior that it cause target 2 to be hit. I have these act-relational intentions even though I know I cannot hit both targets. Still, Wilson does not suppose that *all* intentions escape the demand for strong consistency.[10] Rather, he thinks that even though future-action intentions are subject to these consistency demands, act-relational intentions are not.

This shows that for me to intend (in Wilson's case) of *b* that it cause *G* is only for me to act with the intention, in the *weak* sense, of causing *G*. To intend of *b* that it cause *G* is to *aim* or *direct* my behavior, *b*, toward bringing about the goal, *G*.[11] What Wilson calls "act-relational intention" is, then, similar to what I have been calling endeavoring. And an act-relational intention to bring about *G* need not involve an intention—of the sort tied to coordinating plans—to bring about *G*.

But now there seems to be a lacuna in Wilson's framework. In my terminology, his framework includes future-directed intention and endeavoring, but not present-directed intention. What might have appeared to be present-directed intention—that is, Wilson's "act-relational" intention—turns out not to be intention, strictly speaking, for it is not subject to appropriate demands for consistency. Suppose I had earlier decided to open the curtains when I got into the room. I walk into the room, see the curtains, and begin to try to open them. Both Wilson and I agree that from the time of my initial decision until just before I began to try to open the curtains I had an intention to open them, an intention subject to demands for strong consistency. On Wilson's view, though, once I begin to endeavor to open them I no longer have an intention to open them that is subject to such consistency demands. But I do not see why we should suppose that my endeavoring to open the curtains rules out an intention to open them beginning now, an intention subject to demands for strong consistency. And in the normal case it seems to me I will both endeavor and intend so to act. Of course, it is possible to endeavor to open them without intending to open them; that is the lesson of the video-games example. But that does not mean that endeavoring to open them precludes a present-directed intention so to act. If this is right, we will want at least to supplement Wilson's framework with something like what I have been calling present-directed intention.

The distinction between weak and strong notions of 'with an intention' also helps clarify an aspect of Donald Davidson's work on intention. In his 1963 paper, "Actions, Reasons, and Causes," Davidson wrote, "The expression 'the intention with which James went to church' . . . is syncategorematic and cannot be taken to refer to an entity, state, disposition, or event. Its function in context is to generate new descriptions of actions in terms of their reasons."[12] Suppose James went to church with the intention of (thereby) pleasing his mother. Davidson's proposal, I take it, is that this does not involve a special state or event of James's intending to please his mother. Rather, talk of the intention with which James went to church is a way of alluding to some desire, goal, aim, or purpose— some "pro-attitude"—which is part of James's reason for going to church, and so allows us to describe his action in terms of that reason.

Now, in this early paper Davidson did not see a need for a notion of intending distinct from those of desire and belief. Later, in his 1978 paper, "Intending," Davidson changed his mind on this issue.[13] He has remarked that this change in his views "partially undermined" his treatment, in his 1963 paper, of 'with an intention'.[14] But the distinction between weak and strong notions of acting with an intention allows us to save an insight included in Davidson's early view even while recognizing the distinctiveness of intention. Just as Davidson suggested in his early paper, it may be true that James acts with the intention (in the *weak* sense) of pleasing his mother even though he has no distinctive attitude of intending to please her. James may merely be acting in order to please her and may merely want, desire, care about, or have some such other pro-attitude toward pleasing her. And this pro-attitude will be part of James's reason for churchgoing. In such a case, 'the intention with which James went to church' should not be taken to refer to any special event or state of intending.

Finally, the distinction between weak and strong notions of acting with an intention allows me to complete my defense of the demand for strong consistency of intentions and beliefs, a defense begun in Chapter 3. Recall the worry about this demand mentioned at the end of Subsection 3.4.2. This worry was based on an argument of the following sort: I might rationally try to move the log even though I believe I will fail. So I might rationally intend to move the log while believing I will fail. So the demand for strong intention-belief consistency is unacceptable.

When fleshed out, such an argument involves an inference from

(1) I try to move the log.

to

(2) I act with the intention of moving the log.

and then from (2) to

(3) I intend to move the log.

But if I am right about the need to distinguish weak from strong readings of 'with an intention', this pair of inferences involves an equivocation on 'with an intention'. We must read it in the weak sense in order for the inference from (1) to (2) to go through; but then we must read it in the strong sense for the inference from (2) to (3) to work. As long as we keep track of these two senses of 'with an intention', we need not allow such an argument to force us out of our acceptance of the demand for strong consistency.

9.3 The Standard Triad

I am now in a position to expand my account of the structure that is typically present when one acts intentionally. In a typical case of intentionally *A*-ing three things are true:

(a) One intends to *A*.
(b) One endeavors to *A*.
(c) One intentionally *A*'s.

Call this *the standard triad*. Let us speak of the phenomena of intending, endeavoring, and acting intentionally as the *elements* of this standard triad. In typical cases we have all three elements of the triad. Granted, there may be occasional exceptions to this generalization. One possible exception has already been mentioned in Chapter 8. Perhaps when I spontaneously but intentionally catch the ball you throw me, I endeavor to catch it, and catch it intentionally, but do not thereby execute a relevant intention. A second possible exception arises when we consider cases of intentionally refraining from doing something. I might intend not to respond to your greeting, and so intentionally refrain from responding. But do I *do* anything with the intention of refraining from responding? It seems that I may not; it seems that there may just be a nonoccurrence of my responding, a nonoccurrence appropriately explainable by my intention. In such a case we have intention, and intentional refraining, but no endeavoring.[15] Still, I think that in the overwhelming majority of cases of intentional action performed by planning agents like us all three elements of the standard triad will be present.

Let us call *what* is intended, *what* one endeavors to achieve, and *what* one does intentionally, the *intentional objects* of the elements of the standard triad. In typical cases of intentional action we not only have all three elements of the standard triad, but we also have a *match* in their intentional objects: what is intended, what one endeavors to achieve, and what one does intentionally, all match. The point I want to make here, however, is that even when all three elements of the standard triad are present there will not always be such a match in their intentional objects.

In the video-games example I endeavor to hit target 1, and I hit that target intentionally; yet I do not intend to hit target 1. I do intend to do something—to shoot at that target, say—but the consistency demands on intentions give us reason to doubt that what I intend includes hitting that target. The consistency demands on intentions, then, can drive a wedge between the intentional objects of (b) and (c), on the one hand, and of (a), on the other hand.

We can make a related point by using the notion of *rational agglomerativity*.[16] Given the role of intentions in coordination, there is rational pressure for an agent to put his various intentions together into a larger intention. If I both intend to hit target 1 and intend to hit target 2, there will be rational pressure for me to intend to hit both targets. But the same is not, in general, true about endeavoring. I may both endeavor to hit target 1 and endeavor to hit target 2, and yet not be under rational pressure to endeavor to hit both targets. Indeed, in those cases in which I know that I cannot hit both targets I am under strong rational pressure not to endeavor (not to try) to hit them both. Again, I may do one thing with the intention (in the weak sense) of hitting target 1, and at the same time do another thing with the intention (in the weak sense) of hitting target 2, and yet, rationally, not do anything with the intention of hitting both targets (which I know not to be possible). So, considerations of agglomerativity apply differently to the intentional objects of (a) and (b):

what I intend is subject to a rational pressure for agglomeration in a way in which what I endeavor to achieve is not.

With respect both to consistency and to rational agglomerativity, what I do intentionally is like endeavoring and unlike intending. The psychological conditions needed for me intentionally to *A* and the psychological conditions needed for me intentionally to *B* may both rationally be present even though I believe I cannot do both.[17] This is a lesson of the video-games example. And these psychological conditions may both be present without imposing rational pressure on me to satisfy the psychological conditions for intentionally doing both. I endeavor to hit target 1, and (roughly) that is why I hit target 1 intentionally if I do succeed in hitting it. And I endeavor to hit target 2, and (again roughly) that is why I hit target 2 intentionally if I succeed in hitting it. But even if it turns out that I was wrong about the impossibility of hitting both targets and in fact hit them both, I still do not intentionally hit them both (though I do intentionally hit each of them).

Thus, endeavoring to achieve a certain goal—acting with an intention, in the weak sense—is closer in these respects to intentional action than to intending to act. Demands for consistency and agglomeration drive a wedge between the intentional objects of intending, on the one hand, and of endeavoring and intentional action, on the other hand. But in a different respect endeavoring is closer to intending. Recall the example in which I intend to run the race and believe that I will thereby wear down my sneakers. When I actually run the race, all three elements of the standard triad are present, and all include *my running the race* among their intentional objects. Yet not only do I intentionally run the race, but I also, given my belief about my sneakers,[18] intentionally wear my sneakers down. Or so, anyway, I have urged. What I do intentionally seems in this way to be *belief-extendable*. In contrast, we have noted that what I intend is not belief-extendable in this way; for my belief about my sneakers does not extend my intention to run the race to an intention to wear down my sneakers.

What about my endeavoring (acting with the intention, in the weak sense) to run the race? Is this extended by my belief about my sneakers to an endeavor to wear them down? Clearly not. What I endeavor to achieve, like what I intend to achieve but unlike what I do intentionally, is not belief-extendable. Belief-extendability drives a wedge between the intentional objects of (a) and (b), on the one hand, and the intentional objects of (c), on the other. I wear down my sneakers intentionally, but I neither intend nor endeavor to wear them down. In this respect endeavoring is closer to intending than to intentional action.

Endeavoring, then, stands poised between intending and intentional action. On the one hand, what I endeavor to achieve is not extended merely by my beliefs about the upshots of my actions. In this respect endeavoring is like intending. But, on the other hand, endeavoring is not subject to the same demands for consistency and agglomeration as is intending.

What can we say by way of explanation of this pattern of similarities and differences? First, consider the differences with respect to belief extendability. In Chapter 8 I conjectured that our inclination to extend what I do intentionally, in the light of my belief about my sneakers, is grounded in our interest in the ascription of responsibility. Our scheme for classifying actions as intentional is shaped in part by an interest in locating paradigm actions for which agents are to be held responsible.[19] And my awareness that I am now wearing down my sneakers by intentionally running the race seems sufficient, in the context, to make my wearing down my sneakers such a paradigm. In contrast, to allow what I intend to do to be shaped in this way by concerns with responsibility would be to undermine important regularities. For example, it would undermine the regularity that an intention to bring about E involves a disposition to reason about means to bringing about E.

A similar point can be made about endeavoring. To allow what I am endeavoring to do to be shaped in this way by concerns with responsibility would also threaten important regularities. For example, if I am endeavoring to achieve p by A-ing and I see that my A-ing does not achieve p, I will normally be disposed to endeavor to achieve p in some other way, if I think I can. If at first I don't succeed, I'll endeavor again. But if it turns out that I do not wear down my sneakers by the end of the race, I will have no disposition, say, to rub the sneakers against the pumice stone I have with me, with the intention of wearing them down. If my belief that I will wear down my sneakers were to extend what I am endeavoring to do, the cited regularity would be undermined.

Both endeavoring and intending involve clusters of regularities, regularities that underlie commonsense psychological explanations and predictions. Both clusters resist the introduction of a principle that allows intending or endeavoring to be belief-extendable. In contrast, our classification of actions as intentional appeals to a much looser range of considerations, and is shaped by an interest in responsibility. In this domain a principle of belief-extendability seems quite natural.

Turn now to the second question: why isn't endeavoring subject to the same demands of consistency and agglomerativity as is intending? A quick answer might be that it just is not, and this is what marks the difference between endeavoring and present-directed intending. But this response would miss the real issue. Is there some deeper rationale for our "cutting up" minds—both our own and others—in this way? Is there some deeper rationale for making this discrimination in our understanding of normal psychological functioning?

I think the distinction between endeavoring and intending reflects an important capacity we have, a capacity to distinguish between those practical conflicts we must resolve in order to get on with our lives in a coherent way, and those conflicts which we do not need to resolve. This capacity has an obvious pragmatic rationale, given our limits. I proceed to explain.

The first step is to expand the problem. When I endeavor to *A*, I act in order to *A*, my aim or purpose in acting includes *A*. Even if I do not, strictly speaking, intend to *A*, I do desire to *A*, either as a means or for itself, or both. Further, I do not *merely* desire to *A*. My desire is guiding my attempt to *A*: it is a *guiding desire*. Now, in this case my guiding desire guides present conduct. But a desire may also be a guiding desire by virtue of guiding planning for the future. Consider an example similar in structure to the video-games example. I very much want to marry Susan, and I very much want to marry Jane. I live in Utah at a time when it is possible to marry them both. So I set about planning how to persuade each of them to marry me. Then comes a change in the law: I can no longer marry them both but can marry only one. So now I face a serious conflict. One way of reacting to this conflict would be to reach a decision in favor of one of these women rather than the other. But I might also proceed by continuing to plan on ways of persuading each of them to marry me and let the "world" (that is, Susan or Jane) resolve my conflict. If I proceed in the second way, I will construct a subplan guided by the desire to marry Susan and a subplan guided by the desire to marry Jane. I will want to ensure that the components of each of these subplans are compatible with those in the other subplan; for the idea is to carry them both out. For example, I will not want to plan to cook a dinner for Jane on the same evening as I plan to cook a dinner for Susan. But the guiding desires of the two subplans will not be consistent, given my beliefs. Nor am I under rational pressure to desire to marry them both. So there can be guiding desires that guide both planning and intentional action and yet are not subject to the same demands of strong consistency and agglomerativity to which intentions are subject.

So we can enlarge our question about the difference between endeavoring and intending. We can ask: why should rational agents like us have the capacity to have *both* ordinary intentions (subject to demands for consistency and agglomeration) *and* guiding desires (which are not subject to these demands)? I have supposed that our planning and intentional conduct are typically controlled by our intentions, that these intentions are subject to demands of consistency and agglomerativity, and that these demands are grounded largely in our needs for coordination. But sometimes our planning and intentional conduct are controlled by a guiding desire that is not similarly subject to these demands. Our concern with coordination typically obliges us to form intentions, and not merely to allow our desires to control our planning and conduct. This is not always the case, however: intention formation is but one of several different strategies for the resolution of practical conflicts.

For an agent to perform an intentional action many potential conflicts must somehow be resolved. Some get settled at the level of habit—for example (in a normal case), with which foot to step out of a car door. Some get settled at the level of fairly specific intentions—for example, whether to stop the car at this restaurant or to go on driving. Some others must get settled for the agent to reach the more specific intentions required for present action—for example, whether to meet Howard before or after dinner. But sometimes there are conflicts that need not be settled *by the agent* for her to proceed. Instead, she can "let the world decide." In such cases she need not settle the conflict with an intention in favor of one or the other of the conflicting elements. She can just let her desire for each element guide corresponding planning and action—though, as we have seen, this further planning will itself normally require the formation of various intentions, intentions subject to demands for consistency and agglomeration.

So, on the one hand, the capacity for having a guiding desire to *A* without having an intention to *A* is useful to us in part because it allows us to avoid settling conflicts that we need not settle in order to get on with our actions and our lives. On the other hand, there are many conflicts that we do need to settle in order to get on with our lives—in order to coordinate our pursuits of important goals, both individual and social; in order not to keep tripping over ourselves and others. And that is a major reason why our capacity for forming intentions and partial plans is so important to us. The capacity to react in these different ways to practical conflict is useful to agents like us, agents who have limited resources to devote to difficult issues of conflict resolution. The distinction between intending and having a guiding desire (and so between present-directed intending and endeavoring) enables us to mark these different ways of reacting to practical conflict. The distinction is important to us in part because the capacity to react in these different ways is important to us.

chapter 10

Intention and Expected Side Effects

WE normally distinguish what a person intends from those things she merely expects to bring about as a result of doing what she intends. We sometimes make this distinction even when the merely expected upshot was one that the agent explicitly saw as importantly relevant to her decision as to what to do, and so explicitly considered in her deliberation. Although such a distinction seems firmly embedded in our common-sense understanding of intention, it can also appear problematic upon reflection.

An examination of this distinction is doubtless well motivated in a book on the nature of intention, not least because of the role it sometimes plays in moral philosophy. But I also have a further reason for turning to this distinction here. I have so far focused largely on the roles of prior intentions as inputs to further practical reasoning. But, of course, intentions are also typical outputs of practical reasoning. Reflection on the distinction between what is intended and what is merely expected as an upshot of what is intended will help shed light on this latter aspect of intention.

We have already seen in Chapters 3 and 8 some illustrative examples of the distinction of interest here. But it will be useful to introduce a further example, one drawn from the recent literature.[1] Both Terror Bomber and Strategic Bomber have the goal of promoting the war effort against Enemy. Each intends to pursue this goal by weakening Enemy, and each intends to do that by dropping bombs. Terror Bomber's plan is to bomb the school in Enemy's territory, thereby killing children of Enemy and terrorizing Enemy's population. Strategic Bomber's plan is different. He plans to bomb Enemy's munitions plant, thereby undermining Enemy's war effort. Strategic Bomber also knows, however, that next to the munitions plant is a school, and that when he bombs the plant he will also destroy the school, killing the children inside. Strategic Bomber has not ignored this fact. Indeed, he has worried a lot about it. Still, he has concluded that this cost, though significant, is outweighed by the contribution that would be made to the war effort by the destruction of the munitions plant.

Now, Terror Bomber intends all of the features of his action just noted: he intends to drop the bombs, kill the children, terrorize the population, and thereby weaken Enemy. In contrast, it seems that Strategic Bomber only intends to drop the bombs, destroy the munitions plant, and weaken Enemy. Although he knows that by bombing the plant he will be killing the children, he does not, it seems, *intend* to kill them. Whereas killing the children is, for Terror Bomber, an intended means to his end of victory, it is, for Strategic Bomber, only something he knows he will do by bombing the munitions plant. Though Strategic Bomber has taken the deaths of the children quite seriously into account in his deliberation, these deaths are for him only an expected side effect; they are not—in contrast with Terror Bomber's position—intended as a means.[2] This, anyway, seems to be the commonsense view.

This supposed difference between the two bombers is thought by some to make an important moral difference. In particular, according to the principle of double effect this difference might make a crucial difference in the moral permissibility of the bombings.[3] According to this principle it is sometimes permissible knowingly to bring about (or allow) some bad effect in the course of achieving some good end, even though it would not have been permissible to bring about (or allow) that bad effect as one's intended means to that good end. So it might be permissible for Strategic Bomber to bomb the plant and yet impermissible for Terror Bomber to bomb the school, even though in both cases it is known that the children will be killed and even though both bombing missions make the same contribution to weakening Enemy.

Of course, one can recognize the commonsense distinction between intending some means and merely expecting some side effect without supposing that this distinction can bear so much moral weight. My primary interest here is not in the moral principle but in the commonsense psychology that underlies it; however, I will return briefly to the principle at the end of this chapter.

10.1 Three Roles of Intention

My theory of intention supports the commonsense distinction between intending some means and merely expecting some side effect. To see why, recall three roles of intention that have been central to the discussion so

far. Two of these roles concern the relation between future-directed intentions and further practical reasoning, and they partly constitute the
reasoning-centered dimension of commitment. These are the roles of
intention in posing problems for further reasoning and in constraining
other intentions. The third role concerns the relation between intention
and endeavoring and partly constitutes the volitional dimension of commitment. This is the tendency of intention to issue in corresponding
endeavoring. Let us take up these roles in turn.[4]

Return to Terror Bomber. He intends to kill the children as a means
to promoting military victory. This intention to kill the children will play
two important roles in his further practical reasoning. First, it will pose
a problem, namely: how is he going to kill them? Terror Bomber must
figure out, for example, what time of day to attack and what sorts of
bombs to use. He must solve various problems about means to killing
the children; he must engage in appropriate means-end reasoning.

Second, his intention to kill the children will constrain his other intentions. To see this, let us develop the example further. Suppose that
after settling on his plan to terrorize Enemy by killing the children (but
before his bombing run), Terror Bomber (who is also commander of a
small battalion) considers ordering a certain troop movement. He sees
that this troop movement would achieve certain military advantages. But
then he notices that if the troops do move in this way Enemy will become
alarmed and evacuate the children, thereby undermining the terror-bombing mission. That is, the option of moving his troops has an expected
upshot (evacuation of the children) that is incompatible with an intended
upshot of the bombing mission he already intends to engage in. So the
option of moving the troops is blocked by the prior intention to terror-
bomb, given the bomber's beliefs. Terror Bomber's prior intention to
terror-bomb, together with his beliefs, creates a screen of admissibility
through which options must pass in later deliberation. And the option
of moving the troops does not pass through this screen. So Terror Bomber's prior intention to kill the children stands in the way of his forming
a new intention to order the troop movement.

Now consider what happens when Terror Bomber begins to execute
his intention. An intention to bring about p will normally give rise to
one's endeavoring to bring about p: one will act in order to bring about
p. Endeavoring to bring about p involves guiding one's conduct accordingly. In the normal case, one is prepared to make adjustments in what
one is doing in response to indications of one's success or failure in
promoting p. So Terror Bomber can be expected to guide his conduct in
the direction of causing the deaths of the children. If in midair he learns
they have moved to a different school, he will try to keep track of them

and take his bombs there. If he learns that the building they are in is heavily reinforced, he may for that reason decide on a special kind of bomb. And so on.[5]

Of course, this all depends on his retaining his beliefs about the connection between killing the children and the goal of military victory. If he finds out in midair that the war is over, or that the children in the school are prisoners Enemy would like to see killed, he will not continue to guide his conduct by the children's deaths.

Now what about Strategic Bomber's attitude toward killing the children? It seems clear that his attitude toward killing them will not play a similar trio of roles. Strategic Bomber will not see himself as being presented with a problem of how to kill the children: he will have no disposition to engage in such means-end reasoning. Nor will he be disposed to constrain his further intentions to fit in with killing them. If he were later to consider the troop movement just described, and if he were to note the resulting likelihood of evacuation, this would not block his option of moving those troops. Indeed, it would give him reason to move them. And, finally, even after he is in the plane engaged in the bombing mission, he will not endeavor to kill the children. In the normal case this means he will not guide his activity by keeping track of the children and their deaths.[6] Rather, he will just keep track of the munitions plant and its destruction.

Further, there is good reason for Strategic Bomber to resist having an attitude toward killing the children that would play these three roles. Having such an attitude would not normally help him achieve the goals he wants to achieve, and might well prevent him from achieving some of those goals. For example, it might prevent him from considering the advantageous troop movement, given that option's expected incompatibility with his killing the children.

Since Strategic Bomber does not have an attitude toward killing the children that plays the trio of roles characteristic of intention, he does not intend to kill the children. This is the conclusion to which my theory of intention leads. In response to this conclusion it might be suggested that Strategic Bomber, although he does not *directly* intend to kill the children, does *obliquely* intend to kill them.[7] And you can say this if you like; the *word* 'intention' is not the issue. The roles characteristic of intention, three of which I have been emphasizing, are what matter. Oblique intention does not guarantee the presence of an attitude that plays these roles. For that reason, I think that talk of oblique intention is likely to mislead. But as long as we are clear that oblique intention is not intention, in the sense of 'intention' that is tied to roles of the sort I have been emphasizing, the issue is merely a verbal one.

So the commonsense view about the difference between the two bombers seems to be both intuitively plausible and supported by my theory of intention.

10.2 The Problem of the Package Deal

Strategic Bomber's attitude is, however, open to the following challenge: "In choosing to bomb the munitions plant, you knew you would thereby kill the children. Indeed, you worried about this fact and took it quite seriously into account in your deliberation. In choosing to bomb, then, you have opted for a package that includes not only destroying the plant and contributing to military victory, but also killing the children. The bombing is a package deal. Having chosen this overall package, how could you fail to intend one of its parts? How could you fail to intend to kill the children?"

This is *the problem of the package deal.*[8] This problem raises the following general question: Suppose a rational agent believes his *A*-ing would result in a bad effect, *E*, seriously considers *E* in his deliberation about whether to *A*, and yet still goes on to make a choice in favor of *A*-ing. How could such an agent fail to intend to bring about *E*?

As we have seen, both common sense and my theory of intention support the view that Strategic Bomber may well not intend to kill the children. It is but a short step to the claim that Strategic Bomber need be guilty of no serious irrationality in failing so to intend. Once we grant that Strategic Bomber need not intend to kill the children, it seems strained, at best, to insist nevertheless that when he does not intend to kill them he is criticizably irrational. But at this point we are challenged by the problem of package deal.

Let us spell out the problem more explicitly. To do this it will be useful to borrow from a natural model of practical reasoning sketched by Wilfred Sellars in his essay "Thought and Action."[9] Strategic Bomber intends to weaken Enemy and proceeds to reason about how to do so. Sellars would see his reasoning as having three main stages.[10] First, there is the stage at which he lays out the larger "scenarios" between which he must choose. Each of these scenarios will include both his weakening Enemy and those other features of his competing courses of action that are to be given serious consideration in his deliberation. To keep things simple, let us suppose that our example admits these scenarios:

> (S1) Bomb the munitions plant, destroy the munitions plant, weaken Enemy, and kill the children.

(S2) Bomb the rural airport, destroy the airport, and weaken Enemy.

Second, he will evaluate these scenarios "as wholes" and thereby arrive at a "complex intention." In our example this will be the complex intention to bomb the munitions plant, kill the children, and weaken Enemy (and not bomb the airport). Finally, he will be led from this complex intention to the simpler intention to bomb the plant. And, though Sellars does not emphasize the point, it seems that Strategic Bomber will also just as easily be led from his complex intention to the simpler intention to kill the children.

Now, this model has some plausibility; and I think versions of it are rather common in our thinking about practical reasoning.[11] But as long as this is our model of Strategic Bomber's practical reasoning, we will have great difficulty in explaining how he can rationally refrain from intending to kill the children. On the model, the initial conclusion of Strategic Bomber's practical reasoning will be a complex intention which includes killing the children. And once he has reached this conclusion, it is difficult to see how he could fail to intend to kill the children.

We can develop the point further by noting a quartet of principles to which this model of practical reasoning seems committed. All these principles concern the situation in which the practical reasoning of a rational agent has been successfully completed and has issued in an intention. There is, first, the idea that such practical reasoning should issue in a conclusion in favor of a scenario *taken as a whole,* where such scenarios include *all* factors given serious consideration in the reasoning. Strategic Bomber, for example, should draw a conclusion in favor of one of the total packages under consideration: (S1)-and-not-(S2), or (S2)-and-not-(S1). Second, there is the idea that this conclusion is a *practical* conclusion, one tied tightly to action. We may express this idea by saying that this practical conclusion is a *choice* of a total scenario. Strategic Bomber, then, should choose one of the total packages under consideration; he cannot choose simply to drop the bombs. The third principle goes on to associate such a choice in favor of an overall scenario with the formation of a complex *intention* in favor of that overall scenario: Strategic Bomber must *intend* a total package. Finally, the fourth principle connects such an intention in favor of an overall scenario with intentions to perform each of the actions included within that scenario that the agent knows to be within his control.

Let us state these principles more precisely. We begin with

> *Principle of the holistic conclusion of practical reasoning*
> If I know that my *A*-ing will result in *E*, and I seriously consider this fact in my deliberation about whether to *A* and still go on to

conclude in favor of *A*, then if I am rational my reasoning will have issued in a conclusion in favor of an overall scenario that includes *both* my *A*-ing *and* my bringing about *E*.

For short, I will call this the *principle of holistic conclusion*. Note that this principle does not require that my conclusion in favor of *A* include all upshots I expect *A* to have. It must only include my bringing about those expected upshots that, in fact, I seriously consider in my deliberation.

The remaining three principles may usefully be expressed along the following lines:

> *Principle of holistic choice*
>   The holistic conclusion (of practical reasoning) in favor of an overall scenario is a *choice* of that scenario.

> *The choice-intention principle*
>   If on the basis of practical reasoning I choose to *A* and to *B* and to . . . then I *intend* to *A* and to *B* and to . . .

> *Principle of intention division*
>   If I intend to *A* and to *B* and to . . . and I know that *A* and *B* are each within my control, then if I am rational I will both intend to *A* and intend to *B*.

It is clear that once we accept this quartet of principles we are faced with the problem of the package deal. Strategic Bomber does (quite appropriately) seriously consider the fact that by bombing he will be killing the children. So the principles of holistic conclusion and holistic choice together require that (if rational) Strategic Bomber choose to bomb and to bring about the deaths of the children and . . . But then, by the choice-intention principle, he must intend to bomb and to bring about the deaths and . . . But Strategic Bomber knows, we may assume, that it is up to him whether to bomb, and also that it is up to him whether to kill the children. He knows that his performance of each type of action is within his control.[12] So by the principle of intention division Strategic Bomber, if rational, will intend to kill the children. And this conclusion is in serious tension with both common sense and my planning theory of intention.

10.3 Some Failed Solutions to the Problem of the Package Deal

The problem of the package deal argues for the conclusion that Strategic Bomber, if rational, will intend to kill the children. Both common sense and my planning theory argue strongly that this conclusion should be rejected. But it is one thing to know that an argument issues in an unacceptable conclusion and quite another to diagnose where the argument goes wrong.

The inference from the four principles to the unacceptable conclusion seems valid. So we must reject at least one of the principles. Which one?

In this section I will discuss attempts made to reject the principle of intention division and the principle of holistic conclusion. I shall argue that both attempts fail to solve our problem. Then I shall turn to my own solution in the next section.

10.3.1 Chisholm's Rejection of Intention Division

In the second chapter of *Person and Object*, Roderick Chisholm suggests that we can solve the problem of the package deal by rejecting the principle of intention division. Chisholm does not pose the problem in precisely the way I have. But he does face a similar problem, one posed by his acceptance of "the principle of the diffusiveness of intention": "If a rational man acts with the intention of bringing about a certain state of affairs p and if he believes that by bringing about p he will bring about the conjunctive state of affairs, p and q, then he *does* act with the intention of bringing about the conjunctive state of affairs, p and q."[13] Now, Chisholm regularly assumes that if I act with the intention of bringing about p then I intend to bring about p.[14] So Chisholm's principle of the diffusiveness of intention tells us that, if rational, Strategic Bomber must intend to bring it about that both the munitions plant be destroyed and the children die. And this may seem already to grant the main thrust of the problem of the package deal.

But Chisholm suggests otherwise; for he also accepts "the principle of the nondivisiveness of intention": "From the facts that (i) there is a certain state of affairs p such that a man acts with the intention of bringing it about that p occurs, and (ii) that state of affairs p entails or includes a certain other state of affairs q, and furthermore (iii) the man in question knows or believes that p entails q and (iv) he is completely rational, it does *not* follow that (v) he acts with the intention of bringing it about that q occurs."[15] Now, as stated, Chisholm's principle of the nondivisiveness of intention is, in fact, compatible with my principle of intention division. This is because my principle of intention division is a rather limited principle. It applies only when the initial intention is an intention to A and to B, the derived intention is an intention to A (or, an intention to B), and the agent knows that A and B are, each of them, within his control. Chisholm's principle of the nondivisiveness of intention is, in effect, the rejection of a much stronger principle, one that applies whenever what is intended "entails or includes" something else. This stronger principle that Chisholm is rejecting applies whether or not what is entailed or included is the agent's performance of an action he knows to be within his control. So, strictly speaking, we could grant Chisholm's principle of the nondivisiveness of intention and yet still accept my principle of intention division.

Nevertheless, it is clear from Chisholm's discussion that he means to reject my more limited principle of intention division as well.[16] So I think it is clear that Chisholm would insist that, though (if rational) Strategic Bomber will intend to bring about both the destruction of the plant and the deaths of the children, it does not follow that he will intend to bring about the deaths of the children. And this is how Chisholm would try to solve the problem of the package deal.

Is this an adequate solution? I think not. The first problem is that Chisholm says little that would justify a rejection of my principle of intention division. Chisholm's main defense of his principle of the nondivisiveness of intention is in the form of an example. He urges that I may intend to go to Washington while the President is there, know that this requires the President to be in Washington, and yet not intend to bring it about that the President is in Washington.[17] And Chisholm seems right about this, and about the support it provides for his principle of nondivisiveness, *as that principle has been stated*. The example does support Chisholm's rejection of a very strong principle of intention division, one that applies whenever what is intended "entails or includes" something else. But such an example does *not* by itself support the rejection of my rather limited principle of intention division. This is because in the example my initial intention is *not* both to go to Washington and to *bring it about* that the President is there; and I do not suppose that it is *up to me* whether the President will be there. So *my* principle of intention division does not apply to the example Chisholm uses to defend his principle; and Chisholm's defense of his principle does not actually challenge my principle of intention division. Further, when Chisholm's example is changed so that my principle of intention division *does* apply, the conclusion to which this principle leads seems quite plausible. If my initial intention is both to go to Washington and to bring it about that the President is there (say, by inviting her to a party), and if I really do know that in each case it is up to me whether I so act, then I think I *would* (if rational) intend to bring it about that the President will be there.

More important, it seems to me that in accepting his principle of the diffusiveness of intention, and insisting that Strategic Bomber intends both to destroy the plant and to kill the children, Chisholm has already granted too much; for we would normally want to allow that Strategic Bomber may well not even intend to kill the children *as a part* of such a larger intention. Consider what is involved in intending both to *A* and to *B*, when one knows that each way of acting is in one's control. Such a complex intention will play the trio of roles I have been emphasizing. First, if in such a case I intend to *A* and to *B*, I will normally be disposed to reason about how to do both *A* and *B*. But Strategic Bomber will only be disposed to reason about how to destroy the munitions plant, rather than about how both to destroy the plant and to kill the children. Second, the intention to *A* and to *B* will normally tend to issue in one's endeavoring to do both. But Strategic Bomber will only be disposed to endeavor to destroy the plant, rather than both to destroy the plant and to kill the children. If Strategic Bomber were to destroy the plant but (unexpectedly) discover that the children had survived, he would not suppose that he had *failed* to do something he was trying to do. Finally, if in such a case I intend both to *A* and to *B*, I will treat as inadmissible other options whose expected upshots are incompatible with my both *A*-ing and *B*-ing. Yet it is clear that Strategic Bomber can be expected *not* to treat as inadmissible other options whose expected upshots are incompatible with his killing the children. For example, Strategic Bomber may later go ahead and seriously consider ordering the troop movement.

I think these observations show that once we grant Chisholm's principle of the diffusiveness of intention we have already diverged from both common sense and my planning theory of intention.

On the one hand, then, Chisholm's main defense of his principle of the nondivisiveness of intention does not directly attack my limited principle of intention division, but only supports the rejection of a much stronger principle. On the other hand, even if we were to follow Chisholm in rejecting our principle of intention division, this would still not suffice to save the commonsense conception of intention. Too much violence has already been done to that conception by the principle of the diffusiveness of intention.

10.3.2 *Harman's Rejection of "Holism"*

In a recent paper Gilbert Harman addresses a problem that is similar to the problem of the package deal and argues that to solve the problem we should reject what he calls a "holistic view of decisions."[18] Cast in terms of my quartet of principles, Harman's suggestion would seem to be that we should reject the first principle—the principle of holistic conclusion. But it turns out that the kind of "holism" that is Harman's primary target is much stronger than my principle of holistic conclusion.

Though Harman is, I think, justified in rejecting his version of holism, his reasons for doing so do not support the rejection of my more limited principle of holistic conclusion. So Harman's argument against his version of "a holistic view of decisions" leaves intact the problem of the package deal. Or so, anyway, I now proceed to argue.

Here is how Harman describes a holistic view of decisions:

> In a holistic view, all foreseen aspects of your action are part of what you intend, because you have to accept them all when you decide to act. In deciding what to do, you must consider all foreseeable effects, consequences, and other aspects of your decision, and you must evaluate them as a total package. Good or bad "side" effects and consequences affect the desirability of your decision in exactly the way that good or bad ends or means do. All parts of the story are intended, because
>
> (1) your intention comprises that conclusion you reach as the result of practical reasoning and
>
> (2) [in holistic view] your conclusion should include the acceptance of everything you know about your action, its foreseen side effects and consequences just as much as a certain end and means.[19]

It is clear that this version of holism leads to the conclusion that Strategic Bomber, if rational, will include his killing the children as "part" of what he intends. On this holistic view Strategic Bomber should consider, among other things, the bad effect of the deaths of the children. But then, given (2), this bad effect should be accepted by Strategic Bomber in his practical conclusion. And so, given (1), this bad effect (and so, his bringing about this bad effect) should be part of what is intended.

Now, this is not quite so strong a conclusion as that with which the problem of the package deal threatened us; for it is not yet asserted that Strategic Bomber should intend to kill the children *simpliciter*. It is only asserted that his killing them should be a part of what he intends. This is just to say that Harman does not concern himself here with the principle of intention division. But, as I have just indicated in my discussion of Chisholm, I do not think this should give much solace to the defender of our commonsense conception of intention. Even without the principle of intention division, holism (in Harman's sense) seems seriously to challenge that conception.

Though close to our problem of the package deal, Harman's problem about holism differs in an important way, for Harman's holism is much stronger than my principle of holistic conclusion. To be sure, Harman's holism does entail that principle. But Harman's holism also entails the further, and extremely demanding, requirement that in practical reasoning one "must consider all foreseeable effects." Now, one may satisfy my principle of holistic conclusion without satisfying this last, extremely demanding requirement: one may include in one's conclusion all effects that are *both expected and seriously considered,* without seriously considering all foreseeable (or even, foreseen) effects. So criticism of the last requirement as too demanding need not touch the principle of holistic conclusion, as I have stated that principle.

Indeed, the requirement that one consider all foreseeable effects of actions one considers in deliberation has no special relevance to the problem of the package deal. That problem is not posed because Strategic Bomber must consider all foreseeable effects of his bombing in his deliberation. The problem is posed, rather, because he does in fact quite seriously consider certain undesirable effects and yet, it seems, still does not intend to bring about those effects.

This is important, for many of Harman's remarks about why holism is wrong are directed at this last, very strong requirement. Harman argues that, given the limitations on our capacities for calculation and reflection, "there must be certain procedures you can use without extensive reflection, methods that yield satisfactory results most of the time."[20] He goes on to sketch such a procedure, a procedure whose "rationale . . . lies in its cost effectiveness."[21] "The basic idea, then, is to try to keep things simple. You try to limit yourself to considering a single way of obtaining a single end of yours. If there is a salient complication [for example,] a sufficiently unhappy side effect . . . then you try to determine whether this is sufficient to overcome your reason for doing the simple action. If it is not sufficient to overcome that reason, you simply disregard the complication."[22]

In endorsing such a procedure Harman is endorsing a procedure in which we many times do not consider all foreseeable upshots of actions that are up for consideration; for not all foreseeable upshots (or even all foreseen upshots) will be, as Harman says, "salient." As I have noted, however, such a rejection of the requirement to consider all foreseeable effects does not itself touch my principle of holistic conclusion, or the problem of the package deal.

Still, Harman sometimes writes as if he thinks such considerations of "cost effectiveness" also challenge my principle of holistic conclusion. Harman seems to suppose that if Strategic Bomber really does conclude that he should go ahead and bomb the munitions plant, despite the cost in children's lives, he should just "disregard the complication" of the deaths of the children in the conclusion of his practical reasoning. His conclusion should be simply in favor of bombing the plant, and not in favor of the more complex scenario of bombing the plant and (thereby) killing the children.

But why does Harman believe this? Perhaps the idea is that if all the undesirable upshots of *A*, which are both foreseen and seriously considered in deliberation, are included in the conclusion of practical reasoning, this would make such conclusions too complex. But I do not see why we should believe this. The major costs incurred would seem to be in the consideration of the foreseen effect in deliberation; and these costs have, we are now assuming, already been incurred. So why shouldn't these considered effects be included in the conclusion of that deliberation?

Further, Harman's suggestion that Strategic Bomber should just "disregard" such complications runs the risk of underwriting a strategy of Divide and Ignore. To see the problem, suppose Strategic Bomber really does go on to disregard the deaths of the children after seriously considering them in his deliberations. Later, but before the bombing mission, he learns of a Red Cross hospital near the munitions plant. So he asks himself whether this is sufficient to overcome his reason for bombing the plant. He concludes that, though a serious matter, it is not enough to block the bombing mission. So he goes on to disregard the Red Cross hospital. Yet later he learns of a prisoner of war camp near the munitions plant, weighs the cost to the prisoners of war against the benefits of the destruction of the plant, and decides to go ahead and disregard those costs. And so on. It is clear that something has gone wrong. If Strategic Bomber really is to disregard an unhappy side effect once he judges it to be outweighed by his reasons for the bombing mission, he may never consider whether all these unhappy side effects *taken together* are sufficient to overcome his reason. He is following a strategy of Divide and Ignore. To avoid engaging in Divide and Ignore, Strategic Bomber needs to keep track of the various bad effects that are seriously considered in his prior deliberation. And a natural way to keep track of such expected bad effects is to include them in one's practical conclusions.

It seems to me, then, that we have not been given persuasive reasons for rejecting the principle of holistic conclusion. Further, this principle really does seem a plausible principle of good reasoning. What the principle requires is only a certain clearheadedness and intellectual honesty— an absence of "bad faith," if you will. Once I seriously consider *A*'s anticipated effect, *E,* in my deliberation about whether to *A,* I should see that the issue for my deliberation concerns a complex scenario, one that includes, inter alia, *A together with E*. If I am clearheaded and intellectually honest about this, my conclusion should concern this complex scenario, and not merely my *A*-ing *simpliciter*. All this is compatible with a due recognition of the limits on our capacities for reasoning and reflection. Granted, these limits will constrain the extent to which various foreseen or foreseeable effects should be given serious consideration in our deliberation. But such constraints do not touch the principle of holistic conclusion, for that principle concerns only those foreseen effects that have in fact already been seriously considered.

So, given that Strategic Bomber really does seriously consider the fact that by bombing he will kill the children, there is good reason to insist that, if rational, he will reach a conclusion in favor of the complex scenario that includes both the bombing and the killing. So we are as yet without a solution to the problem of the package deal.

Granted, Harman has explained how we may sometimes not intend an expected side effect of our intended actions. When an expected side effect is not one we actually consider in the deliberation leading to our intention, we may, Harman is right to note, not intend it. And in endorsing certain cost-effective strategies, Harman has legitimized such nonconsideration, and so given us reason to reject holism as he understands it. But this does not save Strategic Bomber from the problem of the package deal; for he does seriously consider in his deliberation (and rightly so) the bad upshot he nevertheless seems not to intend.

10.4 Intention and Choice

Our problem arises from the apparent conflict between backward-looking and forward-looking pressures on what we intend. On the one hand, intentions are typically grounded in prior deliberation. Once deliberation enters the picture, however, plausible standards of clearheadedness and intellectual honesty are engaged. This leads to pressure for practical conclusions to be holistic and so, it seems, for intentions to be holistic. This pressure is backward-looking, for it is grounded in the connection between intention and prior deliberation. The problem of the package deal exploits this backward-looking pressure by exploiting the demand for holistic practical conclusions to which it leads.

On the other hand, intentions, once formed, play complex roles in further reasoning and action. In particular, they play the trio of roles I have been emphasizing in this chapter. This is not only true of a relatively simple intention to drop bombs, but also of a more complex intention to drop bombs and kill the children. But it seems that Strategic Bomber, for example, can rationally refrain from having an attitude toward killing the children that plays such roles in further reasoning and action. So there is pressure against forcing intentions to be holistic. This pressure is forward-looking, for it depends on the characteristic roles of intention in guiding further reasoning and action. And it is this forward-looking pressure to which I have appealed in defending the commonsense view that Strategic Bomber need not intend to kill the children.

In focusing on the commitment characteristic of intention—as I have through most of this book—I have focused on the roles of prior intentions in *further* reasoning and action. But, of course, intentions are themselves frequently an upshot of *prior* reasoning. The problem of the package deal is the problem of how to reconcile the conflicting pressures (forward-looking and backward-looking) that these different roles exert on what a rational agent intends.

Both Harman and Chisholm try to resolve the conflict by blocking one of the sources of pressure. Harman tries to appeal to considerations of cost-effectiveness to block the backward-looking pressure for holistic practical conclusions. Chisholm tries to block the forward-looking pressure against holistic intentions by undermining their connection with relatively simpler intentions. For reasons I have explained, I think neither strategy works. My alternative strategy is to grant both pressures, but deny that they apply to the same thing.

The problem of the package deal depends on identifying (or, anyway, linking very tightly)

> (1) the conclusion of practical reasoning that is subject to pressures for holism (pressures based on standards of clearheadedness and intellectual honesty in reasoning),

and

> (2) the intention in which practical reasoning issues.

This identification (or tight linkage) derives from the combination of the principle of holistic choice and the choice-intention principle. The former identifies (1) with a holistic choice; the latter connects such a choice with (2). The rejection of either one of this pair of principles would undermine the tight connection between (1) and (2). This would allow us to say that the backward-looking pressure for holism, though it applies to certain conclusions of practical reasoning, that is, to (1), does not similarly apply to the intentions in which the practical reasoning issues, that is, to (2). And in this way we could block the problem of the package deal.

I propose then that we challenge one of these principles: holistic choice or choice-intention. But which one?

It is tempting to think that we should just reject the principle of holistic choice. The idea behind this temptation is that we should see the holistic conclusions of practical reasoning—those that favor overall scenarios— as *merely evaluative conclusions*. They are just conclusions that a certain overall scenario is superior to its competitors. Strategic Bomber must reach such an evaluative conclusion in favor of the overall scenario that contains both the bombing and the killing of the children. This is required by standards of clearheadedness and intellectual honesty. But this does not mean that he must *choose* such an overall scenario. So the problem of the package deal can be blocked; for Strategic Bomber need not choose, and so need not intend, a scenario that includes killing the children. He just must value the total scenario containing the bombing and the killing of the children more highly than he values its competitor.

This is not very convincing, however. The same considerations that support the demand for a holistic conclusion of practical reasoning seem also to argue for a holistic *choice* as a conclusion of such reasoning. After all, Strategic Bomber does not merely assess overall scenarios; he is not merely a fly on the wall. He is an agent, one who must plump for one scenario over others. Indeed, he sometimes must plump for one scenario over another even though he thinks both equally desirable. If he is clearheaded about what he is doing, he will plump for an *overall* scenario. And this amounts to *choosing* that overall scenario.[23]

This leaves the choice-intention principle. This principle links holistic choice with an attitude toward future conduct that plays the trio of roles characteristic of intention. It is this link that I propose to reject. We need to distinguish what is chosen on the basis of practical reasoning from what is intended; for these are differently affected by standards of good reasoning, on the one hand, and concerns with further reasoning and action, on the other.[24]

Return to Strategic Bomber. He is obliged by a plausible principle of good reasoning to include the deaths of the children in the total package which he chooses on the basis of his reasoning. But it does not follow that his attitude toward these deaths must play the roles in further reasoning and action that are characteristic of intention. Nor does it follow that it would be somehow irrational of him to fail to have his attitude toward these deaths play these further roles.

Strategic Bomber does, we may assume, choose to kill the children: their deaths are included in the total package in favor of which he chooses. But the notion of choice at work here is one tied tightly to prior deliberation. The demand to include the deaths of the children in what is chosen comes from a demand for clearheadedness in one's reasoning and choice—a demand to confront clearly and honestly the important features of what one will be doing in plumping as one does. It is this demand that leads to the pressure for choice to be holistic. But this demand does not force one's *intentions* to be holistic; for one's intentions are tied not only to prior deliberation but also to our trio of roles concerning further reasoning and action. Nothing in the ideal of clearheaded reasoning forces one to have the dispositions concerning *further* reasoning and action that would be characteristic of holistic intention. Though clearheadedness obliges Strategic Bomber to choose (inter alia) to kill the children, it does not oblige him later to screen out options incompatible with killing them, or to endeavor to kill them. So choice and intention can diverge. For Strategic Bomber not only to have chosen to kill the children but also to *intend* to kill them, he would need to have an attitude toward killing them that plays the trio of roles I have been emphasizing. And he doesn't.

It is natural to assume that whatever one chooses one thereby intends.[25] But reflection on the problem of the package deal strongly suggests that we should reject this assumption. What one chooses is constrained by holistic pressures—pressures grounded in standards of clearheadedness in reasoning—in a way in which what one intends is not. And what one intends is tied to further reasoning and action in a way in which what one chooses is not.

But then how exactly are choice and intention related? One's choice in favor of an overall scenario will involve one's coming to have some intentions or others—intentions that will guide further reasoning and action. This is what distinguishes a choice of a scenario from a mere preference or positive evaluation in its favor. But *which* intentions? Having rejected the choice-intention principle, we need to put something in its place.

10.5 A New Approach to Intention and Choice

10.5.1 *Three Principles*

We have so far been neglecting structure that is implicit in the scenarios chosen by Strategic Bomber and Terror Bomber.[26] We have supposed that Strategic Bomber chooses the scenario:

> (S1) Bomb the munitions plant, destroy the munitions plant, weaken Enemy, and kill the children.

But further structure is implicit in (S1). One way we might try to get at this further structure is to use the notion of a means-end relation and represent the chosen scenario as:

> (S1a) Bomb the munitions plant as a means to destroying the plant, as a means to weakening Enemy, even though I will thereby kill the children.

The idea is that bombing and destroying the munitions plant are related as means to the intended end of weakening Enemy, whereas this is not true of killing the children. In contrast, the scenario chosen by Terror Bomber cites killing the children as a means to the intended end of weakening Enemy. Once we make this structure explicit we may seem to have available a natural and straightforward view of the relation between choice and intention, namely: a rational agent intends all and only those elements of a chosen scenario that are either the intended end of that scenario or are cited as means to that end.

This suggestion is on the right track in appealing to further structure within chosen scenarios. But it will not do as it stands. The problem is that the notion of a means is either too tightly tied to that of intention or the present proposal gives us the wrong results. To clarify this point, let me add an episode to the story of Strategic Bomber. Suppose he is told that once he kills the children there will in fact be a terrorizing effect on the enemy populace, and so that by killing the children he will be weakening Enemy. This is an important fact, one he is likely to note in his deliberation. But now his chosen scenario will include the fact that killing the children will causally contribute to weakening Enemy. Does it follow that within his chosen scenario his killing of the children is a *means* to weakening Enemy?

There is a dilemma here. On the one hand, it might plausibly be insisted that this does not follow. Just because killing the children is now supposed to contribute causally to the intended end, it does not follow that it is to be seen by Strategic Bomber as one of his *means* to that end. But why not? The answer seems to be that, though Strategic Bomber sees the causal relation between the children's deaths and a weaker Enemy, he still may not *intend* to bring about the latter by bringing about the former. For example, if the children were to leave the site of the munitions plant, he would not follow them with his bombs as a way of ensuring that he would weaken Enemy. But the problem with this answer is that it makes the notion of what is one of an agent's means to some end depend on what that agent intends. So we cannot use this notion of a means in a noncircular way in a new choice-intention principle.

On the other hand, we might say that the notion of means needed here is simply that expressed by 'by' in 'he will weaken Enemy by killing the children'. In cases such as these the relevant notion of means has a straightforward causal interpretation: A is a means to bringing about B just in case A would contribute causally to B.[27] So in the modified version of the Strategic Bomber case his killing the children is a means (in this causal sense) to his intended end. But now the problem is that, on this interpretation of the notion of a means, the suggested account of the relation between choice and intention will force a rational Strategic Bomber to intend to kill the children. And that seems wrong. By itself the acquisition of the additional information about the causal connection between the deaths of the children and a weaker Enemy should not force Strategic Bomber to intend to kill the children.

As a first step toward a solution let us put aside the notion of an agent's means as being too closely tied to the notion of intention. In its place let us simply use the notion of doing one thing *by* doing another, in a sense of 'by' that is independent of the agent's intentions.[28] Thus, in the modified case Strategic Bomber does weaken Enemy *by* killing the children, even if killing the children is not one of his *means* to weakening Enemy. We then introduce the notion of a *by-chain* in a scenario in the following way: Suppose an agent intends to promote E and chooses a scenario that includes promoting E by B-ing and B-ing by A-ing, where the agent believes he can A. Then we say that E-B-A constitutes a *by-chain* within that scenario.

The lesson of the modified case of Strategic Bomber is that a rational agent may choose a scenario containing by-chain E-B-A and yet not intend that by-chain. In light of this observation, how can we use the notion of a by-chain to solve the problem about choice and intention?

I want to propose three principles concerning the relation between choice and intention. Together these principles impose certain requirements and certain constraints on one's intentions, given one's choice and one's other intentions. They do not, however, uniquely determine what a rational agent will intend, given what she has chosen.

The first principle has already been anticipated:

> (P1) If on the basis of practical reasoning I choose scenario S in the pursuit of intended end E, then I will intend at least one by-chain in S.

But what if scenario S includes more than one by-chain? I think that there is a general, *but defeasible,* presumption in favor of intending by-chains within a chosen scenario, a presumption that has a reasonably clear pragmatic rationale. The most straightforward source of support for this presumption is simply that it is normally by coming to intend such by-chains that one's plans come to be means-end coherent. And there is a strong pragmatic rationale for means-end-coherent plans: plans that are means-end incoherent are typically doomed to failure. But the pragmatic support for a defeasible presumption in favor of intending such by-chains goes beyond the need for means-end coherence. Intending such by-chains will normally help the agent get what she wants, even if such an intention is not needed for means-end coherence.

To see this last point, return to the original cases of Terror Bomber and Strategic Bomber. Terror Bomber's intention to kill the children plays the trio of roles in his further reasoning and action. And it seems clear that this will normally help promote Terror Bomber's goals, given that his beliefs are true. For example, given Terror Bomber's beliefs it will help his efforts to weaken Enemy if he keeps track of where the children are and follows them with his bombs; and it will also help if he treats as inadmissible those options which, like the troop movement, are incompatible with his killing the children. In contrast, in the case of the original Strategic Bomber the action of killing the children, though in the chosen scenario, is not part of a by-chain in that scenario. And it would *not* help promote Strategic Bomber's goals, other things equal, for him to intend to kill the children. Indeed, such an intention might well interfere with his goals. If, for example, he were to screen out options incompatible with his killing the children, he might well needlessly block from consideration an advantageous troop movement. The point seems a general one: it is normally conducive to an agent's ends for him to intend the by-chains in the scenarios he chooses, whereas this is not so for the merely expected elements in such scenarios. And this provides pragmatic support for a general presumption in favor of intending such by-chains.

Now, Terror Bomber's intending the by-chain that includes killing the children is what makes his plan for weakening Enemy means-end coherent. A similar point cannot be made about Strategic Bomber in the modified case. To achieve means-end coherence Strategic Bomber need only intend the by-chain of weakening Enemy by destroying the munitions plant (by dropping bombs). Still, there remains a presumption (in the modified case) in favor of Strategic Bomber's also intending the by-chain that includes killing the children. After all, in an uncertain world two potentially successful means are better than one, other things equal. (You might call this the Insurance Principle.)

So we have a second principle concerning the relation between a rational agent's choices and intentions:

> (P2) If on the basis of practical reasoning I choose scenario *S*, and *S* contains the by-chain *E-B-A*, there is a general but defeasible presumption in favor of my intending this by-chain.

Given this general presumption in favor of intending such by-chains, how is it that in our modified case Strategic Bomber may still not intend to kill the children? I will focus on one important way in which this could happen.

Begin by reflecting on what would be involved (in the modified case) in Strategic Bomber's intending the by-chain containing his killing of the children. Among other things, this would involve his having a disposition to endeavor to kill them, and so a disposition to keep track of where the children are and systematically to adjust his behavior in light of such information. It would also involve his having a disposition to treat as inadmissible such options as the troop movement. In contrast, neither such disposition need be associated with the mere expectation of killing the children.

Now, a reflective person might be committed to refraining from the patterns of thinking and acting that would be manifestations of these dispositions. He might be committed to refraining from endeavoring to kill innocent people and to refraining from filtering his options by their incompatibility with his killing innocent people. Such a person would presumably judge that killing innocent people is a very bad thing. But his commitment to refrain from the cited patterns of thinking and acting need not involve the same commitment to refrain from killing innocent people when these killings do not involve such patterns of thinking and acting.[29]

Suppose that Strategic Bomber (in the modified case) is such a person. He strongly disapproves of his killing the children. But, beyond that, he is committed to refraining from the patterns of thinking and acting that would be involved in his *intending* to kill them. This commitment might naturally be embodied in a personal policy not to engage in such patterns of thinking and acting: a general intention not to endeavor to kill children and not to filter his options by their incompatibility with his killing them. Such a general intention need not, of course, be irrevocable or unblockable.[30] But it may still play a significant role in further reasoning and action. For want of a better label, let us call this Strategic Bomber's *self-governing* intention—or, for short, his SG-intention. This SG-intention will block the defeasible connection between choosing the by-chain involving killing the children and intending that by-chain.

How? Not simply by way of the demand for intention-belief consistency. Given his beliefs, Strategic Bomber's SG-intention would not be inconsistent, strictly speaking, with an intention in favor of the by-chain that includes killing the children. It is possible, given Strategic Bomber's beliefs (in the modified case), for him successfully to perform both by-chains in his chosen scenario without either endeavoring to kill the children or filtering out options on the grounds of incompatibility with killing the children. Indeed, this is just what Strategic Bomber expects to happen. Still, there remains a kind of incompatibility between an intention in favor of the by-chain that includes killing the children and the SG-intention. We need to say in what this incompatibility consists.

What is needed here is the idea that different intentions, though consistent, might still be *functionally incompatible*. If Strategic Bomber intended the by-chain that includes killing the children, he would thereby be disposed both to endeavor to kill them and to filter out options incompatible with killing them. But Strategic Bomber's SG-intention involves dispositions not to endeavor to kill the children and not to filter out such options. Such dispositions are in obvious conflict. Yet they are part and parcel of the characteristic functional roles of the cited intentions. These intentions are *functionally incompatible* in the sense that their characteristic functional roles cannot both be fully realized in the same person and at the same time.

Strategic Bomber's SG-intention is functionally compatible with his belief that he will be weakening Enemy by killing the children. So there is no special problem with his having both this intention and this belief. But there is a problem with his having this SG-intention and the intention to weaken Enemy by killing the children; for these intentions are functionally incompatible. In general, we should expect a rational agent not to have functionally incompatible intentions. If in the modified case Strategic Bomber has the cited SG-intention, then even if he chooses a scenario containing the by-chain involving killing the children, he should not be expected to intend that by-chain, and this despite the (defeasible) presumption in favor of intending such by-chains. We can capture this idea in a third principle governing the intentions of a rational agent:

(P3) I will not both intend by-chain *E-B-A* and also have an intention that is functionally incompatible with the intention in favor of that by-chain.

Principles (P1)–(P3) together constitute a partial replacement for the choice-intention principle that originally figured in the problem of the package deal. Note that (P1)–(P3) are not offered as principles of *reasoning*, for we should not assume that having chosen an overall scenario one must engage in yet further reasoning in order to figure out what to intend. Rather, in a typical case one's choosing an overall scenario will itself involve one's coming to have dispositions characteristic of certain intentions. What principles (P1)–(P3) aim at is a partial account of the intentions that a rational agent will come to have in arriving at certain choices on the basis of practical reasoning.

10.5.2   *Terror Bomber, Strategic Bomber, and Double Effect*

Let us see how these principles work for certain important cases. Begin with the original pair of cases. Terror Bomber's scenario includes killing the children within its lone by-chain, whereas Strategic Bomber's does not include killing the children within a by-chain. This difference in their scenarios can naturally result, on (P1)–(P3), in a difference in what is intended. We may suppose that Terror Bomber has no intention that would be inconsistent or functionally incompatible with his intending the lone by-chain in his scenario—the by-chain that includes his killing of the children. (If he did have such an intention, the combination of (P1) together with either (P3) or the demand for intention-belief consistency would prevent him from choosing this scenario.) So, if Terror Bomber is rational and chooses that scenario, he will intend this lone by-chain, and so intend to kill the children. In contrast, Strategic Bomber chooses a scenario that does not include killing the children as part of a by-chain, but does include an appropriate by-chain that does not contain his killing the children. So he may satisfy the demands of (P1)–(P3) and still not intend to kill the children.

Notice how this account of the original case of Strategic Bomber differs from that suggested by Harman. Harman would say that Strategic Bomber need not intend to kill the children because he need not consider that upshot in his deliberation. And pragmatic considerations are offered in defense of this claim that a limited agent need not consider such upshots. On the view presented here, this mislocates the rationale for the absence of such an intention on the part of Strategic Bomber. We may assume that Strategic Bomber will in fact consider this bad upshot in his deliberation and so will choose a scenario containing that upshot. But he still need not intend that upshot. This is because in choosing a scenario a rational agent will normally intend only certain elements of that scenario; and this limitation on how much of a chosen scenario is intended is itself supported by a pragmatic rationale. Pragmatic considerations enter Harman's account at the point of justifying a kind of blinders: at the point of justifying the nonconsideration of certain upshots. In contrast, pragmatic considerations enter my account at the point of justifying patterns of connection between choice and intention.

Of course, this does not tell us whether or not Strategic Bomber would also go ahead and bomb if his bombing option were precisely that of Terror Bomber's. The difference between Strategic Bomber and Terror Bomber in the original case lies in the options with which they are presented; it need not involve a difference in inclination to plump for terror-bombing if that is the only bombing option available. This raises an interesting question: what features of Strategic Bomber's psychology might lead him to eschew terror-bombing if that were the only bombing option available?

One answer takes us back to the idea of an SG-intention. Suppose that Strategic Bomber does in fact have the SG-intention not to endeavor to harm innocent people and not to filter options by their incompatibility with causing such harm. This SG-intention need not prevent him from choosing strategic bombing, but it will block terror-bombing. To see this, suppose that Strategic Bomber, with his SG-intention, were presented with Terror Bomber's scenario: weaken Enemy by killing children by dropping bombs. On (P1) if a chosen scenario contains only one by-chain, then the agent will, if rational, intend that by-chain. So a choice of Terror Bomber's scenario would involve intending to kill the children. But this intention would be functionally incompatible with the cited SG-intention.[31] On (P3), then, as long as Strategic Bomber retains his SG-intention,[32] he will not be able rationally to choose Terror Bomber's scenario. His SG-intention will screen this choice.

This shows the need for a further complication in my treatment of option admissibility. Roughly speaking, we have seen so far that an option is admissible if intending it would lead to no new violation of the demand for intention-belief consistency. But now we see a way in which an option may pass this test and yet fail to be admissible. Strategic Bomber does not have intentions that are, strictly speaking, inconsistent with a new intention to terror-bomb. He does not, for example, intend not to kill children. (If he did, he would also find strategic bombing to be inadmissible; and he doesn't.) Still, his general SG-intention does block the option of terror-bombing from consideration. This is a consequence of principles (P1)–(P3). So these principles result in an extension of the screen of admissibility—an extension beyond consistency, strictly speaking, and in the direction of the need to avoid functionally incompatible intentions.

Return now to the principle of double effect. Notice that as a result of his general SG-intention Strategic Bomber's rational choices will exhibit the pattern endorsed by that principle: he will sometimes choose to act in ways that he knows will have certain bad effects, though he would not have chosen to act in those ways if that had involved his intending to cause those bad effects. This pattern is a consequence of the way in which his general SG-intention structures the relation between his choices and intentions, given principles (P1)–(P3).

Now, one worry that is sometimes felt about the principle of double effect is that it seems to see a moral agent as reasoning about her intentions in reasoning about what to do. But, it might be urged, in practical reasoning whose direct concern is to guide our conduct, we do not reason about our intentions but about what to do; and it is by reasoning about what to do that we shape what we intend. This worry is expressed by Jonathan Bennett in the following passage: "In my opinion, it is a mistake to think of first-order morality—morality for the guidance of deliberating agents—as making any use of the concept of the deliberator's future intentions. The morality I consult as a guide to my conduct does also guide my intentions, but not by telling me what I may or may not intend. It speaks to me of what I may or may not do . . . and in that way it guides my intentions without speaking to me about them."[33] Our model of the role of intentions in practical reasoning helps us defuse this worry about the principle of double effect. Strategic Bomber does not reason about his intentions: he reasons about what to do. But his prior intentions, commitments, and policies—in particular, his cited SG-intention—nevertheless help determine what options he can coherently reason about. And that is why his rational choices display the pattern endorsed by the principle of double effect. This suggests that the principle of double effect may best be treated as a description of a pattern that will be displayed by the choices of rational agents who have appropriate SG-intentions.

Of course, this is not yet a defense of the principle of double effect. Such a defense would require a serious argument for having the SG-intention not to engage in the patterns of thinking and acting characteristic of an intention to cause or allow certain bad effects (such as harm to innocent people). And this defense would need to justify such an SG-intention without also justifying an analogous general intention simply not to cause or allow those bad effects. Such an argument is beyond the scope of this book. Nevertheless, we have made some progress. We have uncovered structure in the relation between the choices and intentions of a rational agent; and this structure may shed some light on the principle of double effect.

10.6 A Mean between Extremes

Central to my solution to the problem of the package deal is the distinction between what one chooses on the basis of practical reasoning and what one thereby comes to intend. This distinction puts us in a position to characterize in a useful way both the similarities and the differences between the attitudes of Terror Bomber and Strategic Bomber (in the original case) concerning killing the children. Both have made a choice that includes killing them; but only Terror Bomber intends to kill them. In contrast, if we were to identify the scenarios favored by practical conclusion, choice, and intention, we would not be able to do this. We would be forced to say one of two things: Strategic Bomber simply does not reach a practical conclusion in favor of (inter alia) killing the children; or, Strategic Bomber really does intend (inter alia) to kill them. In the former case we would fail to capture an important similarity between Strategic Bomber and Terror Bomber; we would fail to capture the sense in which both plump for an option known to involve killing the children. And in the latter case we would fail to capture an important difference between Strategic Bomber and Terror Bomber; for, after all, Strategic Bomber does not guide his further reasoning and action in the way he would if, like Terror Bomber, he intended to kill the children. The framework I have been sketching allows us to avoid both these extremes, and usefully to characterize both the similarities and the differences between these two agents. These characterizations in hand, we can face the vexed question of whether, despite these similarities, the differences make an important moral difference.

chapter 11

Conclusion

I HAVE approached intention by way of the phenomena of future-directed intentions and partial plans. I have tried to locate these phenomena in a plausible model of limited rational agency, a model that articulates some of the main ways in which future-directed intentions and partial plans help support coordination and extend the influence of practical reasoning over time. I have tried to understand the impact of this model on various of our assessments of the rationality or reasonableness of actions and agents. And I have argued that this model has important implications for our understanding of what it is for an action to be performed intentionally or with a certain intention, for we must do justice to both faces of intention.

On the model I have sketched, prior intentions play a central role both as inputs and as outputs of practical reasoning. As inputs, intentions structure deliberation: they pose problems for deliberation and constrain solutions. And they play these roles in part because of their characteristic stability. As a characteristic output of practical reasoning, intention is tied to further reasoning and action in ways in which choice need not be: that is why we do not intend everything that is an element in what we choose. And intentions control conduct—though the relations between intending to do something and doing something intentionally (or with a certain intention) are complex. Future-directed intentions, then, influence later conduct in ways that involve neither action at a distance nor irrevocability. And these modes of influence are so central to the functioning of limited but intelligent agents like ourselves that there is little reason to worry that the formation of such intentions is a waste of time. So our model of intention and agency seems clearly to avoid the horns of the trilemma mooted in Chapter 1. Finally, my sketch of standards for the assessment of the rationality of an agent for her intentions and intentional actions has included a historical dimension, a historical dimension motivated by the role of intention in reliably extending the influence of practical reasoning over time.

I believe that one of the virtues of my account is that it sheds some light on the relationships between certain problems in the philosophy of mind and action, the theory of rationality, and moral philosophy, problems that can too easily be cut off from each other and treated piecemeal. Perhaps this account will also help to combat the tendency in the philosophy of mind to focus primarily on perception and belief and to ignore the central place of intention and action in our understanding of mind and intelligence.

It is my hope that in future research this approach to intention can be deepened in a variety of ways. Let me sketch three. First, I have spoken of habits of reconsideration that are reasonable of an agent to have. And I have urged that we take a broadly consequentialist approach to such matters. But except for some brief remarks I have said little about just what habits are likely to be reasonable for agents like us. It should be possible to say more, in a systematic and detailed way, about just what such reasonable habits are. In particular, it should be possible to say more about the kinds of situations that should be taken by the agent as posing problems for her prior plans.

Second, I have said that the background of prior intentions and plans also involves flat-out beliefs. And I have said a bit about how such beliefs function as part of this background framework. But there are large questions here about the nature of flat-out belief and its relation to degrees of confidence and subjective probabilities, questions I have largely skirted. I believe it should be possible to develop the approach sketched here in a way that addresses these further issues.

Finally, there are suggestive parallels between the roles of prior plans in practical reasoning and the roles that deontological constraints are supposed to play, according to their defenders, in moral reasoning. There is a parallel, for example, between the way in which a deontological constraint on killing innocent people is supposed to screen out certain options as morally impermissible and the way in which prior plans impose a screen of admissibility on options. I explored related matters in my brief discussion of the principle of double effect toward the end of Chapter 10. But many questions about the extent and the usefulness of this parallel remain open.

Let me note one question in particular. A deontological constraint on killing innocent people is not a demand to minimize such killings. Indeed, it would normally be a violation of such a constraint for you to kill one person in order to prevent the killings of two other people—even if these two other killings would be performed by you. And this may seem odd.

As Robert Nozick once put it: "How can a concern for the nonviolation of [constraint] C lead to the refusal to violate C even when this would prevent other more extensive violations of C?"[1]

Once we recognize the parallel between deontological constraints and prior plans we may have some leverage on this question. After all, in providing a screen of admissibility on options our prior plans do not enjoin us to minimize plan violations. An option that is incompatible with my prior plans, even though its performance would improve my ability to construct and execute consistent plans, would normally still be inadmissible. Perhaps a recognition of the pervasiveness of such structures even outside the distinctively moral sphere would go some way toward demystifying deontological constraints. The suspicion that there is a special problem about deontological constraints may depend in part on an overly simplified view of the structure of practical reasoning, one that fails to come to grips with the complex roles of future-directed intentions and partial plans.

I close where I began: with the observation that we use the concept of intention to characterize both mind and action. To understand the mental state of intending we need to locate it in a model of limited, intelligent agency, a model that takes seriously the phenomena of partial plans and planning. When we turn to the characterization of action as done intentionally or with a certain intention we must not assume too simple a relation to the state of intending. In particular, concerns about responsibility shape our characterizations of action in a way in which they should not shape our characterizations of mind. By recognizing both faces of intention we put ourselves in a position to treat the state of intending as a distinctive and central element in our conception of intelligent agency.

Bibliography

Adams, Robert. "Motive Utilitarianism." *Journal of Philosophy* 73 (1976): 467–481.

Allman, W. F. "Staying Alive in the Twentieth Century." *Science 85* (October 1985): 31–37.

Anscombe, G. E. M. *Intention*. Ithaca: Cornell University Press, 1963.

——— "Modern Moral Philosophy." *Philosophy* (1958): 1–19.

Audi, Robert. "Intending." *Journal of Philosophy* 70 (1973): 387–403.

Aune, Bruce. *Reason and Action*. Dordrecht: Reidel, 1977.

Austin, John. *Lectures on Jurisprudence,* vol. I. London: John Murray, 1873.

Austin, J. L. "Three Ways of Spilling Ink." In *J. L. Austin: Philosophical Papers,* 2nd ed., ed. J. O. Urmson and G. J. Warnock. Oxford: Oxford University Press, 1970.

Baier, Annette. "Mixing Memory and Desire." *American Philosophical Quarterly* 13 (1976): 213–220.

Beardsley, Monroe. "Intending." In *Values and Morals: Essays in Honor of William Frankena, Charles Stevenson, and Richard Brandt,* ed. Alvin Goldman and Jaegwon Kim. Dordrecht: Reidel, 1978.

Bennett, Jonathan. "Morality and Consequences." In *The Tanner Lectures on Human Values,* ed. Sterling M. McMurrin. Cambridge: Cambridge University Press, 1980.

Bentham, Jeremy. *An Introduction to the Principles of Morals and Legislation.* London: Methuen, 1982.

Block, Ned. "What Is Functionalism?" In *Readings in Philosophy of Psychology,* ed. Ned Block, pp. 171–184. Cambridge, Mass.: Harvard University Press, 1980.

Brand, Myles. *Intending and Acting*. Cambridge, Mass.: MIT Press, 1984.

Brandt, Richard. "The Concept of Rational Action." *Social Theory and Practice* 9 (1983): 143–164.

——— *A Theory of the Good and the Right*. Oxford: Oxford University Press, 1979.

Bratman, Michael. "Castañeda's Theory of Thought and Action." In *Agent, Language, and the Structure of the World: Essays Presented to Hector-*

Neri Castañeda, with His Replies, ed. James E. Tomberlin. Indianapolis: Hackett, 1983.

—— "Davidson's Theory of Intention." In *Essays on Davidson: Actions and Events,* ed. Bruce Vermazen and Merrill B. Hintikka. Oxford: Oxford University Press, 1985. Reprinted with an added appendix in *Actions and Events: Perspectives on the Philosophy of Donald Davidson,* ed. Ernest LePore and Brian McLaughlin. Oxford: Basil Blackwell, 1985.

—— "Intention and Means-End Reasoning." *The Philosophical Review* 90 (1981): 252–265.

—— "Personal Policies." Working paper prepared for a Workshop on Risk and Rationality, sponsored in 1985–86 by the University of Maryland Center for Philosophy and Public Policy.

—— "Simple Intention." *Philosophical Studies* 36 (1979): 245–259.

—— "Taking Plans Seriously." *Social Theory and Practice* 9 (1983): 271–287.

—— "Two Faces of Intention." *The Philosophical Review* 93 (1984): 375–405.

Castañeda, Hector-Neri. "Conditional Intentions, Intentional Action, and Aristotelian Practical Syllogisms." *Erkenntnis* 18 (1982): 239–260.

—— "Reply to Michael Bratman." In *Agent, Language, and the Structure of the World,* ed. James Tomberlin. Indianapolis: Hackett, 1983.

—— *Thinking and Doing.* Dordrecht: Reidel, 1975.

Chisholm, Roderick M. *Person and Object.* La Salle, Ill.: Open Court, 1976.

Churchland, Paul. "The Logical Character of Action-Explanations." *The Philosophical Review* 79 (1970): 214–236.

Darwall, Stephen. *Impartial Reason.* Ithaca: Cornell University Press, 1983.

Davidson, Donald. *Essays on Actions and Events.* New York: Oxford University Press, 1980.

—— "Actions, Reasons, and Causes." In *Essays on Actions and Events.*

—— "How Is Weakness of the Will Possible?" In *Essays on Actions and Events.*

—— "Intending." In *Essays on Actions and Events.*

—— "Reply to Michael Bratman." In *Essays on Davidson: Actions and Events,* ed. Bruce Vermazen and Merrill B. Hintikka. Oxford: Oxford University Press, 1985.

Davis, Wayne. "A Causal Theory of Intending." *American Philosophical Quarterly* 21 (1984): 43–54.

Dennett, Daniel. "Three Kinds of Intentional Psychology." In *Reduction, Time, and Reality,* ed. R. Healey. Cambridge: Cambridge University Press, 1981.

Dewey, John. *Human Nature and Conduct: An Introduction to Social Psychology.* New York: Random House, 1957.

Elster, Jon. *Ulysses and the Sirens.* Cambridge: Cambridge University Press, 1984.

Farrell, Daniel. "Intention, Reason, and Action." Unpublished manuscript. Department of Philosophy, Ohio State University.

Foot, Philippa. "Morality, Action, and Outcome." In *Morality and Objectivity,* ed. Ted Honderich. London: Routledge & Kegan Paul, 1985.

—— "The Problem of Abortion and the Doctrine of Double Effect." *Oxford Review,* no. 5 (1967).

Fried, Charles. *Right and Wrong.* Cambridge, Mass.: Harvard University Press, 1978.

Gauthier, David. "Afterthoughts." In *The Security Gamble: Deterrence Dilemmas in the Nuclear Age,* ed. Douglas MacLean. Totowa, N.Y.: Rowman & Allenheld, 1984.

—— "Deterrence, Maximization, and Rationality." In *The Security Gamble: Deterrence Dilemmas in the Nuclear Age,* ed. Douglas MacLean.

Gibbard, Allan. "Attainable Rationality in Action: An Analysis." Paper presented at the 1984 Stanford Conference on Planning and Practical Reasoning.

Goldman, Alvin. *A Theory of Human Action.* Englewood Cliffs: Prentice-Hall, 1970.

Grice, H. P. "Intention and Uncertainty." *Proceedings of the British Academy* 57 (1971): 263–279.

—— "Method in Philosophical Psychology (From the Banal to the Bizarre)." *Proceedings and Addresses of the American Philosophical Association* 48 (1974–75): 23–53.

Grisez, Germain. "Toward a Consistent Natural-Law Ethics of Killing." *The American Journal of Jurisprudence* 15 (1970): 64–96.

Hampshire, Stuart, and H. L. A. Hart. "Decision, Intention, and Certainty." *Mind* 67 (1958): 1–12.

Harman, Gilbert. *Change in View.* Cambridge, Mass.: MIT Press, 1986.

—— "Practical Reasoning." *Review of Metaphysics* 29 (1976): 431–463.

—— "Rational Action and the Extent of Intentions." *Social Theory and Practice* 9 (1983): 123–141. Revised version in *Change in View,* chap. 9.

—— "Willing and Intending." In *Philosophical Grounds of Rationality,* ed. R. Grandy and R. Warner. Oxford: Oxford University Press, 1986.

Hart, H. L. A. *Punishment and Responsibility.* Oxford: Oxford University Press, 1968.

—— and A. M. Honoré. *Causation in the Law.* Oxford: Oxford University Press, 1959.

Hobart, R. E. "Free Will as Involving Determination and Inconceivable without It." *Mind* 43 (1934): 1–27.

Jeffrey, Richard. *The Logic of Decision,* 2nd ed. Chicago: University of Chicago Press, 1983.

Kaplan, Mark. "Rational Acceptance." *Philosophical Studies* 40 (1981): 129–145.

Kavka, Gregory. "Some Paradoxes of Deterrence." *Journal of Philosophy* 75 (1978): 285–302.

—— "The Toxin Puzzle." *Analysis* 43 (1983): 33–36.

Lewis, David. "Psychophysical and Theoretical Identifications." *Australasian Journal of Philosophy* 50 (1972): 249–258.

Lubow, Neil. "Acting Intentionally." Unpublished manuscript. Department of Philosophy, University of New Hampshire.

McCann, Hugh. "Rationality and the Range of Intention." *Midwest Studies in Philosophy* 10 (1986): 191–211.

McGuiness, Frank. "Thinking-to-be and Thinking-to-do." In *Hector-Neri Castañeda,* ed. James Tomberlin. Dordrecht: Reidel, 1986.

Mele, Alfred R. "Intending and the Balance of Motivation." *Pacific Philosophical Quarterly* 65 (1984): 370–376.

Miller, George, Eugene Galanter, and Karl Pribram. *Plans and the Structure of Behavior*. New York: Holt, Rinehart and Winston, 1960.

Nagel, Thomas. *The View from Nowhere*. New York: Oxford University Press, 1986.

Nozick, Robert. *Anarchy, State, and Utopia*. New York: Basic Books, 1974.

—— *Philosophical Explanations*. Cambridge, Mass.: Harvard University Press, 1981.

O'Shaughnessy, Brian. *The Will*, vol. II. Cambridge: Cambridge University Press, 1980.

Perry, John. "A Problem about Continued Belief." *Pacific Philosophical Quarterly* 61 (1980): 317–332.

—— "The Problem of the Essential Indexical." *Nous* 13 (1979): 3–21.

Putnam, Hilary. "The Nature of Mental States." In Putman, *Mind, Language, and Reality: Philosophical Papers*. Cambridge: Cambridge University Press, 1975.

Raiffa, Howard. *Decision Analysis*. Reading, Mass.: Addison-Wesley, 1968.

Rawls, John. *A Theory of Justice*. Cambridge, Mass.: Harvard University Press, 1971.

Raz, Joseph. *Practical Reason and Norms*. London: Hutchinson, 1975.

—— "Reasons for Action, Decisions, and Norms." *Mind* 84 (1975): 481–499.

Robins, Michael. *Promising, Intending, and Moral Autonomy*. Cambridge: Cambridge University Press, 1984.

Ryle, Gilbert. *The Concept of Mind*. London: Hutchinson and Company, 1949.

Savage, Leonard J. *The Foundations of Statistics*, 2nd ed. New York: Dover, 1972.

Schelling, Thomas. "Ethics, Law, and the Exercise of Self-Command." In Schelling, *Choice and Consequence*. Cambridge, Mass.: Harvard University Press, 1984.

—— "The Intimate Contest for Self-Command." In *Choice and Consequence*.

Searle, John. *Intentionality*. Cambridge: Cambridge University Press, 1983.

Sellars Wilfred. "Thought and Action," In *Freedom and Determinism*, ed. Keith Lehrer. New York: Random House, 1966.

—— "Volitions Re-Affirmed." In *Action Theory*, ed. Myles Brand and Douglas Walton. Dordrecht: Reidel, 1976.

Sidgwick, Henry. *The Methods of Ethics*, 7th ed. London: Macmillan, 1907.

Simon, Herbert. "Rationality as Process and as Product of Thought." *American Economic Review (Papers and Proceedings)* 68 (1978): 1–16.

—— *Reason in Human Affairs*. Stanford: Stanford University Press, 1983.

—— *The Sciences of the Artificial*, 2nd ed. Cambridge, Mass.: MIT Press, 1981.

Smart, J. J. C. "Extreme and Restricted Utilitarianism." In *Theories of Ethics*, ed. Philippa Foot. Oxford: Oxford University Press, 1967.

Strawson, P. F. "Freedom and Resentment." *Proceedings of the British Academy* 48 (1962): 1–25.

Ullmann-Margalit, Edna, and Sidney Morgenbesser. "Picking and Choosing." *Social Research* 44 (1977): 757–785.

Velleman, J. David. "Practical Reflection." *The Philosophical Review* 94 (1985): 33–61.

Vermazen, Bruce. "Negative Acts." In *Essays on Davidson: Actions and Events,* ed. Bruce Vermazen and Merrill B. Hintikka. Oxford: Oxford University Press, 1985.

Von Wright, Georg Henrik. *Explanation and Understanding.* Ithaca: Cornell University Press, 1971.

Williams, Bernard. "Ethical Consistency." In Williams, *Problems of the Self: Philosophical Papers 1956–1972.* Cambridge: Cambridge University Press, 1973.

Wilson, George. *The Intentionality of Human Action.* Amsterdam: North Holland, 1980.

Wright, Larry. *Teleological Explanations: An Etiological Analysis of Goals and Functions.* Berkeley: University of California Press, 1976.

Notes

1. Introduction

1. The example, and the main point of this paragraph, come from Anscombe's monograph: G. E. M. Anscombe, *Intention* (Ithaca: Cornell University Press, 1963).

2. This has been a main theme of Herbert Simon's work. See, for example, *The Sciences of the Artificial,* 2nd ed. (Cambridge, Mass.: MIT Press, 1981).

3. A point long ago impressed upon me in conversation by Josie Teitel.

4. The importance of the idea of commitment to our understanding of intending has recently been emphasized by Michael Robins in his *Promising, Intending, and Moral Autonomy* (Cambridge: Cambridge University Press, 1984).

5. This may be the view of Miller, Galanter, and Pribram when they write: "What does it mean when an ordinary man has an ordinary intention? It means that he has begun the execution of a Plan and that this intended action is a part of it . . . The term ['intent'] is used to refer to *the uncompleted parts of a Plan whose execution has already begun."* See George Miller, Eugene Galanter, and Karl Pribram, *Plans and the Structure of Behavior* (New York: Holt, Rinehart and Winston, 1960), p. 61.

6. At least the first two horns of this trilemma are hinted at by the nineteenth-century philosopher John Austin. See John Austin, *Lectures on Jurisprudence,* vol. I (London: John Murray, 1873), lecture XXI, pp. 450–452. My talk of a ghostly hand is borrowed from R. E. Hobart's essay, "Free Will as Involving Determination and Inconceivable without It," *Mind* 43 (1934): 1–27.

7. Anscombe, *Intention,* esp. p. 9.

8. Alvin Goldman, *A Theory of Human Action* (Englewood Cliffs: Prentice-Hall, 1970).

9. See Donald Davidson, *Essays on Actions and Events* (New York: Oxford University Press, 1980), especially essays 1–5. I discuss some of the complexities of Davidson's treatment of intention in these essays in "Davidson's Theory of Intention," in Bruce Vermazen and Merrill B. Hintikka, eds., *Essays on Davidson: Actions and Events* (Oxford: Oxford University Press, 1985). This essay is reprinted with an added appendix in *Actions and Events: Perspectives on the*

Philosophy of Donald Davidson, ed. Ernest LePore and Brian McLaughlin (Oxford: Basil Blackwell, 1985).

10. Goldman does make significant use of the notion of an "action-plan." But it is clear from his discussion that this is not a psychological element over and above desires and beliefs but is, rather, constituted of various desires and beliefs. See, for example, *A Theory of Human Action,* pp. 56–57.

11. We might also be led to a version of (2) by way of a natural interpretation of subjective expected utility theories, of the sort developed by Leonard J. Savage in *The Foundations of Statistics,* 2nd ed. (New York: Dover, 1972), and by Richard Jeffrey in *The Logic of Decision,* 2nd ed. (Chicago: University of Chicago Press, 1983). Such theories attempt to describe an agent's relevant attitudes in terms of appropriate probability and utility functions. They then go on to recommend as rational decisions in favor of options whose "expected utility" is maximal. Now, one is not forced to interpret such theories as supposing that the only attitudes relevant to the rationality of decision and the intentionality of action are those described by such utility and probability functions. (Indeed, it may be possible to locate such theories within the planning framework to be developed in this essay. See Chapter 3, note 12.) But such an interpretation is nevertheless a natural one. And if that is the way we understand these theories, they will seem to involve a sophisticated version of thesis (2).

12. Austin, *Lectures on Jurisprudence,* I, 450.

13. Robert Audi, "Intending," *Journal of Philosophy* 70 (1973): 387–403; Monroe Beardsley, "Intending," in *Values and Morals: Essays in Honor of William Frankena, Charles Stevenson, and Richard Brandt,* ed. Alvin Goldman and Jaegwon Kim (Dordrecht: Reidel, 1978); Paul Churchland, "The Logical Character of Action-Explanations," *The Philosophical Review* 79 (1970): 214–236; Wayne Davis, "A Causal Theory of Intending," *American Philosophical Quarterly* 21 (1984): 43–54.

14. George Wilson, *The Intentionality of Human Action* (Amsterdam: North Holland, 1980). See my discussion in Chapter 9.

15. See especially Davidson, "Intending," in his *Essays on Actions and Events,* and my discussion in "Davidson's Theory of Intention."

16. As Philip Temko once put it in discussion.

17. In H. L. A. Hart, *Punishment and Responsibility* (Oxford: Oxford University Press, 1968). The quote to follow is from p. 117.

18. See, for example, H. P. Grice, "Method in Philosophical Psychology (From the Banal to the Bizarre)," *Proceedings and Addresses of the American Philosophical Association* 48 (1974–75): 23–53; David Lewis, "Psychophysical and Theoretical Identifications," *Australasian Journal of Philosophy* 50 (1972): 249–258; Ned Block, "What Is Functionalism?" in *Readings in Philosophy of Psychology,* ed. Ned Block (Cambridge, Mass.: Harvard University Press, 1980) pp. 171–184; and Hilary Putnam, "The Nature of Mental States," in his *Mind, Language, and Reality: Philosophical Papers* (Cambridge: Cambridge University Press, 1975), vol. II. As will be clear from this varied list, I include in the functionalist tradition philosophers with different views about the relation between functionalism and physicalism. In this book I take no position on that issue.

19. These will typically not be strict regularities, but rather of a sort involved in what Grice calls "*ceteris paribus* laws." See Grice, "Method in Philosophical Psychology."

20. Later we will need to make a distinction between internal and external norms. But for now we can safely ignore this complexity.

21. See, for example, Herbert Simon, *Reason in Human Affairs* (Stanford: Stanford University Press, 1983), esp. chap. 1.

22. Another philosopher who has attempted to tie these two issues together is Gilbert Harman. See especially "Rational Action and the Extent of Intentions," *Social Theory and Practice* 9 (1983): 123–141, a paper I will be discussing in Chapter 10. (A revised version of this paper is Chapter 9 of Harman's *Change in View* [Cambridge, Mass.: MIT Press, 1986].) Harman has also discussed related matters in "Practical Reasoning," *Review of Metaphysics* 29 (1976): 431–463, and in "Willing and Intending," in *Philosophical Grounds of Rationality*, ed. R. Grandy and R. Warner (Oxford: Oxford University Press, 1986). Although my views about intention differ from Harman's in a variety of ways (some of which I will be noting in the chapters to follow), I have benefited from studying this trio of papers.

23. Edna Ullmann-Margalit and Sidney Morgenbesser, "Picking and Choosing," *Social Research* 44 (1977): 757–785. By the way, Ullmann-Margalit and Morgenbesser report that "Buridan's own position on this matter . . . is not known. In fact, the story about the ass is not to be found in his writings" (p. 759n).

24. An example modeled after one of Ullmann-Margalit and Morgenbesser's in "Picking and Choosing."

25. In writing this paragraph I was helped by comments from Amy Lansky.

26. See Jon Elster, *Ulysses and the Sirens* (Cambridge: Cambridge University Press, 1984). See also Thomas Schelling, "The Intimate Contest for Self-Command," and "Ethics, Law, and the Exercise of Self-Command," both in Thomas Schelling, *Choice and Consequence* (Cambridge, Mass.: Harvard University Press, 1984). In writing this paragraph and the next I benefited from a conversation with Paul Dietrichson.

27. Roderick M. Chisholm, *Person and Object* (La Salle, Ill.: Open Court, 1976), chap. 2.

2. On the Way to the Planning Theory

1. Austin, *Lectures on Jurisprudence*, vol. I, lecture XXI, p. 452.

2. I will be returning to questions about the relation between intention and belief in Chapter 3.

3. For a different sort of objection to understanding intention in terms of predominant desire see Alfred R. Mele, "Intending and the Balance of Motivation," *Pacific Philosophical Quarterly* 65 (1984): 370–376.

4. A point I will be developing further in Chapter 3.

5. For a recent, subtle defense of an approach along these lines see Wayne Davis, "A Causal Theory of Intending," *American Philosophical Quarterly* 21 (1984): 43–54. Myles Brand criticizes such reductive approaches to intention in

his *Intending and Acting* (Cambridge, Mass.: MIT Press, 1984), chap. 5, sects. 1–2, and chap. 6, sect. 1.

6. See Richard Brandt, *A Theory of the Good and the Right* (Oxford: Oxford University Press, 1979); and Stephen Darwall, *Impartial Reason* (Ithaca: Cornell University Press, 1983).

7. In describing this decision as arbitrary I do not claim that it is not explainable. I only claim it is not explainable in terms of my reasons for preferring route 101 to route 280.

8. Ditto for reasoning from a prior intention to a more specific intention, or to an intention concerning preliminary steps.

9. A view along these lines can be found in Bruce Aune, *Reason and Action* (Dordrecht: Reidel, 1977), chap. 3, esp. p. 122. Joseph Raz holds that a decision to *A* provides a reason for *A*-ing, but does not extend this view to intentions not arrived at by decision. See Joseph Raz, "Reasons for Action, Decisions, and Norms," *Mind* 84 (1975): 481–499, esp. 494; and also Joseph Raz, *Practical Reason and Norms* (London: Hutchinson, 1975). Raz also sees the decision to *A* as providing an "exclusionary reason" to disregard reasons against *A*-ing. In my remarks in this section I do not consider this further aspect of Raz's complex and subtle views.

10. I should make it clear that this first objection is addressed only against the intention-based-reasons view as I have formulated it in the text. It is not intended as an objection to the theories of Aune and Raz; for each of them develops the view in a way that avoids this particular worry. My second objection is, in contrast, intended to be an objection to the views of both of these philosophers.

11. Ned Block has pointed out that one might avoid this conclusion by seeing intention-based reasons as lexically ordered *behind* desire-belief reasons. One checks to see if the desire-belief reasons balance out, and only then turns to prior intentions. But this would mean that intentions would play an even weaker role in practical reasoning, and so the first problem for the intention-based-reasons view would be even more severe.

3. Plans and Practical Reasoning

1. See, for example, the trio of papers by Gilbert Harman referred to in Chapter 1, note 22; Wilfred Sellars, "Thought and Action," in Keith Lehrer, ed., *Freedom and Determinism* (New York: Random House, 1966); Bruce Aune, *Reason and Action* (Dordrecht: Reidel, 1977); Annette Baier, "Mixing Memory and Desire," *American Philosophical Quarterly* 13 (1976): 213–220; Myles Brand, *Intending and Acting* (Cambridge: MIT Press, 1984); and Hector-Neri Castañeda, *Thinking and Doing* (Dordrecht: Reidel, 1975). I discuss Castañeda's views at length in my "Castañeda's Theory of Thought and Action," in James Tomberlin, ed., *Agent Language and the Structure of the World* (Indianapolis: Hackett, 1983).

2. So the plans I want to focus on are not the total strategies that Savage envisages in his "Look before you leap" principle. As Savage says: "In view of

the 'Look before you leap' principle,· . . . [t]he person decides 'now' once for all; there is nothing for him to wait for, because his one decision provides for all contingencies." (See Savage, *The Foundations of Statistics*, 2nd ed., p. 17.) Savage, of course, does not suppose that limited agents like us ever really reach such "once for all" total decisions.

It is important not to confuse the partiality of plans with their revocability in the face of later difficulties. If I am not mistaken, Donald Davidson makes this mistake in his "Reply to Michael Bratman," in Bruce Vermazen and Merrill B. Hintikka, eds., *Essays on Davidson: Actions and Events* (Oxford: Oxford University Press, 1985), pp. 195–201, esp. p. 200. He suggests there that he has noted the partiality of plans in an earlier essay. The relevant passage of that essay that he quotes is, "[My] present intention with respect to the future . . . is based on my present view of the situation; there is no reason in general why I should act as I now intend if my present view turns out to be wrong." But this passage does not describe the partiality of plans, but rather their revocability.

3. I do not think that these brief explanations of the relevant notions of consistency are without their difficulties. As Joseph Almog once emphasized in conversation, there are deep problems here analogous to problems that arise when we try to say, for example, in what sense our beliefs about the morning star (that is, the evening star), or Cicero (that is, Tully) should be consistent. But I think this gloss on consistency will suffice for my purposes here. Serious pursuit of these problems would take us into thorny issues about the semantics of attitude reports. And my strategy in this book is to go as far as I can without getting embroiled in such issues. This is because it seems to me that the main points I want to make about the distinctiveness of intentions and their roles in our lives do not turn on these semantical issues.

4. To avoid misunderstanding let me note that I use the term 'means-end coherence' here because I find it more suggestive than just speaking of plan coherence. But it should be clear from the text that I mean to include under the demand for means-end coherence not just a demand to settle on appropriate means. I mean also to include demands to settle on appropriate preliminary steps and on needed specifications of relatively general ends.

5. There is an interesting issue here that is not settled by the demand for means-end coherence. Increased detail in my plan may be seen by me not as necessary for successful execution, but only as increasing the chances of success. Since the further deliberation required to add such detail will have its own costs, there is here a trade-off about which I might deliberate. Frequently, however, we do not bother to deliberate about whether to engage in deliberation concerning a certain level of detail in our plan, but just go ahead and do (or do not) deliberate at that level. In Chapter 5 I address a special case of this general issue of when to (or not to) deliberate.

6. An example suggested by Lawrence Becker.

7. I think this is a point Bruce Aune mistakenly ignores. This is what leads him to the view that if I intend to *A* and believe that if I *A* then I *B*, then I have a "good reason" to intend to *B*, and "should be willing" so to intend. (See Aune, *Reason and Action*, pp. 148–153.) On this view, if I intend to go to sleep and

believe that if I do so I will snore and annoy my wife, then I have a good reason to intend to annoy her, and should be willing so to intend. But this seems wrong. The truth seems rather to be only that I cannot consistently add an intention not to annoy her. I discuss related matters in Chapter 10.

8. In writing the last three sentences I was aided by discussion with Mark Crimmins and Peter Railton.

9. A point emphasized by Kurt Konolige.

10. Here I was aided by Peter Railton.

11. This notion of framework reasons seems similar in some respects to Raz's notion of an "exclusionary reason," mentioned in Chapter 2, note 9. Raz holds that a decision to A provides both a reason to A and an exclusionary reason to disregard reasons against A-ing. We can get from this idea to something close to ours by way of several changes. First, we drop the claim that decisions are reasons for doing what one has decided to do. Second, we extend the claim about exclusionary reasons to cover intentions generally (a move that Raz himself resists). Third, we substitute our idea of filtering out certain options from one's reasoning for Raz's idea of disregarding certain reasons. These changes leave us with the idea that an intention to A provides reason to filter out from one's reasoning options incompatible with one's A-ing. And this would be similar to one half of my claim that such an intention provides a framework reason. Of course, these changes in Raz's view would not by themselves lead us to my pragmatic conception of these framework reasons—and this pragmatic conception is central to my solution of bootstrapping problems. See Raz, "Reasons for Action, Decisions, and Norms," and *Practical Reason and Norms*.

12. In Chapter 1, note 11, I noted that on one natural interpretation subjective expected utility theory leads to a version of the desire-belief model. Our discussion here suggests the possibility of an interpretation that is instead within the framework of our planning theory. It may be possible to see subjective expected utility theory as an account of how one is to bring to bear, in decisionmaking, utility and probability assignments concerning those options that are relevant and admissible, *given one's background framework of prior plans and flat-out beliefs*. Such a model would help clarify the different roles in practical reasoning of all-or-none belief, on the one hand, and subjective probability, on the other. This would be a response to Mark Kaplan's challenge to provide "a story about how the acceptance of propositions [in contrast with subjective probabilities] impinges upon human practice. We need to know what difference a person's acceptance of a proposition makes to the way she will behave . . ." See Mark Kaplan, "Rational Acceptance," *Philosophical Studies* 40 (1981): 129–145. The quoted passage is from page 136. (Kaplan's response to his challenge is very different from the one suggested here.) My thinking about these matters has been influenced by discussion with Mark Crimmins, David Israel, and Mark Kaplan.

13. Those who endorse the view that intention requires such a belief include H. P. Grice, in "Intention and Uncertainty," *Proceedings of the British Academy* 57 (1971): 263–279; Gilbert Harman, in "Practical Reasoning"; and J. David Velleman, "Practical Reflection," *The Philosophical Review* 94 (1985): 33–61.

Harman discusses the matter further in "Willing and Intending" and in *Change in View,* esp. pp. 90–93.

14. Something like this reply was suggested to me in conversation by Hector-Neri Castañeda, though the reply diverges from his views about conditional intentions and belief in *Thinking and Doing,* p. 279. I once explored—without much success, I now believe—some of these issues about conditional intention and belief in Michael Bratman, "Simple Intention," *Philosophical Studies* 36 (1979): 245–259.

15. Worries along these lines have been offered as criticisms of earlier papers of mine by Hector-Neri Castañeda in "Reply to Michael Bratman," in *Agent, Language, and the Structure of the World,* ed. James Tomberlin (Indianapolis: Hackett, 1983); and by Hugh McCann in "Rationality and the Range of Intention," *Midwest Studies in Philosophy* 10 (1986): 191–211. My exchange with Castañeda is discussed usefully by Frank McGuiness in "Thinking-to-be and Thinking-to-do," in James Tomberlin, ed., *Hector-Neri Castañeda* (Dordrecht: Reidel, 1986). In general, it seems to me that in his reply to my earlier paper Castañeda underestimates the problems created by intention-belief inconsistency for further planning—problems of the sort I have been noting.

16. Thanks to Todd Davies for helping me appreciate the need for these further remarks.

17. I discuss one more complication for my treatment of option admissibility toward the end of Chapter 10.

18. I only say "may well," for the case may be different if I happen intrinsically to desire to do what I intend to do. I was helped in this paragraph by Martha Pollack.

19. This question was impressed upon me by Gilbert Harman in his thoughtful comments on my "Intention and Means-End Reasoning" at the 1981 Eastern Division Meetings of the American Philosophical Association. And my answer was aided by some remarks of Kwong-loi Shun's.

20. Distinguish between two cases in which one has both a relatively general intention to A and an intention in favor of a specification of A. In one case the agent will have begun by forming the more specific intention and will have the more general intention solely by virtue of having settled on the more specific course of action. In the other case the agent will have begun by forming the relatively general intention and then have proceeded to the needed specification. I might begin with an intention to go to your lecture, an intention by virtue of which I intend to go to a lecture. Or I might begin with an intention to go to a lecture, and then settle on your lecture as the one to go to. In saying that the more general intention "lies behind" the more specific intention I mean to indicate that I am considering a case of the second sort.

4. Agent Rationality: Toward a General Theory

1. For a similar notion of rational assessment see Richard Brandt's brief discussion of what he calls "retrospective" judgments of the rationality of an

action or agent, in R. B. Brandt, "The Concept of Rational Action," *Social Theory and Practice* 9 (1983): 143–164. It seems to me that discussions of what Herbert Simon calls "procedural rationality" are mainly relevant to such assessments of the rationality of an agent in intending and acting. See, e.g., Herbert Simon, "Rationality as Process and as Product of Thought," *The American Economic Review (Papers and Proceedings)* 68 (1978): 1–16.

2. A point that Donald Regan helped me to see.

3. The term "primary goods" comes, of course, from John Rawls, *A Theory of Justice* (Cambridge, Mass.: Harvard University Press, 1971).

4. This contrasts with an external, non-plan-constrained recommendation of the action of trying to bring about certain changes in one's habits. Such a recommendation will depend on the expected costs of such changes in the particular case, where the expectations are the agent's.

5. Habits can affect desire-satisfaction in two ways: by affecting one's success in getting what one wants, and by affecting what one wants. This second kind of effect raises important issues, but ones that are beyond the scope of this essay.

6. Sidgwick makes a similar point. See Henry Sidgwick, *The Methods of Ethics*, 7th ed. (London: Macmillan, 1907), p. 492. None of this is to say that it would be rational for you to choose to have habits known by you to be suboptimal if you could just as easily have ones known by you to be optimal.

7. Here I follow Brian O'Shaughnessy, *The Will* (Cambridge: Cambridge University Press, 1980), II, 313.

8. A present-directed intention is not merely an intention to A beginning at *t*, where as a matter of fact *t* is now. To have a present-directed intention to A, I must see that *now* is the time for action. See John Perry, "The Problem of the Essential Indexical," *Nous* 13 (1979): 3–21.

9. Later, in Chapter 8, we will see reason to complicate this picture. But for present purposes we can ignore these complications.

10. To execute the intention to A it is necessary to act with the aim or purpose of A-ing. So, to execute the intention to A one must act with the intention of A-ing. If one successfully executes an intention to A, then one's action is guided by that intention and one thereby does what one intends.

11. Gregory Kavka, "Some Paradoxes of Deterrence," *Journal of Philosophy* 75 (1978): 285–302; Gregory Kavka, "The Toxin Puzzle," *Analysis* 43 (1983): 33–36; Daniel Farrell, "Intention, Reason, and Action" (unpublished manuscript, Department of Philosophy, Ohio State University); David Gauthier, "Deterrence, Maximization, and Rationality," in *The Security Gamble: Deterrence Dilemmas in the Nuclear Age,* ed. Douglas MacLean (Totowa: Rowman & Allanheld, 1984).

12. For a discussion of related matters see John Perry, "A Problem about Continued Belief," *Pacific Philosophical Quarterly* 61 (1980): 317–332.

13. A question raised by David Velleman: Why shouldn't policy-based intentions be treated as a special case of deliberative intentions, analogous to derived intentions in favor of necessary means? I give my answer to this question later in Section 6.4.

14. A brief remark about the time to which my principles are to apply: I

distinguish deliberative from nondeliberative cases on the basis of the presence or absence of relevant deliberation. So we will want the relevant time to be a temporal interval, one long enough for it to be possible—even if not desirable—for at least minimal deliberation to occur.

15. The quote is from Dewey, who writes: "Deliberation is a dramatic rehearsal (in imagination) of various competing possible lines of action." John Dewey, *Human Nature and Conduct: An Introduction to Social Psychology* (New York: Random House, 1957), p. 179.

5. Reconsideration and Rationality

1. I will be making the simplifying assumption that an agent abandons a prior intention only as a result of some form of reconsideration of that prior intention. As Charles Dresser once remarked, this is not quite correct. In an earthquake I might just abandon my prior intention to play bridge tonight without engaging in anything that amounts to reconsideration of that intention. But for present purposes my simplifying assumption will help me keep the discussion from getting too unwieldy.

2. As in my discussion of three kinds of intention, I do not attempt here to provide an exhaustive classification. My concern is only to indicate the types of cases that are of special interest for the ensuing discussion. From now on, the long expression 'reconsideration (or nonreconsideration)' will be shortened to '(non)reconsideration'.

3. I do not mean that there is such implicit reconsideration whenever one considers an option that is incompatible with one's prior intention. I might consider an option that is incompatible with my prior intention to *A*, note this incompatibility, and so drop the option as inadmissible. In such a case my consideration of this option does not involve even implicit reconsideration of my prior intention to *A*.

4. But see the qualification in the discussion of the puzzle in Subsection 5.2.2.

5. It was John Perry who first suggested to me this distinction between reason-changing and reason-preserving nonreconsideration.

6. For example, the agent's general abilities to reason carefully and quickly in the face of the unexpected.

7. An example suggested by a similar example of Allan Gibbard's.

8. This connection between the stability of plans and tendencies to see certain matters as salient highlights the connection between assessments of the stability of plans and issues about education. Such tendencies will be a natural and important concern for any systematic theory of what we should be aiming at in our educational practices.

9. Gilbert Ryle, *The Concept of Mind* (London: Hutchinson and Company, 1949), chap. 2.

10. A point emphasized by Allen Gibbard in his paper "Attainable Rationality in Action: An Analysis," presented at the 1984 Stanford Conference on Planning and Practical Reasoning.

11. In emphasizing the role of problems in triggering reconsideration I echo

Dewey's general emphasis on the role of problems in precipitating deliberation. See Dewey, *Human Nature and Conduct,* Part III.

12. In writing this sentence I was helped by David Israel and John Perry.

13. Thus I agree with the spirit of Michael Robins's remark about intentions: "One can form them arbitrarily . . . but one may not change them at will." See Michael Robins, *Promising, Intending, and Moral Autonomy* (Cambridge: Cambridge University Press, 1984), p. 35. But my approach to explaining why this is so is quite different from Robins's.

14. See Robert Adams's useful discussion of a similar idea in his "Motive Utilitarianism," *Journal of Philosophy* 73 (1976): 467–481.

15. See J. J. C. Smart, "Extreme and Restricted Utilitarianism," in *Theories of Ethics,* ed. Philippa Foot (Oxford: Oxford University Press, 1967).

16. I ignore complications about increased peace of mind on Mondale's part, and similar matters.

17. But keep in mind that the ahistorical theory of Chapter 4 will be challenged and modified in Chapter 6.

6. Agent Rationality: The Historical Theory

1. Rawls, *A Theory of Justice,* p. 29.

2. Recall the explanation of the distinction between reason-preserving and reason-changing nonreconsideration given in Chapter 5.

3. Note that for this historical principle to apply the agent must have actually formed the intention at t_0. It is not enough that if the agent had considered the issue at t_0 it would have been rational for her at t_0 to have formed this intention.

4. Thanks to Richard Lee and Kent Bach for urging me to discuss this case.

5. There is one version of this problem case which might seem particularly challenging for the historical principle. Suppose that the reason it is irrational of me not to reconsider my prior intention to A is as follows: although there has been no relevant change in my external circumstances, I continue to worry anxiously about my original decision; and reconsideration could easily relieve me of this worry. Still, I do not reconsider; and this is irrational of me, even though if I had reconsidered I would have rationally retained my intention. Here the good to be achieved by reconsideration is not some increased likelihood of arriving at a rational decision, but just the indirect psychological benefit of such reconsideration: relief from anxiety. Should the fact that, for such a reason, it was irrational of me not to reconsider from t_0 to t_1 be allowed to block the assessment at t_1 that it is rational of me so to intend? (I owe this objection to Alfred Mele.)

I am inclined to think it should. I have taken a broadly pragmatic approach to the assessment of habits and dispositions concerning reconsideration. On such an approach it is hard to see why some sorts of irrational failures to reconsider should infect the later rationality of the agent for his intentions, and others should not. If, however, you think I am wrong about this, you may make an appropriate qualification to the principle. As far as I can see, the main structure of the principle is not threatened.

6. This way was suggested to me by John Dupré.

7. In this case it is my own action that leads to the change which, when I know of it, newly makes going to concert A advisable from the external perspective. But this dependency on my own action is not essential to my treatment of the case. I would offer a similar treatment of a case in which the relevant changes occur independently of my action. What is essential is that I do not use this new information to provide additional support for my prior intention. Thanks to Warren Quinn for urging me to clarify this point.

8. Pointed out to me by Lawrence Crocker.

9. Thanks to Peter Railton for this apt term.

10. The case in which Mondale's prior intention to attack Star Wars is rational of him to form, but Reagan acts in unexpected ways in the debate.

11. The discussion in this section is based on my working paper, "Personal Policies," prepared for the 1985–86 Workshop on Risk and Rationality sponsored by the University of Maryland Center for Philosophy and Public Policy.

12. An example of Dennis Des Chene's.

13. Sometimes personal policies shade off into habits; this could easily happen, for example, with a policy of buckling up. And sometimes it is natural to think of a policy as merely a rule of thumb—a useful shortcut in figuring out what would be best to do in present circumstances. But I think there is a wide range of cases in which, instead, it is useful to think of such policies as general intentions. And it is such cases that I will be discussing here.

14. Paul Slovic was recently reported, in a popular essay, as suggesting that "if motorists would think in terms of a lifetime of driving rather than single trips . . . then perhaps they would decide once and for all to buckle up." Some of Slovic's observations that are cited in this essay suggest that this may have been unduly optimistic. Nevertheless, you can treat much of my discussion of general policies as a sketch of what it would be for agents like us to "decide once and for all" on such a policy. See W. F. Allman, "Staying Alive in the Twentieth Century," *Science 85,* October 1985, pp. 31–37.

15. So I agree with Wilfred Sellars that "it is essential not to assimilate action on policy to using means to achieve an end." Nevertheless, my treatment of action on policy differs importantly from the one sketched by Sellars. See Sellars, "Thought and Action," pp. 136–138.

16. This approach was suggested to me by Charles Dresser.

17. One whose importance was first impressed upon me by Ned Block.

18. I borrow the verb "negatives" from H. L. A. Hart and A. M. Honoré, *Causation in the Law* (Oxford: Oxford University Press, 1959), chap. 6.

19. An example of Ned Block's.

20. John Fischer and John Perry together led me to think about this case.

21. For needed qualification see the discussion in Chapter 5 of the puzzle about the deliberative case.

22. Emphasized by John Dupré in conversation with me.

23. But see the discussion of complications in the next paragraph.

24. Throughout this section I was aided by Daniel Farrell's helpful comments.

25. Kavka, "The Toxin Puzzle." I think the main points I will make here would also apply to other instances of this general phenomenon. In particular,

they would apply to the cases of deterrent conditional intentions discussed in Kavka, "Some Paradoxes of Deterrence." But by focusing on the "toxin puzzle" I can avoid complications introduced by conditional intentions.

26. A point emphasized by Farrell in correspondence.

27. And this nonreconsideration is reason-preserving.

28. David Gauthier, "Afterthoughts," in *The Security Gamble,* ed. Douglas MacLean (Totowa: Rowman & Allanheld, 1984), p. 159. See also Gauthier's "Deterrence, Maximization, and Rationality," in the same volume.

29. Anyway, this is close enough to the truth for present purposes. We are ignoring the possibility of change in your values from t_1 to t_2, for example.

30. Though it may be that in getting yourself on Tuesday to intend to drink the toxin on Wednesday you will need somehow to hide from yourself such facts about the rationality of reconsideration.

7. Commitment Revisited

1. Roderick Chisholm, *Person and Object* (LaSalle, Ill.: Open Court, 1976), chap. 2.

2. Of course, such external assessments can themselves be made by the agent and then may indirectly influence her practical reasoning about what to do.

3. See Davidson, "Intending," and Stuart Hampshire and H. L. A. Hart, "Decision, Intention, and Certainty," *Mind* 67 (1958): 1–12. J. David Vellemen defends a belief theory in "Practical Reflection," *Philosophical Review* 94 (1985): 33–61. Gilbert Harman sympathetically considers such a belief theory in "Practical Reasoning" and in "Willing and Intending."

8. Two Faces of Intention

1. Philosophers who accept something tantamount to the Simple View include Bruce Aune, in *Reason and Action* (Dordrecht: Reidel, 1977), chap. 2, esp. pp. 89–102; and John Searle, in *Intentionality* (Cambridge: Cambridge University Press, 1983), chap. 3. Searle says (p. 94n) that the rejection of what I have called the Simple View is "a mistake that derives from a failure to see the difference between prior intentions [what I have called future-directed intentions] and intentions in action [present-directed intentions]." But, as will be explained, my objection to the Simple View does not depend on such a failure.

In *An Introduction to the Principles of Morals and Legislation* (London: Methuen, 1982), chap. 8, Jeremy Bentham distinguishes between consequences which are "directly" intentional and consequences which are only "obliquely" intentional. This distinction suggests a view according to which bringing about X may be intentional, even if one does not intend to bring X about, as long as one intends something one expects will (or, will likely) result in X. Such a view is intermediate between the Simple View and the more complex view I will be sketching later. As will become clear, this intermediate view is also subject to the objection against the Simple View to be developed in Sections 8.2 and 8.3. I will be returning to issues raised by Bentham's distinction between direct and oblique intention in Section 8.5 and again in Chapter 10.

The Simple View is rejected in passing by Georg Henrik von Wright in his *Explanation and Understanding* (Ithaca: Cornell University Press, 1971), pp. 89–90. More recently, Gilbert Harman has criticized the Simple View in "Practical Reasoning," *Review of Metaphysics* 29 (1976): 431–463. Later I will discuss Harman's criticism and my reasons for preferring my alternative approach.

2. This explains why I did not include Donald Davidson among those who accept the Simple View, even though he comes close to endorsing the view that if I intentionally start my car then I must intend my particular act of starting it. See his essays "How Is Weakness of the Will Possible?" and "Intending," both in his *Essays on Actions and Events*.

3. See, for example, Charles Fried, *Right and Wrong* (Cambridge, Mass.: Harvard University Press, 1978), esp. pp. 20–24.

4. These examples take off from an example sketched by Robert Audi in "Intending," esp. p. 401.

5. In this last sentence I am indebted to Harman's discussion of such examples in "Willing and Intending."

6. One might even here object to the Simple View if one thought that to intend to hit the target I must believe I will. Later I discuss this line of argument against the Simple View, and why I do not adopt it.

7. This trio of examples is, of course, highly stylized; but that is for reasons of exposition. Similar issues might arise if I applied to two law schools, knowing that they coordinate their admissions and so I can only get into one, or if I pursued marriage with two different women. See my discussion in Chapter 9.

8. See, for example, H. P. Grice, "Intention and Uncertainty," *Proceedings of the British Academy* 57 (1971): 263–279; and Gilbert Harman, "Practical Reasoning."

9. As Harman explicitly notes in "Practical Reasoning," p. 433.

10. In Davidson, "Intending."

11. I am indebted both to Kwong-loi Shun and to the editors of *The Philosophical Review* for urging me to discuss this objection explicitly.

12. Perhaps there are other cases of trying to achieve each of two goals known to be incompatible in which, due to peculiarities of one's character, one really must intend to achieve each goal in order best to pursue each goal. But we need not suppose that my case is like that.

13. Example courtesy of the editors of *The Philosophical Review*.

14. Hugh McCann defends the Simple View against my objection, in his "Rationality and the Range of Intention," *Midwest Studies in Philosophy* 10 (1986): 191–211. McCann's defense is based on a criticism of my views about the irrationality of intention-belief inconsistency, views which I defend in Chapters 3 and 9, as well as in my discussion above of claim (a). Though he rejects the Simple View, Gilbert Harman has also expressed concern about my argument. Harman points out that in saying that I intentionally hit target 1 you might be saying that I intentionally hit target 1 *rather than* target 2; and similarly in saying

that I intend to hit target 1. Call these *contrastive* readings. Harman goes on to suggest that when we deny that I intend to hit target 1, we have this contrastive reading in mind; but "it might be acceptable to say that [I intend to hit target 1] if no such contrast is implied." Harman, *Change in View,* p. 90. I do not, however, see how the distinction between contrastive and noncontrastive readings can block my argument; for the entire argument should be understood in terms of noncontrastive notions of 'intentionally' and 'intends'. The problem is that if I noncontrastively intend to hit target 1, then (by symmetry) it seems that I noncontrastively intend to hit target 2. Given my beliefs, that is what gets me into trouble. In suggesting that "it might be acceptable" to say that I noncontrastively intend to hit target 1, Harman may be challenging the idea that it would then follow, by reason of symmetry, that I also noncontrastively intend to hit target 2. But I do not see what the basis for this challenge is. Granted, since I do hit target 1, I might be said to intend *of* my hitting target 1 that it be a hitting of target 1. And I do not intend *of* my hitting target 2 that it be a hitting of target 2; for I do not hit target 2. But that is a different matter.

15. Anscombe, *Intention,* p. 68.

16. I introduce this further intention to make it clear that I am not just denying that I intend to wear down my sneakers "as an end." I do not intend to get to the track by 9:00 A.M. as an end; but I still do intend to do so. In contrast, I may not intend at all to wear down my sneakers. I will say more about this issue in Chapter 10. For probing discussions of related matters see Jonathan Bennett, "Morality and Consequences," *The Tanner Lectures on Human Values,* ed. Sterling M. McMurrin (Cambridge: Cambridge University Press, 1980), lecture III; and Gilbert Harman, "Rational Action and the Extent of Intentions."

17. Allan Gibbard helped me see this point. Note that I do not say that I run the race *with the intention* of wearing down my sneakers. I will discuss acting with an intention in the next chapter.

18. An example of J. L. Austin's: I insist on payment of a due debt by my debtor even though I know this will ruin him. Austin says I ruin him deliberately but not intentionally. But his reason for saying this seems to be merely an appeal to the Simple View. Austin writes: "At no time did I intend to ruin him; it was never any part of my intention." J. L. Austin, "Three Ways of Spilling Ink," in *J. L. Austin: Philosophical Papers,* 2nd ed., ed. J. O. Urmson and G. J. Warnock (Oxford: Oxford University Press, 1970), pp. 278–279. But we have seen that though I did not intend to ruin him it might still be true that I ruined him intentionally. And that does seem to be a natural description of the case.

19. I hope it is clear that I have not tried here to provide a complete account of these complexities. I do not know how to provide a complete account of necessary and sufficient conditions for an action's being intentional.

20. This raises a question about the intention-action principle of agent rationality. I originally formulated this principle in Chapter 4 under the assumption that when I intentionally *A* my guiding intention is an intention to *A*. But now it is clear that this is not quite right. When I intentionally wear down my sneakers, for example, my guiding intention is only an intention to run the race. A natural

conjecture, one that I will not try to defend here, is that we can extend the intention-action principle along roughly the following lines:

Extended intention-action principle

If it is rational of S to have a present-directed intention to A, and S successfully executes this intention and thereby intentionally B's—where B is in the motivational potential of S's intention to A—then it is rational of S to B.

21. I borrow the term "reactive attitude" from P. F. Strawson's classic paper, "Freedom and Resentment," *Proceedings of the British Academy* 48 (1962): 1–25.

22. Sidgwick, *The Methods of Ethics*, p. 202. For a useful discussion of such matters and their relations to some views of Harman's, see Neil Lubow, "Acting Intentionally" (unpublished manuscript, Department of Philosophy, University of New Hampshire). Also see Anscombe's critical remarks about Sidgwick's proposal, in G. E. M. Anscombe, "Modern Moral Philosophy," *Philosophy* (1958): 1–19.

23. Of course, to play this motivational role my intention need not be an intention to get to the track by 9:00 A.M. It might just be an intention to try, or to get there by then if my old car holds up. Still, if I do intend to get there by 9:00 A.M. (and do not merely expect that I will), my intention will normally play the cited role.

24. I *might* guide my running of the race by keeping track of the state of my sneakers—for example, if I use them as a pedometer. Since even then I would not intend to wear them down, the presence of such guidance does not ensure intention. My point here is only that its absence indicates an absence of intention.

25. So I disagree with Daniel Dennett's remark about our commonsense ("folk") psychology that "one way of distinguishing the good from the bad, the essential from the gratuitous, in folk theory is to see what must be included in the theory to account for whatever predictive or explanatory success it seems to have in ordinary use." See Daniel Dennett, "Three Kinds of Intentional Psychology," in *Reduction, Time, and Reality,* ed. R. Healey (Cambridge: Cambridge University Press, 1981), p. 41.

26. For a useful discussion of such cases by a philosopher who rejects the Simple View and who would, I think, also reject my version of the Single Phenomenon View, see Larry Wright, *Teleological Explanations: An Etiological Analysis of Goals and Functions* (Berkeley: University of California Press, 1976), pp. 122–129.

27. I was helped here by John Perry. The idea that in spontaneous action I might be executing a general intention without executing a specific present-directed intention seems to me to be in the spirit of some remarks of Hector-Neri Castañeda's about the execution of conditional intentions. See Hector-Neri Castañeda, "Conditional Intentions, Intentional Action, and Aristotelian Practical Syllogisms," *Erkenntnis* 18 (1982): 239–260.

28. Note that such cases will not fall under even the *extended* intention-action

principle sketched above in note 20. The natural way of extending the theory of agent rationality to such cases would be directly to extend the principle of policy-based rationality. But I will refrain from pursuing this complexity here.

9. Acting with an Intention

1. J. L. Austin, "Three Ways of Spilling Ink," p. 284. (Thanks to Alan Donagan for reminding me of Austin's discussion.)

2. Harman seems to suggest a similar distinction in *Change in View,* pp. 93–94.

3. Chisholm, *Person and Object,* chap. 2.

4. This is Chisholm's sense of both locutions (ibid., p. 74). As far as I can see, Chisholm has, in his theory, no notion of an intention that is not presently involved in what one is endeavoring to do; he has no notion of an intention that is not an intention in action. This is a serious lacuna.

5. These distinctions in hand, should we go back to (1) and make an analogous distinction between a weak and a strong notion of acting with a *further* intention? Suppose I take the glove off my left hand as a preliminary step to hitting target 1. I do not, strictly speaking, intend to hit target 1. But do I, in a *weak* sense, act with the *further* intention of hitting target 1? I am inclined to answer that there is no such weak sense of acting with a further intention: there is no sense of acting with a further intention such that I act with the further intention of hitting that target. But this is merely a verbal dispute. If you disagree, then you should suppose there are four notions of acting with an intention, notions that result from the combination of the distinctions between acting with an intention and acting with a further intention, and between weak and strong readings. You should then understand my remarks about acting with a further intention to be about acting with a further intention, in the strong sense.

6. Philosophers in this tradition include Bruce Aune and Hector-Neri Castañeda. See Aune, *Reason and Action,* chap. 2, sect. 4; and Castañeda, *Thinking and Doing,* p. 277. Searle's use, in *Intentionality,* of the notion of "intention in action" suggests that he too identifies present-directed intention and volition. His initial arguments for the presence of an "intention in action" in all intentional action—for example, James's case of the anesthetized patient who mistakenly thinks that he is raising his arm (p. 89)—are arguments for the presence of some volitional element. By labeling this volitional element "intention in action" Searle seems to take the further step of identifying it with present-directed *intention.*

7. Grice, "Intention and Uncertainty."

8. See Chapter 8.

9. Published in Amsterdam by North Holland, 1980.

10. As he kindly made clear in private correspondence.

11. On Wilson's view we should say *consciously* aim.

12. Reprinted in Davidson, *Essays on Actions and Events* (New York: Oxford University Press, 1980). The quotation is from p. 8.

13. Reprinted in Davidson, *Essays on Actions and Events.* See also the dis-

cussion of the development of Davidson's views in my "Davidson's Theory of Intention."

14. See the introduction to Davidson, *Essays on Actions and Events,* p. xiii.

15. For a useful discussion of the last sort of case see Bruce Vermazen, "Negative Acts," in Vermazen and Hintikka, eds., *Essays on Davidson: Actions and Events.*

16. This terminology is derived from Bernard Williams's discussion of "the *agglomeration principle*" concerning ought judgments in his paper, "Ethical Consistency," in his book, *Problems of the Self* (Cambridge: Cambridge University Press, 1973).

17. Here I am, of course, confining myself to those psychological conditions that do not themselves require the performance of the action in question. This excludes, for example, knowledge that I am *A*-ing.

18. And perhaps some other conditions; see the discussion in Section 8.5.

19. I say only that intentional actions are paradigms of actions for which we hold people responsible, not that they are the only such actions. For example, we also hold people responsible for negligently, though unintentionally, causing certain harms.

10. Intention and Expected Side Effects

1. See, for example, Bennett, "Morality and Consequences."

2. In saying this I do not deny that Strategic Bomber kills the children *intentionally*. See Chapter 8.

3. For discussions sympathetic with the principle of double effect see, for example, Germain Grisez, "Toward a Consistent Natural-Law Ethics of Killing," *The American Journal of Jurisprudence* 15 (1970): 64–96; and Thomas Nagel, *The View from Nowhere* (New York: Oxford University Press, 1986), chap. 9. A ground-breaking paper is Philippa Foot, "The Problem of Abortion and the Doctrine of Double Effect," *Oxford Review,* no. 5 (1967). In this paper Foot considers the principle of double effect sympathetically, but in the end rejects it. In a more recent paper, Foot changes her mind and argues for the need for some version of this principle. See Philippa Foot, "Morality, Action, and Outcome," in *Morality and Objectivity,* ed. Ted Honderich (London: Routledge & Kegan Paul, 1985).

4. The reader will note that I am ignoring here the characteristic inertia of intention. This is because it does not bear on the present problem.

5. In the terminology of Robert Nozick, then, Terror Bomber's conduct "tracks" the children's deaths. See Robert Nozick, *Philosophical Explanations* (Cambridge, Mass.: Harvard University Press, 1981), esp. chaps. 3 and 4.

6. I say "in the normal case," for there are cases in which Strategic Bomber might guide his activity by keeping track of the children and their deaths, and yet still not endeavor to kill them. Suppose he wasn't dropping a single bunch of bombs but was launching missiles one at a time, aimed at the munitions plant. The only way he has of knowing whether he has hit the plant is to listen to Enemy radio for an announcement of the deaths of the children. After each missile is launched, he waits for a radio announcement. In its absence he launches yet

another missile, and so on until he hears of the deaths of the children or somehow comes to change his opinion concerning the link between the destruction of the munitions plant and their deaths. Still, he does not launch his missiles *in order to* kill the children. Nor does he engage in means-end reasoning concerned with how to kill the children, or screen his other options for their compatibility with his killing them. So he still does not intend to kill them.

7. As I noted in Chapter 8, note 1, this is Jeremy Bentham's terminology. See Bentham, *An Introduction to the Principles of Morals and Legislation,* chap. 8.

8. Throughout this section I benefited from Gilbert Harman's examination of a related but different problem in his "Rational Action and the Extent of Intentions." In Section 10.3 I explain how my problem differs from Harman's and why I reject important features of his solution.

9. Wilfred Sellars, "Thought and Action," in *Freedom and Determinism,* ed. Keith Lehrer (New York: Random House, 1966), pp. 105–139, esp. 131–136. See also Sellars's later discussion in "Volitions Re-Affirmed," in *Action Theory,* ed. Myles Brand and Douglas Walton (Dordrecht: Reidel, 1976), pp. 47–66, esp. sects. 3–4. Bruce Aune seems to endorse the features of Sellars's theory that are of interest here. See Aune, *Reason and Action,* pp. 135–136. As far as I know, Sellars has not offered a solution to the problem posed by the case of Strategic Bomber.

10. Actually, Sellars does not assume that the reasoning will begin with a prior intention. I have focused on such a case so as to indicate the connection of such reasoning to the sort of ongoing planning that I have been emphasizing in this book. Another qualification is that Strategic Bomber might begin with only a guiding desire to weaken Enemy, rather than an intention, strictly speaking. (See my discussion in Chapter 9.) But for simplicity I will be assuming that he has an intention so to act.

11. Versions of this model seem to be common in discussions by "decision analysts" who attempt to use expected utility theory as part of a recommended procedure for making decisions. See, for example, Howard Raiffa, *Decision Analysis* (Reading, Mass.: Addison-Wesley, 1968).

12. Granted, he also knows that it is *not* in his power to bomb *without* killing the children. But that does not affect the present point.

13. Chisholm, *Person and Object,* p. 75.

14. So Chisholm does not make the distinction I urge in Chapter 9 between a weak and a strong reading of 'with an intention'.

15. Chisholm, *Person and Object,* p. 74.

16. See his example, ibid., p. 75.

17. Ibid., p. 74.

18. Harman, "Rational Action and the Extent of Intentions."

19. Ibid., p. 124. The brackets are in the original text. This passage is somewhat modified in the revised version of this paper that appears as chap. 9 in Harman's *Change in View.* (The relevant passage is on pp. 98–99.) Although I believe that these modifications do not touch the main points I make here, these modifications came to my attention too late for me to incorporate them into this

chapter. The other passages quoted from Harman's essay remain essentially unchanged in the revised version.

20. Ibid., p. 132.

21. Ibid., p. 134.

22. Ibid., p. 133.

23. Of course, evaluation and choice can diverge—as in certain cases of weakness of will. But here we are limiting our attention to the practical reasoning of an agent who is not guilty of irrationality.

24. Sidgwick tells us that "undesired accompaniments of the desired results of our volitions are clearly chosen or willed by us." And from this he seems to infer that these "accompaniments" are intended. But we now see that this inference is at best questionable; and on the approach I take here to the relation between intention and choice the inference is mistaken. See Sidgwick, *The Methods of Ethics*, p. 202.

25. See, for example, Aune, *Reason and Action*, p. 115.

26. Throughout this section I am much indebted to a series of helpful comments from Charles Dresser and Martha Pollack.

27. In other cases of *B*-ing by *A*-ing, such a straightforward causal interpretation will not be available, for example: endorsing a check by signing it. But I put aside such complications here.

28. This distinction between 'means', in a sense tied to intention, and 'by', in a sense that is not tied to intention, helps sort out issues raised by the following commonly discussed example: A knowledgeable neurophysiologist might raise her arm in order to fire the neurons whose firing is a cause of her arm's rising. What we can say about such a case is that raising her arm is the neurophysiologist's *means* to causing the neurons to fire; but she does not cause the neurons to fire *by* raising her arm.

29. *Why* one might have such commitments is not an issue to which we can do justice here. That one might be so committed is something that I will take for granted for purposes of the present discussion.

30. See the discussion of personal policies in Chapter 6.

31. Assuming Strategic Bomber does not block the application of his general policy to this particular case. See the discussion in Chapter 6.

32. And does not block its application to this case.

33. Bennett, "Morality and Consequences," p. 97.

11. Conclusion

1. Robert Nozick, *Anarchy, State, and Utopia* (New York: Basic Books, 1974), p. 30.

Index